POWER & ILLNESS

POWER & ILLNESS

The Political Sociology of Health and Medical Care

Elliott A. Krause

Elsevier · New York

NEW YORK · AMSTERDAM · OXFORD

ELSEVIER NORTH-HOLLAND, INC.
52 Vanderbilt Avenue, New York, New York 10017

ELSEVIER SCIENTIFIC PUBLISHING COMPANY
335 Jan Van Galenstraat, P.O. Box 211
Amsterdam, The Netherlands

Third Printing, 1978

Pages 237–258 and 274–293 of this volume appeared in two
articles in the *International Journal of Health Services*, vol. 3, no. 3
and vol. 5, no. 4. They are reprinted here by permission of the
publisher. Copyright 1973 and 1975 by Baywood Publishing Company, Inc.

Library of Congress Cataloging in Publication Data

Krause, Elliott A
   Power and illness: the political sociology of health
   and medical care
   Bibliography: p.
   Includes index.
   1. Social medicine. 2. Social medicine—United
States. 3. Medical policy—United States. I. Title.
[DNLM: 1. Delivery of health care—United States.
2. Quality of Health care—United States. 3. Politics
—United States. 4. Sociology. 5. Health. W84 AA1
K9p]
RA418.K72   362.1′0973   77-317
ISBN 0-444-99037-2

Manufactured in the United States of America

Designed by Loretta Li

For Andy, Carol, and Theodora

Contents

Preface

This book is not primarily about the details of health and health service, although many of these details are included. Rather, *Power and Illness* is a work of general political sociology showing how an essential resource—health—and an essential service—health care—are intimately involved with the political, economic, and social struggles of the present day. In effect, it is a study of the context of health and the context of care—with special reference to power.

Power is presently being used by those who possess it against the interests of the majority of citizens, and yet most people are only dimly aware of what is going on. Thus, the approach used is critical of the present system, employing the findings of several generations of research to show the ways in which health care and the level of health itself are a problem for the majority. It is different from some approaches in this area in that it has the perspective of the critical left but also uses the data of the liberal center. That is, this book is an analysis of the situation of health; it is not a tract.

Because of family, school, and college experience, I early developed a continuing interest in the health field; medical sociology thus became a research field of genuine importance to me. At first my understanding of the health-care situation was fragmented and eclectic: though there was a pattern in the neglect, I was only able to describe it in parts, not grasp it wholly. It was to be the personal impact of the onrush of social events in the sixties, rather than isolated academic theorizing, that finally resulted in my choice of the theoretical perspective that informs much of this book.

In my first book, on occupations, I began to use a directly political perspective and critical approach. I gradually edged away from formal medical sociology, at least of the sort I had been exposed to earlier, and went into the study of political sociology and political economy. Action work—as a consultant to the Community Action Program headquarters of the OEO in Washington—taught me a brutal lesson on the irresponsibility of some well-meaning professional reformers, and the consequent smashing of the hopes of the poor and helpless. From time to time I would examine the new books and articles in the sociology of health. With every passing year the gap grew between the outrages described by the Health Policy Advisory Center, the Health Research Group, the Medical Committee for Human Rights, or the Women's Health Movement, and the dull, increasingly irrelevant drone of much of the professional literature. Thus about four years ago, I began work on this book.

The first job was to make some kind of order out of the action, scholarship, and pamphleteering that characterized the field then, as it does to some extent today. One theoretical perspective—that of modern Marxian theory—seemed superior to the others for establishing a broad background and point of view. But, an early decision was made not to deal extensively with the technical vocabulary of Marxian analysis for fear of limiting the audience. Secondly, I decided to use an historical perspective as much as possible in hope of giving the reader a sense that the issues were all in flux and would ultimately be decided as a consequence of the winning or losing of real struggles.

Another decision to be made concerned the organization of the book. I would work from the well-investigated center to the less-investigated periphery by beginning with a major section on the workers in the workplace, then moving toward the delivery system, and finally into the society-wide political processes affecting health and health service systems. The *context* of health and service would be inspected for what it could yield in the way of explanation; the ground would be inspected for what it could tell us about the figure.

My last chapter, *Who Will Make the Future?*, suggests that there is an alternative to the present system of service and insurance—an American National Health Service. But neither "alternative one" (tinkering with the present system) nor "alternative two" are perfect, and some may be angry with me for not solving all their problems and coming up with the perfect set of recommendations in the last chapter. But it is precisely the message of this book that the answer will be fought out—with power, money, political organizations and ideologies—out there, in the society. What I *can* do—and I think it is a service—is to lay it all out bare, with no Emperor's clothes on, for all to see.

I have been fortunate in having the time, care, and comments of a number of colleagues: sociologists, health service workers, students, and others from many walks of life. For detailed commentary and sociological insight as they read versions of this manuscript, I would especially like to thank Irv Zola, Alex Inkeles, Julius Roth, Jerome Myers, and Peter New. During the period when I worked on the last version of the book, the East Coast Health Discussion Group provided many new insights into the complex problems of relating Marxian theory—itself in flux—to the problems of the health field. Among the members of this group, I would particularly like to thank Len Rodberg, Vicente Navarro, Sander Kelman, Dit Talley, Grace

Ziem, and Joe Eyer, who were patient with someone whose theoretical interest differed from their own. From the standpoint of a practicing physician and political liberal with years of experience in the politics of health, I would also like to thank my father, George Krause. His point of view differed from mine consistently, but the care and attention this work received at his hands made a special difference to me. Of course none of the above are responsible for the errors and interpretations in the following pages.

The staff and facilities of several libraries were especially helpful: those of the Countway Medical Library, the Schering Library of the Center for Community Health and Medical Care, and the Law School Library, all of Harvard University; the Northeastern University Library; the Rotch Library at MIT; and the small but excellent library of the Lawrence General Hospital near my home and its librarian Sandy Clevesy. I am also indebted to the staff at Elsevier, particularly my longtime friend and present editor, Bill Gum. They helped to make this book far better than I would have been able to by myself. Finally, the three people to whom this book is dedicated were a source of sustenance, cheer, and welcome distraction throughout the long battle to place it before the reader.

E.A.K.

POWER
&
ILLNESS

A Point of View

No person is an island. Neither is a sector of the economy, or social institution. Yet if such an institution—the health care system for example—is consistently viewed in isolation, if those who study it refuse to explore systematically the myriad ways it is tied into the power and control systems of the wider society, then a disservice is done to those whose basic interests are at stake. For an absence of such an understanding—on the part of citizens who get sick or who pay health insurance while well—guarantees the system's persistence in something like its present form, or at least limits changes to the outcomes of private infighting. The central organizing thesis of this book is that a persistent and comprehensive study of the existing system of health care in America, within its social context, will demonstrate that this system plays an integral part in maintaining social inequality and the persistence of disease—that it is at least as much a part of the problem as it is of the solution.

1

In the following pages, we will inspect the historical trends in the meaning of patient experience, the architectural evolution of systems for delivering care, and the continuity of power relations between those who own and control the production of health goods and services and those who work within the system as employees or who "consume" its "products". Throughout history, to a marked degree, health services have reflected in miniature the achievements and failures of the societies in which they have existed. Otherwise put, the place to understand the functioning of the health care system is primarily outside of its narrowly conceived boundaries. One can gain some understanding of Nazi Germany, for example, by studying relations between guards and inmates within the concentration camps, but no one would assert that the primary social and political explanation for this phenomenon lay there, or, for that matter, the primary explanation of the quality of guard-inmate relations. In just this fashion we will explore the careers, experience, and world view of the servers and the served within health care organizations. But our primary investigation must necessarily be elsewhere—in the relations between this direct experience and the pattern of power relations which characterize the wider society. Here and only here can we see the other end of the strings that tie the health care field down, like a Gulliver in Lilliput, thrashing but helpless.

Two perennial controversies are relevant to this book: the "advocacy-versus-objectivity" debate and the problem of scope of analysis as this relates to the significance of the topic on the one hand and the thoroughness of the proof on the other. In a recent study of the foundation of the American economics profession, Furner demonstrated that the economists formed their American academic style in the late 1800s by eliminating from leadership positions those who took strong public stands for change in the ways the corporations were controlling governmental areas of operation, ostensibly within the sphere of citizen control. Richard T. Ely, by no means a radical but someone who refused to limit the scope of his investigations to supply-and-demand theory, was removed from his offices in the American Economic Association, an organization he founded. Other economists, such as Ross, were driven into sociology (a fate they and others perceived as exile). Their sin was twofold—they cared and they were willing to say so publicly in print, both in books and in speeches. They were accused of "lack of objectivity" and of "not doing economics". Most learned their lesson. Furner notes that by 1900,

> Only rarely did professional social scientists do what no one else was better qualified to do: bring expert skill and knowledge to bear on cosmic questions pertaining to the society as a whole . . . The academic professionals, having retreated to the security of technical expertise, left to journalists and politicians the original mission—the comprehensive assessment of industrial society that had fostered the professionalization of social science.[1]

In the early seventies, after building an outstanding reputation as a teacher and after the publication of an influential series of critical articles and monographs on the political economy of American education, Sam Bowles was denied tenure in the economics department at Harvard, over the protests of Nobel laureate Wassily Leontief and John K. Galbraith. To no avail—his sin, according to the departmental decision, was that while his work was valuable, "it wasn't economics".[2]

The majority of my colleagues in medical sociology may not place this study within that field as it is presently conceived for two main reasons: the proconsumer, proindividual, and left-critical stance of the analysis and the scope of the topic as defined here. The value issue is complex, but its essentials have been considered by many within the sociological profession in recent years, to the point where it is becoming accepted within some of the specialties that a value-committed stance is not necessarily antithetical to honest use of the existing data.

3

But the left-critical perspective and the proconsumer orientation is a rather new one within the sociology of health care as presently defined in America. It is not a new one, I hasten to add, among the activists working for change in the occupational health and safety of miners, in the publications of the Health Policy Advisory Center, in the pamphlets of the Medical Committee for Human Rights, and in the emerging series of self-help manuals and patient rights books being published by professional and consumer activists, such as the members of the women's health care movement. But as the chaos escalates in the health worker area and in the health care settings, as the lines of the present two-class system of care harden even further, and as costs escalate out of reach of the average citizen, it would seem to be time for a systematic analysis using some of the better-tried concepts of theoretical sociology, but focused constantly on the field of health care for the purposes of assessing the existing balances and imbalances of power and control between the ill (or the potentially ill) on the one hand and the owners and controllers of the delivery system, on the other. This kind of analysis could be useful not only to the student within the liberal arts tradition—in medical sociology, political sociology, the sociology of human services—but it might also serve as a realistic introduction to the actual world of practice, where the forces delineated must be coped with on a daily basis. Here it could be of some use along with the more cut-and-dried description of the existing system that often dominates the health professional's courses in practice.

Thus the viewpoint of this book is that changes need to be made, and that this book should be one of the useful planning tools for such changes. Part of the burden of the book, of course, will therefore be to point out what the inequities are. But if the entire text were devoted to this, then we would never get around to the why of the inequities and the ways the system resists attempts at change. We will be constantly

4

concerned with the activist's way of analyzing situations—the neces-
sity of knowing what the strong and weak points are in the existing
system, assessing the field of forces from the gladiatorial pit itself, the
way it looks to the gladiators, rather than in remote isolation in the
stands. Ultimately, of course, one either buys Max Weber's idea that
we can have a value-free sociology, or one does not. We have been
explicit as to the stance this book will take. Hopefully neither the
theoretical frameworks used nor the value commitment will lead to
major blind spots in the analysis of data or the reasoning pursued.

    A second controversy—so closely related to the first that it is almost
an intellectual sibling—is the controversy over the scope of analysis.
A symbol of this problem lies in the finding of a study a few years ago
by Pilisuk and Hayden. They set out to examine the role of the
military-industrial complex within American society, and concluded
that they couldn't mark off any significant economic, sociological, or
political boundary between the "military-industrial complex" and the
rest of the economy. Instead, they concluded, America was not
controlled by a military-industrial complex, America was a
military-industrial complex.[3] *If one company made submarines,*
forty companies made the nuts and bolts for them, and all forty-one
would campaign in Congress to keep the defense budget up. The
Marxian critique in general terms will be used in this study primarily
as a guide to questions and as a director of analysis, rather than as a
dogmatic or ideological procrustean bed in which to cram findings.
For example, we will use the phrase "interest group", which is
common in liberal, non-Marxian sociology, but it will be used only at
the level of specific battles between specific groups. We will not employ
the conservative ideology that often accompanies the use of this term.

    Inevitably we will need a general analytical framework for the
relationship between state power, corporate interests, the organized
health-field groups, and the citizen. This is the broad-scale analysis

referred to above—the relationship between the national political economy and the narrower topics usually considered in isolation, such as the day-to-day process of care, the decisions on the layout of the delivery system, and the true functions of planning, legislation, regulation, and environmental safety activity.

This broader scale of analysis is in fact finally becoming an issue even within medical sociology. At two recent national meetings of the sociology profession, in 1974 and 1975, there were debates among these specialists about renaming the specialty section "health and society" or some similar title. This debate reflects the dissension in the ranks between those who want to keep the narrow focus and those who, parallelled with the efforts of this book, insist that only in the wider perspective can the phenomena truly be understood (in contrast to simply being described).

But with a broadened scope come increased risks. C. Wright Mills put it this way.

Is there any necessary tension between that which is true but unimportant, and that which is important but not necessarily true? A better way to ask the question is: For what level of verification ought workers in social science be willing to settle? We could of course become so exacting in our demands that we should necessarily have nothing but very detailed exposition; we could also become so inexacting that we should have only very grand conceptions indeed.[4]

This book is conceived on a grand scale, and accordingly the risks are such. In addition, there is what could be called a "data legitimacy problem", a problem with overtones that are both academic and political in nature. Medical sociology, as presently constituted, has focused heavily on the treatment roles and relationships within the organizational setting of care, plus statistical studies of incidence and prevalence of illness in which the sociologist acts as the "social factors" analyst, often in partnership with the epidemiologist. The

6

result conclusively demonstrates again and again that the poor are sicker than anyone else, primarily as a result of their living conditions. The ways this illness is treated or not treated—particularly the patterning of facilities in the community—is not for sociologists a regular topic, though an interdisciplinary "medical care" field is growing up which concerns itself with these problems. But the literature of community sociology or political sociology is strikingly unrelated, to date, to this problem; health care is seldom viewed as a problem of general sociology. There are some possible explanations. Grant funds during the golden fifties and early sixties, in medical sociology's great expansion period, were primarily made available for studies of patient care and improving the functioning of hospitals— findings intended to grease the wheels of the existing system. Naturally the patterns of care, and especially investigations of the power role of interest groups in affecting it, were seldom funded by either government or the foundations; when it did happen the recipients were carefully screened beforehand. Others who write on the architecture and function of service systems and on the role of state power do so from widely varying perspectives—from the radical activist critiques mentioned earlier to the academic medical elite planners; from the AMA's economists to perhaps the most important group politically if not scientifically, the journalists and politicians with their quickly written, lively, and often deeply flawed and incomplete critiques, full of unchallenged assumptions about the possible.

We will be treating this material carefully, as data, with as much cross-checking as possible from different points of view, and will be using special theoretical frameworks at each level of analysis of the problem. Government statistics, so prevalent in many areas and even voluminous in the health area, nevertheless turn out to be quite sparse in precisely some of the areas we would like to have them in detail— e.g., illness rates by race, occupational disease by plant, state by state, and so on. When we realize the trend of government to become

7

more directly involved in the delivery and regulation of care, how-
ever, it is not so surprising that those inside are not eager to make
universally available the existing data they possess, or even in some
cases to gather it in the first place.[5]

As a result, this book has depended on data from many sources
quite outside the standard sources in sociology, or even the field of
health care analysis as practiced in medical schools and schools of
public health. Some sources will strike the more politically conserva-
tive as unreliable. They have, at times, struck the author so as well,
even when he agreed in basic philosophy and value commitment with
the analysis presented. Thus if a liberal university press monograph
and a radical critique from one of the activist organizations both state
that "X" is going on in most American cities, and the standard source
has better documentation, it is likely to be quoted first. This is not to
deny that the activists cannot analyze the situation in its essentials,
but rather that like gladiators, they make their decisions quickly and
for action purposes, without the time to polish data and take the last
step to guarantee an airtight case. But their hypotheses often make
good street sense, and when the first "standard" studies begin to point
in the same direction, the verification level at which we are going to be
working will be approached. With reservations stated if need be, an
analysis will be made. A systematic analysis of this scope is by
necessity a form of risk-taking behavior and in the rapidly changing
field of health care, always runs the special risk of obsolescence to the
extent that current issues are addressed. Ultimately, however, one
either tries or one doesn't.

The Historical Context
of Health

The ownership of the main productive processes of a society provides us with a key to understanding the political power relations in that society. Marx observed that when technological change leads to new means of producing wealth, the new owners of the new processes rise in political power. This type of approach helps us in the analysis of health and service because it asks a series of questions about the political and economic context within which health workers operate, health service systems are set up, and which ultimately cause basic levels of illness to be maintained or alleviated.

The concept of "class struggle" is shorthand, in this type of analysis, for the organized conflict over power and control of resources—including health service and health itself. It is inevitably a conflict between those who own the places in which wealth is produced and those who do not, but who work for those who do. There is nothing automatic about these struggles or about predicting their outcome, for they occur at the level of ideologies which legitimate the status quo as well as at the economic level itself, and thus at the level of individual perception of the legitimacy of any part of a society—most definitely including its system of care for illness. This struggle has its reflection in the behavior of health workers as occupational groups, in the specific shape or pattern of services for treating illness, and in the level of illness itself. A brief review of the record, by way of illustration, can introduce the analytical strategy and the three main topics of the book: the workers, the service system, and the broad social context within which both are set.

HEALTH WORK IN HISTORY: A PREVIEW OF ISSUES

Down through the ages a hierarchy of health workers parallels the social hierarchies of the day. In each era, this "division of labor" is primarily not a technical one, relating to the different tasks of health work, but is a division by class of patient, with a class of practitioner for each patient class in the wider society. Within this occupational hierarchy, of course, one often finds specialization at each level. In general, however, there is regularly a difference between the curers of the masses and the curers of the elite. The important exception to this is the craftsman class in the ancient world, which was usually able to afford community practitioners but not the medicine of the ruling class. Examples of this ancient hierarchy can be found in pharonic Egypt and in Periclean Athens. After inspecting the pattern, it may be helpful to inquire into the relationship between the governing power centers of the nation and these occupations, especially those serving the ruling class. This is all by the way of introduction, however, and should not be taken for definitive historical analysis.

Egypt provides us with the first example of a three-level practice hierarchy. At the top was temple medicine: the ancient god associated with each temple and its group of priests assembled to "cure" the sick. What was practiced in these places was apparently a combination of rest cure and faith healing for the land-owning upper class, the only class which had both the wealth and the leisure to enjoy the treatment. Community practitioners, the next step down, were medical craftsmen operating out of their own homes, practicing fee-for-service medicine.[1] Herodotus observed: "Each physician is a healer of one disease, and one only. All the country is full of physicians, some of the eye, some of the head, some of the teeth".[2] At the bottom were the folk curers, from the ancient tribes that had been welded together to form the Egyptian nation.

In Greece, temple medicine operated in ways parallel to the earlier Egyptian case. The leisure class—the aristocracy—patronized the temples. There is evidence, however, that in Greece the temple priests interacted more frequently than in Egypt with the community workers. This may be due in part to the reputation of the Hippocratic community practice group, who were good scientific observers and good bone-setters and wound surgeons, and who did not usually overprescribe the often dangerous medicines of the day.[3] Eventually this craftsman-class medicine became the model for practice in America today, in the form of fee-for-service medicine; perhaps the temple physicians have their functional descendants in the medical school teaching hospitals and pure research institutions of the foundations and the government. It is important for a perspective to single out the second-class status of the community practitioner. He was not a member of the aristocracy:

> As a man who worked for money, who sold his services in the open market, who practiced a *techne*, a craft, much of which was manual, the Greek doctor would not have held a very high social position.[4]

In the ancient world, as in the Middle Ages and the Renaissance, most of the common people, whether of slave, indentured, or free status, could usually afford neither the temple medicine of the class elite nor the craftsman medicine of the small bourgeoisie and merchant class. Consequently folk medicine, often carried from generation to generation by an oral pathway, and often practiced by women, was the only source of care for the majority. Yet the activity is poorly documented and almost unstudied, because it was not the work of the social elites who have been the subject of much past historical research. The few studies available, such as Ehrenreich and English, suggest that much more of importance can be found out about these lower-status workers.[5]

Health occupations, then as now, did not stand in a vacuum but were dependent—especially in the case of the worker elite—on the relations between the ruling economic class and the state, and on the ideology which supported both. Three cases are helpful in introducing this theme: the role of the medieval church with respect to health work; the actions of Henry VIII of England with respect to his health-worker hierarchy; and the actions of the American population in certain social movements in Jacksonian America.

The first of these three periods—the High to late Middle Ages— can give us some idea of the relationship in any society between the legitimating authority, the class structure, and the role of the service professions. The Church sponsored most official health care settings during the early Middle Ages, and with the rise of the universities began to form the degree system in such a way that curriculum and the awarding of the degree had to have official church backing. At the same time the Church worked in tandem with secular property interests and held the political world in balance through its role in legitimating the rule of kings (divine right of the king, coronation by the representative of the Pope). Simultaneously, this very social order bred illness out of the abject poverty of the peasantry, and the order was upheld by the ideology of the Church. One often-quoted passage from 2 Corinthians was "Eiusquisque maneat in vos dignoscatur est", or "Everyone should remain in that calling to which he has been designated" (by God)[6]. The illness bred from the system was then treated in the Church's institutions by nursing nuns and church-degreed physicians.

Replacement of Church hegemony by more secular rule, as when Henry VIII took England out of Catholicism, did not essentially change the basic relationship between elite segments of the profession and state power. Henry personally founded the Royal College of Physicians in 1518, and the College of Barber-Surgeons a few years later.[7] Yet in 1542 he became angry with the barber-surgeons (but not with the physicians) for refusing to serve the poor, and he temporarily revoked their charter.[8] Note, however, that his power legitimated the occupational hierarchy and that he did not use his power to rearrange this hierarchy. And, as 2,000 years earlier, physicians and surgeons were both scarce and expensive:

> In most small towns it was probably the apothecary practicing from his shop who would serve the legitimate medical needs of the neighborhood. There is no doubt, however, that the bulk of day-to-day doctoring in Tudor England, after the dissolution of the monasteries, was carried out by the barbers, itinerant empirics, ignorant quacks, and "wise women", of whom there was no scarcity.[9]

Finally, the example of Jacksonian America is useful. In each of the original thirteen colonies a social class elite had gotten restrictive monopoly licensing laws established just after the Revolution. Yet the scarcity of practitioners, their high fees, and their lack of empirical knowledge, led to revolt. A mass-based populist health movement—the Thompsonian herbalist group—acted in the spirit of the times and organized the rural population, the poor, the other nonorthodox physician and health worker groups, and in all states except Massachusetts (which had the least restrictive laws), the barriers against legal practice were torn down.[10] This era—from 1820 to 1830—was *not* a revolutionary one, but was definitely one of populist uprising, for it saw also the repeal of licensing laws for lawyers and the rise of nonestablished evangelical sect religion. Even if the licensing laws were observed—which they were not because there was no policing—this phenomenon is important as a

13

precedent for present and future action concerning privileged health worker groups.

The rebirth of the American medical profession at the time of America's industrial revolution signifies much that will be of importance to us later in the book. The historical record is clear: private associations slowly grouped together after the licensing debacle of the Jacksonian era, and finally formed, in 1868, the American Medical Association (AMA). But almost half a century elapsed before the medical profession began to gain real power; its role depended to a great degree on its technological effectiveness, a consequence, in turn, of progress in science. The leverage of the modern profession did increase, therefore, at least in part because the ability to cure increased and this began to become obvious to all.[11]

A second factor in the birth of the modern medical profession is more controversial. The thesis has recently been advanced that because the Carnegie Foundation supported the Flexner report and other rationalizing studies—which led to the modern practice of "professional birth control" and extended graduate education—that the capitalist class therefore had a direct interest in the birth of such a profession.[12] Certainly there was some sympathy in each group for the other but the case is not proven. In the present day the two are gradually becoming interrelated, but it is a relation of opposition. Since cost cutting may require greater state control of medical practice, and this cost cutting may benefit some sectors of the capitalist class (e.g., insurance companies), the state may be used more and more against the interests of the basically petit-bourgeois physician group. In any case, it is in this wider field of forces that we can understand the trends for any occupational group in health, in the present as in the past.

To sum up, these examples illustrate that the existing record is incomplete, especially with respect to the nature of health work by the majority of health workers with the majority of the population.

14

The history of elites serving elites, however, indicates close relations between such groups within the profession and within the state and the owning and controlling class. In the struggle over resources and control of life directions, the health-worker elite often served a custodial or supportive role, gaining much of its influence and power from the groups which sponsored it. Occasionally, however, history provides us with examples of people gaining more control over their lives, their government, and the productive process itself. At these times the consequences for health occupational elites have been marked. Their existing system of practice and their method of operation have in such times come under direct challenge.

SERVICE SYSTEMS: THE POLITICS
OF ARCHITECTURE

Any society needs support to keep it functioning, and the health service system is usually one of the more critical of these supports. Since most societies through history have been divided at least in major outline between a primary class of "haves" and a far larger class of "have-nots", the maintenance of this unequal status quo can in part be related to each functional support of the system. We should not be surprised, therefore, that whatever the type of political economy and whatever the type of technology, the existing service system can be seen to be performing functions that ultimately result in greater support of the position of the "haves", even if in the short run the "have-nots" can, to some degree, benefit from the service. These issues are complex, and in each historical period the precise story is yet to be completely documented. But the overall issue can be introduced using the cases of slavery economies, the imperialism of ancient Rome, and the transition from feudalism to early mercantile capitalism—and that of postrevolutionary France from 1789 to 1848. These cases can supply a few details on the intimate relationships that always exist between a particular form of political economy and the precise shape—the architecture—of the society's health care system.

In the ancient world, slaves had an economic value, a value to be guarded. To some degree the evidence indicates that service systems provided the basic care to keep them productive as laborers. Yet the evidence from Periclean Athens refines our understanding by making the distinction—undoubtedly true for other times and places in the ancient world—between the care given to industrial slaves (such as in the silver mines of Laurium) and the far better care given to domestic household slaves. We should contrast the more personal household slave relationship with that of the mines, where an order far closer to modern capitalism existed, with similar consequences for occupational health and life span.[13] In the slave economy of the American South, on the great rice plantations of Charleston, South Carolina or the cotton plantations of the Mississippi delta, the house physician (if there was one) or the plantation owner himself dispensed medical care to all.[14] Given the economic value of slaves in the southern plantation economy, the care was dispensed in most cases with seriousness. In fact, it became one of the aspects of psychological and social dependency of blacks on the slave owner.

Rome built an empire on the basis of its disciplined army, but maintained it through its administrative skill. The health service system of ancient Rome reflected both the military origins and the imperialist aims of the society and also its efficiency at large public works of engineering. For example, the creation of the field medical paraprofessional role or "medicus" was a Roman army invention, as was the creation of small field hospitals, built across a creek and using the creek as a running water system. These field hospitals, when enlarged, often became the provincial service centers, and had a function in co-opting the local leadership to serve the economic and political interests of the Roman conquerors. According to records, the local field hospitals were offered as services to the indigenous chiefs of the conquered regions, as a kind of side benefit for the local leaders and their family. At home, the massive water system provided free public baths for all, including the un-employed. Health levels were thus higher in this ancient capital than in cities for centuries to come, and the large number of un-employed were at least healthy, as well as entertained by the "bread and circuses" policy of the ruling class. In these ways, the service system supported the power structure in the provinces and colonies of the Empire, while working to support the status quo at home.[15]

The transition from feudalism to early mercantile capitalism provides a third illustration of the complex relationship between a given form of political economy and a given form of health service system. The Church provided a wide range of human services in addition to health care, such as homes for the aged and orphanages. It built "hospices" (the early hospitals) at the site of cathedrals, and rural clinics on the foundations of Roman field hospitals.[16] An important contrast between the actions of Henry VIII in England and the actions of secular authorities on the continent is that the Church did not have a unilateral effect on health care or on the secular world, that in fact it depended upon which nation was in process of formation. For example, in England Henry seized the Church's lands and drove the ill and dependent out of the church service buildings, which he then burned to the ground, allowing the ill and helpless to wander the roads of England.[17] Only Elizabeth I made a formal step to change this situation, but her "Poor Law" was weak indeed by comparison with what the Church had provided. On the continent the accommodation between Catholic kings and the Church remained, and the gradual rise in power by the craftsmen and merchant guilds led to slow relinquishing of major control over human services by the Church, though they often kept a supervisory function and a legitimating one, much as the Church does even today in some Catholic hospitals in western nations. It was the rise in power of the new capitalist class, however, that ultimately spelled the end of church ideological hegemony, and thus of the Church's ability to gain the resources necessary to run the human service system for the old feudal order, itself a casualty of the new rising class.

Hospital Medicine and the French Revolution, 1789–1848

The French Revolution of 1789 brought new ideas to health service. Revolutionary proclamations granted all people citizenship no matter how poor they were, as well as the right to public support in all areas, not just the area of health:

> The French Revolutionaries deserve credit on various counts. They embodied the fundamental right of man to existence as the basic law of the land. They endeavored to set up a national system of social assistance, inclusive of health care. Furthermore, they called attention to the need for assistance inclusive of medical care, in neglected areas and for neglected groups in the population. They endeavored to see the process of assistance as a whole. Finally, they developed ideas on public policy which were to influence France profoundly during the first half of the nineteenth century, and through her other countries.[18]

For the first half of the nineteenth century, Paris became the medical center of the world. New postrevolutionary medical schools were closely integrated with the hospitals. These organizations became the first major academic teaching hospitals in our modern sense, with medical students given clinical instruction on the wards from their first day of medical school. Although Edinburgh and Leyden had preceded Paris in developing voluntary hospitals and clinics, the major difference was the French hospitals were part of a government-owned hospital *system* which was integrated, metropolis-wide, and centrally administered, with specialized hospitals for certain age groups (children, old people) or diseases (kidney, mental illness). This system, and the professors who taught jointly in its hospitals and medical schools—with joint academic appointments—became the mecca for medical travellers. At the same time the Revolution gave further impetus to public health planning, which by the mid-nineteenth century had resulted in an extensive set of health regulations, a centralized public health administration, and a public health system that, in theory if not always in practice, was the first advance in a millennium over the public health system of Imperial Rome.[19]

The revolutionary committees worked with the existing system and deliberately planned to create a rationalized service organization out of scattered parts. For example, some early modifications which remain elements of the system to the present day include:

> (1) Improvement and enlargement of old hospitals (Hotel Dieu, Charite); (2) separation of the medical institutions from the philanthropic ones and the prisons; (3) erection of new, smaller hospitals (many of which were specialized); (4) transformation of confiscated monasteries into hospitals; and (5) government ownership of hospitals and centralization of their administration, which allowed much larger hospitals than private foundations could support.[20]

French health occupations underwent a few changes as a consequence of the post-revolutionary period, but not major change in their ownership situation, since practitioners remained petit-bourgeois owners of their practices. The planners of the new system fused the previously separate occupations of physician and surgeon: the surgeon was now to be a specialist physician. There had been some earlier French precedents for this, as barber-surgeons taught at the famous medieval medical school of Montpellier. But the fusion of surgery and medicine made the hospital, the surgeon's workshop, the focus of the new medicine. Pharmacy had developed its own professional schools at this time, and many new biochemical advances were made by the hospital-based branch of this occupational group. The primary breakthrough of this period was the use of applied science and the stress on practical training—even to the detriment of theoretical work. Pasteur, for example, was ignored at this time, for the comment was made that the microscope was "not practically useful" and those working with it not to be considered seriously.[21]

Lower ranks within the health occupational hierarchy were occupied by *Officers de Santé* (health officers) who were licensed by the state on the basis of practical experience and some apprenticeship training, in somewhat similar fashion and for similar reasons as were the barefoot doctors in the People's Republic of China in a later era. Note that the hierarchy itself was *not* abolished by the Revolution. These were the mass practitioners of the period, and they played somewhat the same role after the Revolution that the barber-surgeons and folk practitioners had played before it. We can estimate the ratio of physicians and surgeons to the population in Paris after 1789 as approaching 1/5,000, with a similar ratio in the countryside between health officers and the people of the rural areas.[22]

The hospital system in Paris was the center of clinical training, even though the medical school was geographically separate. Services were delivered in a centrally planned system: all patients went to a central city admitting office and then were sent to the hospital that specialized in their particular disease. This system allowed for competition by medical students to gain the honored posts of "intern" and "extern" at the Paris hospitals. These became postgraduate positions fought for by medical students from all over the world. On the other hand, medical schools had a very conservative academic structure, and were more rigid in teaching approach than the clinical method used in the hospitals, where the real "action" was. Ackerknecht, a student of this period, concludes:

> It was axiomatic that the hospital was the center of teaching, and of research as well. We might add that a hospital position was also essential politically. A position in the hospital hierarchy was more important than one in the university hierarchy. Best were, of course, simultaneous positions in both. The hospital was a doctor's fortress, his bailiwick, his ward.[23]

This structure, then, even at its birth was beginning to show some of the symptoms of the modern medical center—professional politicking, elitism, unresponsiveness to the community. But for its time it was quite a phenomenon; the world had not seen its likes before. Many of the names in early American medicine—Holmes, Jackson, Bowditch, Bartlett, Shattuck, Clark, and others—studied in these Paris hospitals. On returning they found to their dismay that their own nation was too "backward" to allow them to practice the hospital medicine they had learned in Paris. But they pushed to form the first teaching hospitals on this model, in a few eastern cities.

Rates of illness were first systematically gathered by a nation at this time. Statistical pioneers were active in government planning and successfully demonstrated the need for statistics to assess progress and change. In addition, new and important relationships grew among statisticians, examining physicians in the hospitals, and the postmortem pathologists in these hospitals. These new working relationships allowed the tracing of patterns in epidemics, as well as the rate of infection, and made possible quanitative studies which proved the relationship between observed symptoms and actual pathology, seen in the autopsy rooms of the hospitals. If science is based on reliable measurement, then the Paris hospital was a brilliant pioneer.[24]

Revolutionary ideology pointed toward the need to improve health levels in general, not simply the system of delivering services to the sick. The period of hospital medicine was also a period of action in public health and sanitation. Public health was formed as a medical specialty at this time; other advances included the passage of laws protecting children and expectant mothers, the development of antimalarial swamp drainage projects, and a Paris Public Health Council to deal with epidemics, sewage, burials, factory working conditions, prisons, and hospitals. Within thirty years every city in France had such a council. Public baths increased twenty times from 1789 to 1839. Creches and nurseries were established, along with medical inspection in schools and factories. In *laws* at least, France was now a progressive nation in the field of health care.[25]

A revolution proceeds in stages. In France, it was not until 1789 under the Jacobin dictatorship that the critical centralization of government took place. This centralization in Paris was essentially defensive, to protect the Revolution from internal and external enemies. But it created a trend that made possible, rather quickly, the central governmental control, financing, and planning of the new hospital and public health system in postrevolutionary France. As important as the contributions were the ideological justifications for them: the concepts of "public service", "public interest", and "social utility". Finally, in the revolutionary attempt of 1848, there was the concept of "social medicine", meaning the health of the people depended on the health of the wider society—including the end of economic oppression.[26] But France went through many political changes between these two landmark dates: the militarization under Napoleon, the restoration of the monarchy (1814–1830), the reign of Louis Phillipe, the "bourgeois king" (1830–1848), and then the unsuccessful workers' revolt of 1848. During this period there was some constancy in the new system, but much uncertainty in the careers of individual health workers, based on the highly political nature of appointments in schools and hospitals.

In terms of the process of class struggle, most historians conclude that the Revolution of 1789 ultimately benefitted the middle class more than it did the poor, and when a true workers' revolution was attempted, it was crushed. Marx, in *The Eighteenth Brumaire of Louis Napoleon*, gives us the reason in detail. A new force was loose in France, a new owning class with its own aims about the position of the masses. The proclamation of equality and universal social services—the dreams and the new idealistic laws—did not become reality. Instead, the oppressed peasantry of the old regime was replaced, in the industrial revolution in France, by an oppressed factory proletariat.[27]

Landmark studies on occupational, work-related diseases, such as Villerme's *Physical and Mental Condition of French Textile Workers* related the lifespan and kinds of diseases to conditions in the factories. Other studies indicated the precise correlations between poverty and disease, and also their extent. If the proclamations had stated the rise of equality, the system was still unequal, with the poor and the rural folk at the outposts in the countryside and a private, greedy, and still powerful medical profession in control of the urban hospitals. There had been no creation of a national health insurance. Revolutionary ideology had, of course, led to some marked changes and improvements in the service system, and the first clear statements of goals for the future. But in the underlying processes which produced disease, poverty had not been eliminated, the feudal conditions presided over by the barons of the land were replaced by the even more oppressive living conditions in the urban working-class ghettos and the factories of the new, rising industrial capitalist class.

HEALTH AND THE RISE OF INDUSTRIAL CAPITALISM

Two cases among many potential ones can illustrate the third major theme that will concern us in the chapters to come. The first of these is the environmental issue, seen in historical perspective; the second is the growth of the particularly American form of social insurance in health. Both are concerned with the political and ideological aspects of struggle in the wider society, aspects which have an integral relationship with the level of illness.

The Social Costs of Capitalism: A Footnote from the Lowell Mills

Villerme's studies of the cotton workers of France were a prelude to the carnage that the new capitalist industrial order would unleash

23

everywhere in the world. But the more general issue is not that of the direct consequences of factory life for health, important as they are through to the present day. Rather, the broad social transformation of the fabric of life as a consequence of the rise of industrial capitalism—the concentration of workers in the new industrial slums, the pollution of their living and working environments, and the consequent rise in rates of tuberculosis and typhoid—is the issue. Immigration brought a new industrial proletariat to America, a proletariat driven off the land in Europe after suffering from politically useful famines, such as those of the Irish. These were the workers that flooded into the great cotton mills on the Merrimac River in northern Massachusetts, the first home of America's industrial revolution, especially in the cities of Lowell, Lawrence, and Haverhill.

Here, concentrated in the "company" boardinghouses and in other high-density industrial slum areas, and drawing water from the polluted city water system (there was bottled water for the rich), they suffered in far greater proportion from illness and death in their living environment, than those in the nonindustrial towns. Sedgewick, for example, found an overall typhoid rate in Lowell in 1890–1891 five times that of Boston, and found that mill workers suffered a twenty-five percent higher rate of typhoid than others in Lowell.[28] Mill workers not only drank the polluted city water but the even more polluted canal water. Production pressures in the mills, oppressive heat from the cramped working quarters and the lack of ventilation, and a lack of real provision of clear spring water for many workers (which would have cost more money) often led to the drinking of the sewage-laden canal water that was supposed to be used only for washing and industrial cooling. Sedgewick observed:

In many, perhaps in most, of the rooms this water is delivered by faucets of the ordinary pattern, projecting, as usual, above large sinks. It is generally the most accessible and sometimes the only easily accessible, water; and this circumstance added to the fact that it is often cooler than the pail water, which has perhaps been standing for some time in a heated room, tempts the indifferent or careless to use it for drinking. I discovered one overseer who himself so much preferred canal water for drinking that he did not care to have any other water in the rooms under his care.[29]

Rosenkrantz documents the changing role of public health and the role of the Massachusetts Department of Public Health in a study that encompasses the industrial revolution in this state, or the period from 1842 to 1936. She finds a succession of generations of activists at work: moral reformers at first, then early epidemiologists, and finally medical health professionals—all battling against the industrialists and the politicians in their pocket, battling for environmental reform. But the story is also one of a *narrowing* of the scope of public health services, as the capitalist class combined increasingly with the organized medical profession to keep health services in private hands and to keep industrial health inspection out of the hands of public health reformers and activist physicians. In effect, the absence of a strong, class-conscious working-class organization in the United States led to the result it had along the river.[30]

In no small part, the lack of working-class action was due to successful, organized capitalist action in the area of pushing ideology—such as the Horatio Alger myth. A clear example comes from Thernstrom's study of Newburyport, Massachusetts (just down the river from Lowell and Lawrence) at the time. Thernstrom found the local savings banks defining each factory worker as a "capitalist" (their word) if he invested his pitiful savings in their bank, for they claimed that they as banks in turn invested it in the stock of the mills. Related bank advertising in the local newspaper pictured the factory owner and the worker walking down the street, arm in arm, over the caption, "Fellow Capitalists".[31] Repeated a thousand times a year in city after city, this combination of profit-motivated material neglect and ideological class war had its ultimate effect on both the health of the factory worker and his family and also on his ability to organize a way out of the situation.

Social Insurance, American Style

At the turn of the twentieth century, on the Continent and especially in Bismarck's Germany, the capitalist class worked with the state to create the rudiments of a social insurance system. They did so in response to organized working class action—socialist and Marxist in orientation—and created a system which for a considerable time co-opted working-class opposition. It is also fair to say that the new system created a partial *victory* for the working classes of Europe, for had they not struggled, they would have received nothing.[32] The American case provides us with just such an example, the absence of a strong organized left. Although it was increasingly becoming as industrialized as Germany, the American history of decentralized local government and action through voluntary associations was totally different in ideology from that of Germany. In fact, the ideology of "local self-government" was held by all the actors on the scene: the capitalist factory-owner class, the insurance companies, the elected officials, the public, the labor unions, and the organized medical profession. The line-up of these different groups can be briefly compared on the social insurance issue in three major periods: pre–World War I, the thirties or Depression era, and the late sixties.

In the first, pre–World War I period, academic economists, social workers, sociologists, and other intellectual leaders were the only bloc interested in a German-style national health insurance system. Samuel Gompers, a leader of American organized labor, and most of his followers fought *against* the idea (and against a Marxian or radical position for labor), for they feared that health and pension benefits offered by management would detract from union loyalty. In any case they feared that if labor cooperated with those they called "the professors", then labor would be pushed around by them. The great factory owners of the time were against most forms of health insurance, and the public felt no need for such an alien, "un-American" idea. In case they had any doubts, the rapidly growing private profit-making insurance companies cleared them up. As it became obvious that the United States would go to war with Germany, national health insurance was denounced in the mass media, by insurance company front organizations, as "a German plot to weaken America."[33]

One form of health insurace was instituted in this first era; it created a very limited form of payment for industrial injuries. But as Lubove notes, "Workmen's Compensation laws were administered on a state-by-state basis, and did not include payment for occupation-caused disease" (such as miner's black lung). Instead, the worker had to sign a pledge not to sue the company—which weakened the power of the unions—and these laws too were fought by labor. Second, the private insurance companies could in many states handle the compensation insurance, and thus make money. There were other factors which made the capitalist class support this limited insurance while rejecting and killing all other efforts:

> Employers and insurance companies anticipated advantages in sub-stituting a fixed, but limited, cost for a variable, unpredictable one. Compensation promised to relieve employers and insurance companies of much bitter litigation and mitigate public indignation over the treatment of injured workers. Workmen's compensation was thus a program designed to meet the needs of private business groups as much as those of injured workers.[34]

Finally, the organized medical profession won its first major political battle against national health insurance in this pre–World War I era, and thereby became what it had not really been before–an effective, organized political action group working primarily for doctors' economic interests, instead of a group that combined some interest in monopoly building with a genuine desire to improve standards of training.[35]

The Great Depression, and the Roosevelt era of the New Deal, brought many traditional ideas about freedom and private enterprise under re-inspection, and life chances looked a little different after this time than before. The slight change in the political ideology of the average voter, combined with a strengthening of the vested interests that were present in pre–World War I America, led to the adoption of some social legislation, the growth of voluntary, private health insurance, and the continuing defeat of a national health insurance program. The capitalist class of the nation had become convinced by the potential for radicalism inherent in the Depression, that some form of social security legislation should be passed, and that it was desired by a broad segment of the people. On the other hand, the doctors created a doctor-administered prepaid "doctor-bill" insurance (Blue Shield) and worked with hospitals to form independent, state-to-state, prepaid private hospitalization plans (Blue Cross). These plans, begun in the late thirties, grew to major size after World War II. They had a major political effect on the ability to get national health insurance legislation passed that would last until the present. The poor were not covered by these laws, but that wasn't the point:

> The popularity and effectiveness of the group hospitalization had another result: the progress of medical reform in other areas was retarded for many years. The vocally and politically powerful middle class was pacified by the partial coverage of the plans, and therefore saw no real need to support more radical measures. The reformers who were hoping for middle-class support on programs for the poor as well as for the general population, found themselves largely without allies and doomed to failure.[36]

The Second World War gave to millions of American soldiers their first experience in regular, nationalized health service, as patients in the U.S. Army medical system. In addition, the years after the war saw the size and power of the labor movement growing, as the AFL-CIO increasingly involved itself in prohealth as well as prolabor legislation. The AMA, in the late forties and fifties, put on an increasingly strident campaign to "protect the doctor-patient relationship" and spent millions of dollars trying to fight the passage of new health insurance legislation. They continued to win, but their margin of victory grew smaller and smaller.[37]

Finally, in the sixties, a new political element, in addition to the growing coalition between labor and liberal academic planners, was the citizen activism of older people. The laws in preparation tended with each year to be directed more and more at health insurance for the elderly. The mechanism for paying—the Social Security system—was by now widely accepted by the nation. By the time of the Johnson administration, the political pressure by organized citizen groups, especially of the elderly themselves, was so strong that the politicians could no longer publicly oppose it. Wilbur Mills, who wrote Public Law 89-87 (Medicare) after years of opposing it, was instrumental in manipulating it through Congress. As a consequence, the new alliance of citizen, politician, and academic defeated temporarily the organized medical profession and the insurance industry.[38]

But this story is not without a sequel. After passage, the medical profession managed to utilize the provisions of the act, especially the Medicaid section, in such a way that their income rose instead of falling. Furthermore, costs rose so quickly in comparison to benefits that what was perceived as "revolutionary" when first proposed in the thirties, was, only a few years after passage, inadequate for the middle class and helped perpetuate a two-class medical system that grossly undertreated the poor. Two things happened as a consequence, however, and they probably now overshadow the precise degree of profit or loss, adequacy or inadequacy. At one stroke, federal and state governments became deeply involved in the financing, administration, and regulation of medical care, for the nonprofitable sector of the ill—the chronic, the old, and the poor. At the same time, working in tandem with them unofficially, finance capital—in the form of the large profit-making insurance companies—began to move heavily into health insurance: insurance of the well, the middle class, and thus the profitable. By the mid-seventies they controlled more than sixty percent of the health insurance premium dollar.[39] The modern welfare state, in the field of health, had thus been born in America.

PART ONE

People in Places: The Servers and the Served

1

Control over Work

Control over work has been a political issue since the dawn of time, for such control is effectively a power relationship over an experience that is central to life. In the capitalist era, ownership of the new technology of production encouraged capitalists to organize workers for maximum productivity, splitting up the work tasks to simplify the operations of each worker, all toward the end of greater productivity and thus higher profit. Braverman points out that the socialist world has borrowed the industrial model from the capitalist world, along with its inherent pathologies. If the surplus wealth created by pushing workers in these noncapitalist countries may ultimately revert back to the society at large, things are still pretty bad on the assembly line. This industrial model has been borrowed by modern medicine in both capitalist and socialist nations, and the increase in technology has led to a proliferation of new occupational groups to manage it. Furthermore, the industrial model is increasingly being touted as the future model for medical care.

Yet Marx was not a technological determinist; he never said that technology automatically brought new groups into power and control. Rather, a change in the mode of organizing work afforded opportunities for the rise of a new class. The physician group—the controllers of the old craft technology—have for many years been fighting to maintain their control of a new, more industrial technology, much as the landed gentry in Europe at the dawn of the industrial era tried to gain control of the new technology and the new sources of power enjoyed by the first generation of industrial capitalists who owned and controlled it. We cannot say who will win the struggle in the long run, but at present the physician group—hanging on to a craft model—is also trying to maintain control over a growing field of occupations; as their technology proliferates, so do new jobs and new occupational interests. The physicians are still on top of the pile, but their grip is weakening, as we might expect from the lessons of history.

We can begin the strategies used by the physician group to maintain control over the health care setting, then broaden our perspective to look at the overall structure of the division of labor in health care. Sources of change in the division of labor can be understood by observing the actions of one occupational group (nurses) that has for decades been working toward this end. New functional roles—those of the auxiliaries—can thus be observed against the background we have illuminated. Ideologies which defend the existing structures—and thus their present pattern of ownership and control—will be inspected at the conclusion. For in the world of ideas, as proposed by the struggling groups, eventually the legitimacy of the present division of labor stands or falls.

DIMENSIONS OF DOMINATION

The history of the physician group is perhaps one of the clearest examples of the politics of skill. In Freidson's terms, the physicians' "professional dominance" over their professional organizations,

34

over the division of labor in health, and over the very organizations that are supposed to regulate and police the group in the interests of the community, is a special type of political situation.[21] The key variable is power gained through possession of the medical skill. The power is legitimated—made official—through licensing laws which prohibit others from practicing medicine:

> The foundation of medicine's control over its work is thus clearly political in nature, involving the aid of the state in establishing and maintaining the profession's preeminence. The occupation itself has formal representatives, organizational or individual, which attempt to direct the efforts of the state toward policies desired by the occupational group.[3]

The medical profession has thus far been largely successful in just such control of state policy. But state "protection" of any occupation means ultimately that the sovereign state is in a position to take away what it has given, if those in control of the state want that group's monopoly taken away and are in a position to do so; in a democracy, this power is supposed to reside in the people. In Jacksonian America, though much power was already in the hands of an elite, the power of the people did go far enough to force the delicensing of the medical profession.

The mandate of an occupation is given, in liberal legal theory, by the people, but this gift depends on the perpetuation of a social relationship that relates to the reason why the trust was originally given.[4] In the words of a supreme court judge who found the AMA guilty of working against people's interests in barring certain doctors from membership in their local groups:

> Professions exist because people believe that they will be better served by licensing specially prepared experts to minister to their needs. The licensed monopolies which professions enjoy constitute in themselves severe restraints upon competition. But they are restraints which depend upon capacity and training, not privilege. Neither do they

35

justify concerted action to prevent people from developing new methods of servicing their needs. The people give the privilege of professional monopoly, and the people may take it away.[5]

One way of understanding how the politics of skill have operated in the field of health occupations—in the division of labor—is to consider the past and what pressures are pushing to preserve this past as well as to bring about change. We can do this for the definition of "profession" itself, the meaning and uses of "expertise", the control by the physician of the work setting and over the division of labor itself.[6] A specific case—that of the nursing occupation—will illustrate the strategies. Different relations of other groups to the physician group can then be seen dynamically in terms of how the power balance among the groups in the system would need to be changed to significantly change the present picture.

First, there is the issue of the occupational ideology inherent in the term "profession" itself. What citizens believe the medical profession to be determines how they act in accordance with this belief. For many years social scientists agreed with the general public that a profession, especially the medical profession, was characterized by long training, special skills (expertise), and a code of ethics which was public spirited and unselfish. Such definitions as these meant that a "professional" could be expected to be, *by definition*, well trained, skillful, and public spirited. In the case of medicine, the scientific revolution and organized self-policing efforts increasingly gave some credence to the skill issue, especially by the first half of this century. But as the general educational level rose and the self-interested political action of the AMA increased, the general public began to understand that the term "professional" had an ideological component. Today, a majority of citizens still believe that the medical profession is relatively high in status compared to most occupations, and that it is still a "profession" in the old sense: a calling carried on by morally superior individuals. On the other hand, to the extent that they do *not* think this (the fight by the AMA to kill Medicare helped to change many minds) the Emperor has no clothes and doctors become just another greedy, power-hungry special interest group whom citizens may legitimately and morally fight against, without guilt.

Second, dominance over the health field involves the issue of expertise. Special skill and knowledge certainly exist in the case of the physician. Many complex technical decisions regarding treatment ultimately demand skills and knowledge presently possessed only by this occupational group. Yet this expertise is primarily technical skill and scientific information, for to the extent that the skill is "clinical" (being good at relating to human beings) or "organizational" (being a good administrator of a hospital or a community health project), it ceases being specific to the physician as people have traditionally defined this role. Others, such as housewives, may be better at relating to people, and economists and sociologists may be better at health service planning. Freidson points out that the special expertise of the physician over narrowly technical problems preserves for him a "free zone of operation" even in totalitarian states. His control over the narrow technical details of work is due to the specific technical expertise which put him in a position to do more faster and better for sick people than anyone else in the society.[7]

What *does* vary by political regime is the degree of control over the delivery of services and the economic aspects of the system. In socialist states these are decided, in broad outline, by the government. On the other hand, in socialist states, or in western nations with socialized health care systems, bureaucrats in control of the health sector are usually physicians with a professional loyalty stronger than their bureaucratic one. The budget officer, who may determine whether a new program desired by physicians will operate or how many patients they will have to see per work day, definitely influences the way that medicine is practiced. In turn, the size of the budget is determined by the ruling political party in control of the state apparatus, acting "in the name of all". In a capitalist state with no welfare-state sector, by contrast, the size of the budget, and whether given programs grow or shrink, is often determined through pressuring lawmaking processes (as private insurance companies lobby to be included in a national health insurance program) or by bureaucratic infighting (pushing HEW bureaucrats to "go slow" in setting up a new program, even after it has become law, as the AMA has done with new programs to regulate the practice of medicine).

Although some increase in state power is observable in America in recent years, it still is minor when compared to that found in socialist countries. The American physician still has a great deal of control over work, with the area defined as "doctors' business" often very wide indeed. Control of the wider situation is essential, especially for the older way of practicing medicine: the style of entrepreneurial relations with clients and colleagues, in a fee-for-service system. The public, in any case, cannot judge expertise, for as Peterson has shown, technically incompetent GPs may have just as many patients as do competent ones.[8] And the absence of expertise is concealed by one's colleagues' refusal to "rat". For example, in 1969 the Director of the American College of Surgeons estimated that "one-half of the surgical operations in the U.S. are performed by doctors who are untrained or inadequately trained to perform surgery".[9]

Studies of the actual technical skill of physicians, although few in number because of physician opposition, indicate a widely varying range of competence, including a certain number (at least five–ten percent) whose performance might be considered actively dangerous to patient health.[10] The basically political nature of the definition of expertise, like the public's belief in the unselfish motives of physicians, means that so long as that expertise remains unevaluated by citizens or their hired representatives, it will remain a weapon in the hands of the physician alone, as well as remaining a mystery. But since the state agencies that are supposed to act as watchdogs seldom do so, physicians have practiced unevaluated for generations now.

But factors at work in the immediate present may change this situation. As physicians become involved in more complex ways of delivering services, and financing schemes grow more to involve government, so government and other groups may be in a better position to evaluate the nature of what is being contracted and financed. As this occurs, it may begin to reeducate the public regarding the narrowed scope of expertise to be expected of physicians. If people's expectations are successfully narrowed, this would further limit the physicians' power. In addition, the percentage of physicians in employee status is increasing, so that whatever their salary level and regardless whether they work for a consumer-owned health plan or a government agency, the direct ownership of the "means of medical production" will be less in the hands of physicians. Here especially the skill will be more closely evaluated.

Defensive actions—aimed at resisting these trends or at trying to work with them—have been initiated. For example, medical schools are beefing up their social science and health-planning curriculums, precisely to insure the entry of a new group of MD economists and MD health planners with widened expertise into the physician ranks, to head off attempts at limiting their mandate by other professional groups. Efforts are also being made by the profession to staff the decision-making points within the state where action will be taken affecting their future role as an occupational group.

In general, however, the ownership and control of the setting is the most important factor considered. Changes in the other area can be resisted successfully to the degree that physicians own the place in which they work. Take that away, and their ability to extend their expertise into an ideology controlling more of the society than just direct care will quickly diminish.

A third dimension of physician domination concerns the normal social processes present in all work: training settings, office practice, hospitals, community programs. Domination is perpetuated through the two processes of *insulation from observability* and of *political action to combat legislation which would change the present degree of insulation*.

Insulation from being observed while at work, as Coser noted, is a powerful social fact which allows behavior that others—the general public in this case—would not condone if they knew of its existence.[11] Formal associations protect the physician from observation (thus evaluation and possible sanction) through both their structure and their deliberate nonfunctioning as self-regulatory agencies. And as Freidson has demonstrated, physician groups function informally to combat any popular request—or legal requirement—for a greater evaluative role by citizens or qualified "outsiders".[12]

The decentralized structure of the medical profession means that local groups of doctors (in the local medical societies which are the building blocks of the association) confront each other in matters involving malpractice or complaints. Each local society is supposed to have a grievance committee whose job is to take disciplinary action against their fellow physicians. Yet in 1969, in the entire nation, thirty-two states took no action at all, fifteen physicians were expelled from their societies, and fourteen had their memberships temporarily suspended.[13] In general, the penalty of expulsion from the local medical society has been used more for political reasons, such as disapproval of those going into group practice plans, than for simple incompetence. As Freidson and Rhea pointed out, in a "company of equals", peers are usually unwilling to discipline each other, especially when in some cases they depend on these others to refer new patients to them in the future.[14]

As we have noted, the state is increasingly involving itself in evaluating the nature of health care delivered by physicians, for it is increasingly paying a greater share of the costs. In New York City, the Medicaid evaluation staff of the New York City Health Department evaluates the services provided its clients by physicians. If they are not up to par, in the words of the Director, "No quality, no money."[15] A recent congressional panel investigated this issue of inadequate and unnecessary medical treatment, on a national basis;[16] they found that millions of dollars were being paid out by patients for unneeded operations.

On the other hand, as we have implied, regulatory attempts can be resisted politically by the target group, and evaded or modified so that they do not present a real threat. The AMA has successfully been able to cut out strong regulatory legislation when it is attached to some health insurance bill, and have instead substituted the idea of "peer review" (a group of doctors reviewing other doctors' work) when the patients are paid for with public money. While not quite as much a private club as the local medical society or the state licensing board, the procedure is focused more on the saving of money than on the quality of care, and is not a disciplinary activity which prevents the incompetent practice of medicine.[17]

To sum up, physicians dominate much of the division of labor and certainly the conditions of their own work, and have been reasonably successful in recent years in resisting state attempts to tighten quality control and further discipline the poor performer. But physicians represent only one of a growing family of health occupations. The rapidly growing numbers of nonphysician workers and their wider distribution within the work setting is causing many pressures for change in the traditionally simple hierarchy of physician dominance over all the others. It is to this larger picture that we now turn.

THE DIVISION OF LABOR
EXISTING PATTERNS

Since the time of Egypt there has been a division of labor in health work. In most eras our historical review found that major subdivisions existed among different types of practitioners, but that a hierarchy with one type of physician at the top also existed. The increase in their power to dominate other occupations, physician and nonphysician, came primarily as a consequence of the hospital revolution. Of course, the workshop they created may be gaining more and more independent power and now may be even beginning to turn on the physicians themselves, as we will see below.

At present, health workers are in a form of broad-based occupational hierarchy dominated by physicians, almost completely lacking "upward mobility". (Orderlies cannot become nurses in the setting, nor nurses physicians.) The increase in numbers of auxiliary occupational groups (less than one in ten health workers is a physician if blue-collar workers are not considered; with them included the physician is seen as a small minority) puts pressure on the group to stay on top of a growing mountain. But a combination of real technical expertise, legal requirements for the licensing of health personnel, rules in law concerning the administration of service settings, and the overall societal class system with its built-in tracking, has perpetuated a significant degree of physician dominance over the hospital, and over other settings in which health care is delivered. Since most medical practice is hospital based, and many hospitals are controlled by conservative physicians, the simple increase in numbers does not automatically mean a change in the power structure.

To begin with, health manpower at all levels originates in the overall societal class tracking system of public education. A steady supply of untrained, unskilled blacks and women fill most of the lower posts in this hierarchy, while upper middle class males have the majority of chances for the physician's career. Females are often pushed in the direction of nursing training; there is also some evidence that school recruiters pitch talks about nursing to black females, in predominantly black high schools, primarily in terms of practical nursing, while the same individuals travel to the white suburban high schools and talk about careers leading to an R.N. within a college program. In overall outline, therefore, the social class distinctions of the wider society are reproduced in the way different social groups—by sex, race, and social class—are tracked into the division of labor in health work.

42

The growth of the present hierarchy and the present division of labor have led to the development of five types of health-worker groups, arranged in terms of their relations with the physician group, and of their relations in terms of owner and employee status with respect to the place at which health care is delivered. Four groups relate to physicians in a direct manner: *direct competitors* (osteopathic and chiropractic physicians); *independent nonphysician specialists* (dentists, podiatrists, opticians); *subservient groups* (nurses of all types, most hospital personnel); and *deviant practitioners* (quacks, imposters). A final group—*nonmedical administrators*—are not, in the narrow sense, practicing health workers, but in the broader sense they are, since they relate to the function of the *settings* in which health work is carried out, and constitute a group with rising power relative to physicians, whether or not a physician is the actual occupant of the hospital manager role.

In power terms, the relationship between the physician group and each of these other groups needs to be understood in licensure terms (who has the legal responsibility for whose work); in everyday power terms (including attempts to change present power relations); in terms of recruitment pathways, as these relate to the group's ability to further their position in the hierarchy; and most important of all, in terms of ownership and control of the means of health service production.

Direct competitors to the physician can be considered to be groups that at the present time operate as fully independent generalized health service practitioners with their own licensing boards and at least a medium degree of status in the general communities in which they practice. Osteopathic and chiropractic physicians, less than twenty years ago in the position of marginal professionals, have moved up to the point where both groups have their own licensing boards in the majority of states, and increasingly provide a full range of diagnostic and therapeutic services. Although the orthodox medical profession does not admit them to full membership in most of

43

their societies, osteopathic and chiropractic medical schools and hospitals exist throughout the nation. Of the two, osteopathy moved very close to orthodox medicine, especially in the past decade, while chiropractic remains more set apart in terms of interoccupational politics.

Osteopathic medical students often have more hours of instruction in basic medical sciences than medical students, but the AMA still questions the use of the "special theory" that pertains to what is now only a small part of their curriculum.[19] For students, osteopathic schools are often a second choice, since the majority also appear to have applied to medical school. But the same does not appear to be the case with chiropractic physicians; rather, family influence and previous experience seem to play a stronger role.[20] Community acceptance is wide and growing; in both osteopathy and chiropractic, a mandate exists in the community to match the official license to practice. For example, in the mid-sixties, during the average year more than four million people were seen at least once by a chiropractor; even larger populations are seen regularly by the osteopath. Perhaps part of their success is the great stress placed in training on the importance of the service relationship itself. Studies in both professional groups indicate that great stress is placed on the nature of the relationship between server and served. Skills in this area are not considered as important in the training of the orthodox physician, though some lip service and a short course in psychiatry are usually part of liberal medical school curriculums at present.

These two thriving branches of medical practice, whether or not they are accepted by the medical profession, are groups with their own hospitals and clinics, and are critically important in filling some of the gaps in community care. The shortage of physicians in medium-sized and small towns and in rural areas, for example, has left the field wide open to these two groups. Finally, in some regions of the nation, especially parts of rural New England, the Middle West, and California, *they* and not the physicians constitute the top group, occupying the politically dominant "physician" role in local community politics and in the health service organization. Inside these settings, they order around the nurses and technicians precisely as do physicians in other towns.

Independent nonphysician specialists are a second major group in the health occupational structure. Usually, as in the case of direct competitors to physicians, they own and operate their own offices and control their own licensing boards. Two things characterize these groups: first, they limit their function either to an area of the body (dentist, podiatrist) or to a kind of technological expertise auxiliary to medical practice (optometrist, pharmacist); second, to the extent that they do practice outside of a hospital setting, they are independent of formal *control* by the medical profession though both are limited by law as to the *area* of practice. (Dentists may not treat other parts of the body, pharmacists may not prescribe drugs.) Almost all except dentists are informally though not legally dependent on physicians for referral business (legally in the case of the pharmacist). Some are subservient on the physician's turf and more independent elsewhere. For example, social workers or clinical psychologists in hospital settings are under physician supervision, yet both groups can and do practice in the community.

The line between medical and nonmedical is especially important to recognize in grasping the power relations within the division of labor in mental health areas. Here the expertise itself is not necessarily medical, if it exists at all. Therefore the division between "competitor" and "auxiliary" is far more ill defined, with the affected group campaigning in state after state, in legislatures, for independent licensing boards not packed with psychiatrists. Freud, for example, did not recommend a medical degree for psychoanalysts, and gave reasons against it. But in this country, physicians achieved a legal monopoly and proceeded to expel even European-trained lay analysts from their societies.[21] Only in the recent past has this trend been reversed.

In the *subservient* group—that term is chosen because it cuts through the rhetoric about "independence" and gets to the actual power relations between physicians and those in the group—are most of the remaining health occupations. This group most definitely includes workers who have been fighting for years to get out of it, such as nurses; all the medical-technological occupations, such as the various forms of laboratory workers, x-ray technicians; and also the occupations that are subservient to high-status non-physician practitioners (such as dental hygienists to dentists). The primary characteristic of these occupations in economic terms is, they neither own nor control the means of health service production in the places they work. They are, furthermore, almost always within an employee status, directly under physician supervision or under the supervision of physician influenced settings such as hospitals. In most of these occupations (with the primary exception of nurses) the state occupational licensing board is primarily made up of the supervising group (pathologists on the lab technician board, dentists on the dental hygiene boards) or there is a general state licensing board, with a physician majority and only a few representatives from the affected occupation. On the work setting—and this most definitely includes nurses—their autonomy even when they have some administrative responsibility is only relative. Legally the physician or the service organization is responsible for their actions, in the majority of cases.

Another major characteristic of the subservient groups that characterizes only them and not the direct competitor-colleagues or even the independent limited-practice types, is their official inability to diagnose and prescribe. Note that the *official* (or legal) and the *real* may not be identical. A lot of things happen that aren't supposed to, and sometimes authorities neither know nor care about such details; but in the main, the rule holds. Since diagnosis and prescription of a course of curing action is the reason for the "chain of command" ("I decide, you carry it out"), they may treat under orders but they may not start the treatment without getting orders or getting their opinions approved. New programs which attempt to give greater independence to the higher-status groups within the subservient category—especially things such as community nurse practitioner programs—soon run up against the legal limitations built into the licensing laws, written by physicians or approved by them before passage in state legislatures.

Finally, the subgroup of *deviant practitioners* includes all those who possess neither state-licensed status nor state designated licensing associations, and who do not constitute an integrated element in the network of physicians, physician-competitors, independent limited practitioners, and subservient groups. Faith healers, nostrum vendors, and imposters of members of the other categories are in this category. It is important to note that they all have clientele—sick people do come to them for help. Some of these could not wait in long lines for standard practitioners, or may have incurable illnesses and seek a miracle cure from the ones who will promise anything; some simply want a relationship which can be a base for discussing fears. Here such people as faith healers and Christian Science practitioners may serve a real function. "Imposters", ironically enough, may be better at this personal service activity than "the real thing". For example, Derbyshire documents many cases in which exposed imposters in general medical practice keep their clientele after they have been exposed. They are often found to have been very careful at treating limited illness with limited remedies and also have quite responsibly referred all difficult cases to specialists. This is, of course, a comment on the medical profession in the locales of the successful imposters, as well as on the importance of interpersonal relationships to the ill, when compared with more narrow technical expertise in medical science.

There is one final issue which suggests that even the above categories of practitioners are, in a practical sense, quite artificial. Who actually does what, as against who theoretically or conceptually performs a task in health work, seldom has been studied closely. When it has been, we have seen that overlap in work tasks, especially between the "dominant" and "subservient" categories, is extensive. Politics, in other words, deals in this area with *right* and *legal fiction* as well as with activity per se; nursing, as we noted, is the primary example here. But with that legal right lies the power and leverage of the law, especially the right to persecute and prosecute the nonphysician groups for invasion of territory.

STRUGGLE AGAINST THE HIERARCHY:
THE CASE OF NURSING

Trends which change the position of an occupation from one of the above categories to another depend on a combination of technological and political factors. To gain official, "protected" status through licensure is a political process in the direct sense. Technological change may provide new opportunities to gain independence, as when things get so complex that a physician can no longer follow them, or when a new kind of machine is developed and a new occupation born to run it. But for all the changes in and attempts at changing the power position of a health occupation group, there is a reaction from the group on top. As with Newton's third law of motion, for every action by an occupational group to gain greater power and control over their health work, there is a reaction from the group—the physicians in most cases—that is presently in control of that work. Rather than listing a long series of complex struggles, the writer believes it is more relevant to deal with the most important struggle of this kind, in terms of the implications for flexibility and change in our present service system. This is the struggle of the nursing profession for greater control over their own work.

The Past as Precedent and Burden:
Origins of Subservience

Since the Middle Ages nursing orders of nuns provided the primary bedside care in the hospital systems of Europe. This care, not scientific but personal in nature, was concerned with day-to-day

48

ministration to the needs of the poor. But unlike the medical profession, nursing did not emancipate itself from the Church at the time of the Renaissance; nor has the group emancipated itself from physicians since that time. The reasons provide us with our most important example of physician dominance, and the strategies used by groups to stay on top of the health worker hierarchy.

Florence Nightingale's original definition of the modern professional nursing role clearly made the nurse subordinate to the physician:

> Nightingale . . . refused to allow any of her nurses to undertake to give any service at all on their own initiative. Her nurses' services were to be granted only when specifically requested by the doctors. No nurse could give food to any patient without the doctors' written order. No nurse could soothe or clean a patient without the doctor's order. Nuns were forbidden to engage in religious visiting. Nightingale thus required that what the nurse did for the patient was a function of what the doctor felt was required for the care of the patient. . . . *Nursing was thus defined as a subordinate part of the technical division of labor surrounding medicine.*[22]

Ever since the founding of modern nursing on the Nightingale model, this definition of the central tasks as subservient to the physician, in a direct chain of command, has been the rock on which the ship of "professional autonomy" has foundered. The autonomy conflict in nursing is important because it is a key test case for the ability of hospital-based, medical-technology-related occupations in the health field to gain independent power and control over their work, with respect to the medical profession. Nursing is also numerically one of the largest of the occupations in the health field. By looking at the training process and the strategies used to gain a more independent role, we can illuminate the problem of all the health occupations which are—in one way or another—subservient to the physician.

Training settings are of two major types: hospital or diploma

49

schools, where nurses learn in on-the-job apprentice roles combined with some class work; and academic programs—two- to three-year junior college programs (Associate in Nursing) and full academic college programs (B.A. in Nursing). In the past, the hospital schools were the major training setting, and they remain so everywhere but in the United States. The "academic elite" in the nursing profession, through their primary accrediting agency, the National League for Nursing (NLN), have pressured to eliminate the hospital schools, charging that they exploit nursing students while not providing truly "professional" (i.e., university-based) education. The trend, as a consequence of this pressure group, is away from hospital-based nursing, for the NLN has consistently discouraged the creation of new programs in hospitals.

The aim toward independence from the hospital as a training setting has brought ironic developments. Since far less actual hospital experience is part of the training of academic nurses, they arrive at the hospital for their first job with two strikes against them. First, they are resented by hospital-trained nurses who in fact have better concrete experience through less "nursing theory". Second, since the college nursing schools have to justify the extra years of training—and the stress on social science and management skills given in academic programs—these nurses are sometimes placed in positions of authority over the hospital-trained nurses of a nursing service. The ultimate irony has been the development of "nursing internships"—post-B.A. internships for college-trained nurses to introduce the new graduate to the realities of working in the hospital.[23] In general, the trend away from the hospital as a base of education—regardless of the obvious social dysfunctions for patient care—appears to be motivated primarily by a desire to control the turf on which the training takes place. As with many aspiring occupational groups in the health field, a university base for training programs is preferred to any health-service setting, for on each actual service setting the physician is likely to be in fuller control of the training process and the ends to which it is put.

A further difference in status is found in the tracking system which places some students in nurses' training and others in training for positions below this. In nursing, this tracking process mirrors the educational tracking process of the wider society; it is, of course, a part of that process. Since the new nursing programs are junior college or college based, students from middle- and working-class backgrounds are the only ones who can afford the education. Poor white and most black females either go to work as nurses' aides, with some type of in-hospital in-service training, or aim for the few remaining hospital schools, since tuition is less than in the university programs. In miniature, this process parallels that seen in those who do and do not apply and get into medical school.

Much is made in university programs of the new "administrative" or supervisory role of the hospital nurse. Yet the training process for nurses seems relevant, even today, when it trains for subservience and obedience, irrelevant when it suggests that they are being prepared for situations of real power and responsibility in the health care setting: responsibility without power, perhaps. Nursing at this time does not have significant control over the occupation at work—the personal fate and everyday work experience of the people it trains at the university. If the beginnings of nursing specialization are allowing a few college-trained nurses into ward manager or technical roles (e.g., recovery-room nurse), the schools of nursing still have no power or control over the settings to which they send their graduates. Strauss makes the point that academic nursing schools would need to control the nursing service in a hospital the way doctors in a medical school control a service in the same hospital, if it is a "teaching hospital" for the medical school.[24] But this appears to be a vain hope; for example, at Duke University there was recently an attempt to relate college nurses' training to official roles in ward management. But this plan was not put into effect because of opposition from the doctors and the hospital administrators.[25]

Strategies to Gain Autonomy—and Their Fate

Strategies to gain greater autonomy succeed or fail on the basis of relative power and control over the social field in which the attempt is made. Nurses have tried a series of "gambits", each of which has failed to date. As a consequence they may be turning to a form of action more akin to classic union organizing than to the "professionalizing" of the unsuccessful attempts. Briefly, six strategies have been attempted: the shift to university training; the takeover of physicians' dirty work; the "managerial" ideology; the "outside mover" approach; the "seize-the-technology" strategy; and unionization for greater control over work as well as for higher wage levels. These actions have not been able to free the nursing occupation from dominance by physicians or hospitals. But from their failure, certain lesson can be learned about the limits of change with respect to other groups within the present division of labor.

Basing the occupational training of a group in a university setting is a primary strategy for attempting upward occupational mobility. This is especially true since the academic revolution transformed the universities into just such professional training centers. The status of the university is considered necessary for increasing the status of the occupation trained there. With nursing, however, it is critical to note that the work performed by nurses is not independent, except for the roles of the nursing professions themselves. In general, the only way out of the dilemma would be to gain control of independent health settings, in the same way medical schools have training "services" at local hospitals. This strategy also involves changing laws defining all medical practice as performable only under the supervision of physicians.

Second, a "take-the-dirty-work" strategy has been in effect as a way of gaining authority on the work setting. Manpower shortages have led to nurses taking over many routine medical procedures (intravenous injections, blood pressure measurement, etc.), and in turn nurses passed "their" dirty work on down the line to LPNs and aides. But both the takeover and the pass-down accentuate the validity of the overall structure of the division of labor and the technological hierarchy of occupations in which nursing is not in an autonomous position. Furthermore, if nurses should begin to develop a specialty which is attractive to those above them, as they did at one time with anesthesiology, it can be taken away from above especially if economic gains are visible on the horizon. For example, as anethesiology became more complex what had primarily been a nurse's job became more interesting in profit terms to physicians. A group of them mounted a campaign to "physicianize" the occupation by driving nurses out of it. The pioneer in this activity was Dr. Frank McMechan. He organized physician anesthetist societies and edited journals for physicians in the field, and he also traveled the circuit:

> The room would be darkened immediately before his entrance, and then a spotlight would follow McMechan's figure in the wheelchair as it was slowly rolled to the center of the stage. In a voice resonant with emotion, he would begin his talk. He denounced those who treated anesthesia as a casual incident in the surgical sequence, and declared that human lives should not be placed in the hands of those who had not been trained as physicians.[26]

In rural areas, and in other areas where physician anesthetists are scarce, the nurse still plies her trade. But in all academic medical centers at present, the physician anesthetist with a nurse assistant runs the show. The issue here is a general one: the physician can claim expertise over any and all activities in the health care field, and if the setting is one over which he has actual control, that is that. Attempts to develop "specialist expertise" upon a physician's turf lead to the eventual limitation of the occupation by the group at the top of the technological hierarchy.

A third strategy—used by other groups besides nurses but especially by them—can be called the creation of a "managerial ideology": "Our occupation does not simply do X and Y in a health setting, we *manage* the setting in which X and Y are done". Both hospital administrators and physicians have an easy answer to *this* strategy on the part of any one of the subservient technological occupations: we (the hospital and the physician) are legally responsible for the patient-care process, and therefore we will give the orders. Delegating responsibility temporarily and informally to a group with no legal responsibility for their activities is not the same as seizing and holding responsibility. Since most health settings are bureaucracies, they are hierarchial in structure. Since the prime technological occupation at the top is that of the physician, the combination of legal justification for the structure and power position within it are natural limits on the "management power" strategy of nursing.

Fourth is the "outside mover" strategy—one which in the past has worked for a series of health occupations: chiropractors and osteopathic physicians, podiatrists, dentists, and others. In nursing, there was in the early 1900s a hope that public health nursing and visiting nursing, two groups of nurses engaging in a form of "community practice", would be an avenue for greater occupational autonomy, through practice on a turf not belonging to the physician. But the hospital increasingly became the center for employment, and the physician dominated the hospital. In addition, there was a critical difference between the technology of nursing and that of most independent community practitioners. These practitioners either do general medicine (osteopathic and chiropractic) or they practice on a specific part of the body. The nursing function does not involve diagnosis or prescription, but rather "curing under orders". Legally, even new programs in which a team of nurses work with a pediatrician in community practice require the pediatrician to be legally responsible for the mistakes of the nurses. The definition of the nursing role, built into law, guarantees their ultimate subservience to the physician. Yet attempts to change the law confront the community's frequent support of the status quo and the hierarchy, or

54

cooperation with the medical profession in fighting any major changes in the licensing laws.

Fifth, a "seize-the-technology" strategy has been attempted by nurses and other subservient occupational groups. The idea here is to become an expert in a particular kind of hospital setting (e.g., an emergency room, an intensive care unit, respiratory therapy machines). Often the demands of technology change, and mesh with the aspirations of occupations in the new labor intensive (operator-requiring) technology of modern medicine. Leverage for higher salary exists here in specific settings, once a place becomes dependent on their small cadre of machine and room operators. University training programs, once set up, are then often limited—a form of professional birth control—to make sure the supply of new "experts" does not outrun the demand. Yet there are ultimate limits here: state intervention in health manpower training porgrams could ultimately control the number of specialists so produced, while the fact that the *technology* is almost always owned by the hospital means the workers remain in the employee class rather than the owner class. Physicians, it should be noted, are the only group that can both own and use such technology for profit in the community, such as doctors who privately own a kidney dialysis machine. These avenues to independency and profit through the ownership of technology are usually blocked to others by the passage of laws which prohibit the use of the machine by anyone except as they are "under the supervision of a licensed physician"—similar to the laws on their practice of health care in general. The new technology can bring new occupations with it, but in itself does not constitute a force for change in the power structure within health occupations.

Finally, there is the approach of unionization, for the dual goals of greater bargaining power for wages vis-a-vis employers and greater power to control the direct conditions of work. We will consider unionization of the health worker in the next chapter. But here we will need to observe that a primary limitation on independence, if this is conceived as a goal even in the narrow sense of control over work tasks, is the limitation of the collective bargaining process itself. What is required is a willingness to bargain with an employer in a situation where increased freedom rather than increased wages is requested, and increased wages often become a bribe used by the employer to get the group's mind off the more threatening issues of freedom to control one's own work. The problem lies in the rank-and-file nurses, who will often prefer the raise to the freedom, against the wishes and warnings of the "advanced guard" of their profession.

To sum up, the case of nursing illustrates a problem common to all groups that are legally defined as workers subservient to and under the supervision of physicians. Strategies to gain independence fall up against the barriers created by the existing licensing system, the power structure, the need for partial control by technical "generalists", and the unwillingness of the community to change the laws or otherwise support, in the long run, the efforts of the subservient group to get out from under. Yet, as witness the osteopaths, the chiropractors, the dentists, and the deviant practitioners, it can be done. Perhaps these examples spur on those workers who feel that the supervision is unwarranted and used more for exploitation than for advancing health care; and the public may someday change its mind, and vote new laws into being.

PARAPROFESSIONALS, ASSISTANTS, ASSOCIATES: PROMISE VERSUS REALITY

At present there is a crisis in health manpower supply that is being handled in a way that may be perpetuating the problem as much as it is bringing about change. The use of new "paraprofessionals" and "associates" in health care is an important example of how a real need—that of better distribution of manpower in health services— can be translated into a method for increasing profit by the employers of the new assistants and associates. This is a deflection of the original idealistic aims, one which advances the interests of two medical elites (the academic and the practitioner) without necessarily solving the original problem. They are an example of a "cosmetic solution" to a far deeper problem—one that is ultimately political both in its present arrangement and in terms of its eventual solution.

The analysis of the "new-wave" health-training programs needs to begin with the contrast between de facto "handoffs" of jobs in health care from one group to another, such as doctors giving certain routine tasks to registered nurses and licensed practical nurses, who in turn pass their dirty work off to aides, and specific new programs which deliberately create new roles and attempt to legitimate new occupational categories in the health field as an attempt to solve manpower problems.

The last twenty years have seen everyday adjustments, at first in hospitals but then in doctors' offices, where many physicians increasingly allowed nurses to take over family medicine functions. The "hand-me-down" process occurs in times of manpower shortage because of the functional problem of health settings; an activity has to be done, there are no "Xs" around to do it (no money to hire them, or the hospital is understaffed), so either a "Y" will have to do the medical procedure or it won't get done at all. Since the "Y" group is lower on the hierarchy, it welcomes the new task as a promotion in responsibility, and eventually the actual boundaries of "who does what" begin to change. This is slow, evolutionary occupational culture change that can now be contrasted with a new form of deliberate intervention in the occupational hierarchy that usually occurs in sequence: public perception of a health problem, pressure on politicians; appointment of a joint government-academic elite commission; report of the commission with recommendations for legislation; the passage of legislation which creates a new job title or a new type of career training strategy; the basing of the new program in a government agency (e.g., "New Careers", "Nurse Associate",

"Physician Assistant"); and then grants to the universities, especially to the schools whose professors were active in the original commission. This latter process does several things for certain and one thing with far less certainty: it convinces the public, through heavy mass-media coverage, that something is being done, relieving the pressure both on politicians and the service professionals; it also definitely results in new money for innovative, "exciting" training projects for academic elite members in universities and medical schools. Whether this chain of activity significantly alters the structure of the situation which is causing the problem in the first place, and thus helps the consumer of health services, is something we will need to inspect.

Auxiliary Professionals: Levels of Skill

To begin with, formal *physician assistant* roles are not new, even in modern times: they are at least as old as the "feldsher" dating from late Czarist and early revolutionary Russia, and still present in today's Soviet Union. Feldshers are given two and one-half to three and one-half years of basic medical training, depending on degree of previous education and experience. They function in the city as physician assistants, and in the countryside as "front-line" physicians, handling most everyday problems and referring crises to medical centers.[27] In China a less formally trained person, resident in the village, is called the "barefoot doctor", and in many nations in Africa, the medical officer in the field station has been preserved from colonial days.

In the past decade the new-wave training programs have grown in number, but any discussion of them or their significance must begin with the fact that they are considered experimental even by their sponsors, and do not constitute more than one percent of the new health professionals trained each year. At present, the new programs in the U.S. come under multiple supervision and broad consultation. The usual overseers are the Health Manpower divisions of the AMA and the ANA, the specialist physicians' organizations, and the organizations of health schools (American Association of Medical Educators, National League for Nursing, Association of Schools for Allied Health Professionals), with the Washington funding agency keeping a close watch on the proceedings and the results. Actual programs are carried out on the usual settings for training health manpower: medical schools, nursing schools, schools for Allied Health Manpower.

Three formal levels of skill are postulated and recognized by most of the training programs: first is the top or "associate" level, with some independent ability to practice (diagnose, prescribe, and treat under "standing orders") with physician review of decisions and results; second is the "technical assistant" level, including special skills of an advanced nature but limited to one technial area and under closer supervision; third, is the "aide" level, ranging from existing programs to the paraprofessional types first seen under the New Careers program.

The focus of much of the federal effort, and of the research and evaluation, is on the top level, the two main groups being the physician assistant (more an associate in the above scheme) and the nurse associate. Recruits to date for the physician assistant program come at least in part from the Army's medical corpsmen programs, after the term of enlistment. Nurse associate programs primarily work with RNs having either a hospital diploma and experience or a college degree in nursing. But in all cases there is a premium on some previous practical medical experience with sick people.

It is important to compare the *new* status and skill hierarchy being created by these jobs with the old one. For example, the traditional power, skill, and status hierarchy used to be, in descending order: doctor, nurse, LPN, aide. With the nurse associate we then have, some might say, doctor, nurse associate, nurse, nurse-aide. Or do we? How do physician assistants—primarily male— rate, or rank in relation to the predominantly female nurse associates? How does all of this work out in practice? For example,

Horowitz and Goldstein found that there are major task overlaps in the daily minute-to-minute work of LPNs and aides, or between medical technologists (college degreed) and medical technicians (junior college or high school plus on-the-job training).[28] What are the consequences of the existing set of overlaps in responsibility, between the traditional sets of roles, and the overlap among the new three-way sets, and between the two systems? The long-term findings are not in yet. The few observational studies that have been done on the new associate-assistants at work seem to indicate that their actual tasks vary all the way from true associate to aide, depending on the type of health setting, the attitude of the doctor, and so on. Apparently all that is certain in practice (as opposed to the abstract three-level scheme) is that all levels, new or old, must do what the physician says and may not practice independently of him. Neither the old hierarchy or the new, or their relationships, has ever been studied as a whole in the microscopic manner used by Horowitz. Yet this is a basic need if programs are to be stabilized or credentials made comparable from one place to the next.

Both the physicians' and nurses' programs have medical specialists with a special interest in using the trained individuals because of the nature of their office practice. In the case of physician assistants, the internal medicine specialty and the American Academy of General Practice have been sponsors and prime employers; in the case of nurses, much the same could be said for the pediatricians. The clear sex difference is a controversial problem, especially since both programs were begun well after the passage of legislation on discrimination in training and employment on grounds of sex. Another comparison between the two groups lies in the places where they most commonly practice: physician assistants primarily in medical centers and group practice; nurse associates either in highly technical specialty work within hospitals or in pediatricians' and general practitioners' offices. Also, the length of training differs. Most physician assistants, even those with medical experience in the Armed Forces, have a two-year training period, rather like the clinical years of medical students and often in the same wards of the teaching hospital. By contrast, the nurse associate programs use the three- to five-year nurses' training programs as the basic training in health care, and have much shorter (four to six months on the average) specialty training, for example in pediatric nursing and medicine, for those who will become nurse associates working in a community setting with a pediatrician. In terms of potential for training and length of program, it would appear that the nurse associates have an edge over the physician assistants, for there are far more nurses who have a long training period, the experience, and the skill to be quickly upgraded into the role than there are exmedics or those who will need training from scratch, as physician assistants.

There is one final major difference, at present, between the two groups, and it is probably the most important one. The physician assistant is practically a new role in American health care, whereas the nurse associate role is simply a legitimation of many already existing, de facto semi-independent nursing roles in many community settings. Licensing for the nurse associate, according to legal experts in medicine and nursing, is not a problem and possibly not even a necessity in many states. This is because newer state laws officially allow delegation of most health care responsibilities to nurses as part of the legal definition of the regular nursing role; nursing is often defined in law as activities done for a physician under supervision, period. In theory, therefore, the use of pre-trained manpower, with additional short training programs, would seem to be a possible solution to the lack of manpower and the most efficient use of present physician manpower. A general question, answerable more in terms of interprofessional politics than rational planning, is why we need physician assistants at all, with all the nurses available and retrainable at shorter time periods and less cost.

Social, Legal, and Economic Problems
for the Workers

There are problems for the health workers in these new programs which are characteristic of all minor or "tinkering" attempts to change the health care system without correcting its most basic inequities or its overall function in the social system. For the new training programs, just as for the previous New Careers program and the old job hierarchy, these are: mobility blocks, credentialling problems, economic exploitation, and continuing domination by the physician.

Mobility blocks characterize the reality, if not the theory, of these new programs. For example, in the Soviet Union five to ten percent of the middle-level medical workers—feldshers and nurses—leave the ranks to go to medical school and at least three times that many are taking night courses which serve as credit in this direction. Any middle-level health worker may become a physician by going part-time while staying at his or her present job.[29] More than a hint of sex discrimination is already evident in the new programs. Several observers note that the new male American physician assistants will probably not be satisfied to be perpetual physician assistants and conversely, many physicians in private practice prefer the nurse associate as a helper because of the combination of sexual and occupational deference still taught in most nursing schools. More basically, the male physician assistants are scheduled to be paid significantly more than the predominantly female nurse associates, according to the available evidence.[30] Yet clearly the nurse associates have both more training and more experience, in the majority of cases. In terms of career stages, there has not been any significant change in the opportunity structure; neither the associates nor the assistants can become physicians without returning to get a bachelor's degree in college and then putting in a full or nearly full career in medical school and internship. Talk about such changes is as plentiful today as it was a decade ago in the New Careers program, but talk is cheap. In fact, preparation is made in these careers for near full medical responsibility at permanent second-class pay and status, with vague and unrealized promises of future upward occupational mobility.

Credentialling problems affect these new programs to a major degree. Curran notes that premature licensure—e.g., of physician assistants in Colorado—can often restrict the development of the roles, since the "job description" in the licensing law freezes the role and the details of supervision from that point on.[31] On the other hand, some physician assistants or nurse associates operating without specific laws in states which do not have general "delegation-of-responsibility" plans, could get into trouble in a malpractice suit. Apparently the strategy of the academic elite and the practitioners is to go ahead and handle the problems as they arise.

No one suggests giving the new groups credentials which would give them any real independence of practice outside the supervision of a physician. This leads us to wonder what the new roles provide in the way of responsibility and independence that makes them an improvement over the old, other than the extra training involved for those out in health work already. This is directly parallel to OEO's New Careers program, where new job titles were created for existing jobs, but were not in reality part of a new ladder for job advancement. Created "credentials" that have only minimal acceptance outside the immediate area of training—as opposed to the informal credential of experience over a period of years—may cost more to the society and the trainee than a policy which gives automatic credit for experience if it is combined with refresher courses in special fields.

Physician ownership and control of the settings of practice is critical here. Economic exploitation of the new associates as well as the consumer, appears to be a distinct possibility as a consequence of the way the economic aspects of the innovation are being set up.

For example, Schiff found that on the average one nurse associate to a pediatrician brings in $16,000 extra in average income in the early seventies; yet the average wage being paid to them at this time was less than $8000 per year.[32] If the number of associates is increased and the associate rather than the physician does more of the regular diagnosing in a group practice, while all are kept on nurse-level salaries and the patients are charged doctor-level fees, then using associates can be a way of cutting service costs to the physician without cutting service costs to the consumer. Farris, for example, states that at Massachusetts General Hospital the same fee is charged for service by the nurse associate (usually in the wards that serve the poor) as is charged for physician services, yet no one ever accused Massachusetts General of paying nuses at the same rate as physicians.[32] Thus what appears on the surface to be an innovation in manpower looks more, on deeper study, to be an innovation in profit making, and along classic lines at that.

Finally and most important, the new wave of associate-assistant programs is not likely to change the overall pattern of delivery and nondelivery of health services, any more than the New Careers program made a basic dent in unemployment or restructured and radicalized the social agencies. For physician dominance combined with licensure law and training programs which have been defined and operated by the two medical elites will ensure that the new health occupations will not be able to practice any more independently than the old. The major motivations here are twofold: technological (concerns about half-trained people in crisis situations) and economic. Here is how one fearful practitioner (who is also a medical professor) put it:

Like Frankenstein, present-day physicians who are trying to create a physician assistant cannot picture that *these "paramedical" monsters might one day be an economic threat.* I hold that this is a very real possibility. Once one grants the cloak of "doctor", that person will organize, he will seek to move even farther into the independent practice of medicine. He will reach the ear of a legislator and his organization will lobby for more and more prerogatives.[33]

It is precisely here that the profit-making motivation enters most strongly and leads to the strict controls of supervision, for supervision is informally defined professionally, and *formally* defined legally in many states, as *employment by the superior*. An "associate" who is one's employee cannot be one's competitor; but this in turn reinforces the problem of delivery of services. Since doctors may practice where they want, and to date the public has not forced them to practice where they are needed most, and since the associate-assistants can only practice where the *doctors* are, the ghetto and rural areas are either going to get none of either group, since the doctors don't want to leave the suburbs, or change the two-class medical care system. The result might simply be a modification of the Soviet system. In the city, there would be a one-to-one ratio of physicians and associates, while in the countryside and the ghetto a one-to-thirty ratio, with the latter under de facto supervision and only occasional consultation by the physician supervisor. If we were talking about an army, it would be intuitively obvious that one cannot expect the privates to march where their generals refuse to go. The physicians remain the generals here. Until political forces outside their control change the "marching orders" they give, they will be able to pervert the innovation of auxiliary health workers into simply another way of increasing personal gain without significantly improving the quality or availability of care in the places where it is needed most.

TECHNOLOGY, OWNERSHIP, AND IDEOLOGY

Hughes' basic observation on the close relationship between any social institution and the broader social context within which it is set has been important in understanding not only the existing division of labor in health work, as we have outlined it here, but also the directions in which it is changing.[34] Equally important, and from another perspective making essentially the same point, is Marx's analysis of the relationship between the direction of technological change and the history of ownership of this technology in the settings where it operates. The technological revolution within medicine results in a centralization of people and machines into larger settings, and creates a challenge to the older, decentralized, office-based, simple technology of "storekeeper" medicine. Along with settings of greater size and complexity has come an increasing challenge to the hegemony of the physician group—that is, to the ideology which states that they and they alone have the right to control all medical work.

Challenges to the physicians' ability to maintain this ideological grip, and the occupational dominance which follows from it, come at least in part from precisely these related changes in technology and change in ownership and control of the work-place. Just as the feudal lords in the Middle Ages became increasingly irrelevant to the new order, as industrial production created the opportunities for the rise of a new class which owned and controlled the new technology, so in health services the change toward a more centralized industrial technological organization as the place of health service favors the rise of a new owner and controller class. In this case, they are the professional hospital managers who may or may not be physicians, but who in any case own, manage, and control by virtue of other skills, and who possess other loyalties than to the medical profession.

A history of the division of labor is thus possible. In earlier eras, physician dominance was challenged by setting up independently in the community and ignoring physicians completely; this was the path chosen by chiropractors and osteopaths. They got the community and state legislatures to support their own independent licensing boards. The physician responded by using the growing hospital as a setting for control of occupations; the bureaucratic hierarchy of the hospital conveniently created a chain of command with the physician at the top. But the technological revolution created jobs faster than the physicians could keep track of them, and the bureaucracy itself began to self-consciously organize the new occupations and the new technology directly under *their* (the hospitals') management, rather than under the physician. This battle is still going on, but government intervention is putting more and more weapons into the hands of the administrator, as new laws require review teams composed of more than just physicians.

But this also brings up another question: if physicians are no longer automatically "management" in the hospital, are they becoming a part of "labor"? And speaking of labor means talk of unions. In general, unionization across all occupational groups in health, and especially with respect to the organization and management of hospitals, is so important as an issue that it deserves extensive consideration. It is to this topic— health worker unionization in both its actual and its potential meanings—that we must now turn.

2

Unions: The Past or the Future?

In recent years the American labor movement has entered the health
field and markedly affected life in the vast army of underpaid hospital
workers. The trend toward unionization is spreading to other health
occupations such as the technical specialists, nurses, and even the
physicians themselves. Especially in the unskilled labor area of
hospitals, this has meant a new political framework for the black poor
and for other minority groups as well. To what extent will the action of
labor unions in the health field lead to long-term gains for unskilled
and semiskilled workers, a reform of the present job hierarchy, a
change in the distribution of services to the community, or any other
basic change? We can begin with an inspection of the role that labor
unions have historically played in America, and focus on the present
activity of a leading health workers' union, Local 1199. Next we can
compare unionization and professionalization as completing
strategies when occupational groups use to advance their interests.

Then we will inspect the class position of the workers within the wider society, with class interests inherent in them, as well as their positions in the hospital hierarchy. We will be concerned with the way the positions affect the extent to which their actions lead to cross-occupational action (solidarity in struggle) or to continuing divisions which perpetuate the existing structure. Finally, we will assess the future of unionization across *all* health occupations as this relates to trends in the political action of the insurance industry, the hospital industry, and the state.

A HOSPITAL WORKERS' UNION: 1199

To understand how a labor union can become controversial in an era when labor has long been established on the political scene, it is important to begin with the recent past. In the fifties and early sixties, labor conditions of workers in hospitals were reminiscent of the thirties, the period when labor made its first great gains:

> Hospitals have long been the urban employer of last resort. The newcomers, the discriminated-against, those who are excluded from other jobs are likely to end up as porters, nurses' aides, orderlies, kitchen help, housekeepers, and the like, in the immense and rapidly growing hospital industry. Wages for these jobs, in most of the country, are scandalous. Hours are long, duties dirty and boring, job security nonexistent. Anyone who can get out of a hospital into another job does so; turnover rates often approach 90 percent per year.[1]

Although the first hospital employees' union was organized in 1919 in San Francisco, the thirties were the first period of any significant organizing. But even as late as 1961 less than three percent of American hospitals had collective bargaining agreements with unions.

After 1947 the Taft-Hartley law *exempted* hospital workers from the right to conduct an election which would invite a union in to organize workers. From then on, "hospitals were free to fire or intimidate workers for union activities, to misrepresent the facts in the face of a union drive, to offer selective wage increases to 'bribe' workers away from the union, and so forth."[2] Thus the crushing of union organizing activity was legal in hospital areas in ways it wasn't almost anywhere else.

But several factors made unionization possible in the sixties in spite of these obstacles. First, third-party payment plans (Blue Cross, Blue Shield, Medicare, and Medicaid) took over the majority of the bill-paying duties and hospitals could charge the insurers more for the services if unions demanded higher wages for hospital workers. In turn, the insurers could (and did) pass the increased cost on to the consumer. Second, a new professional managerial class of hospital administrators, trained in labor arbitration and expecting to work with unions, replaced the virulent union haters of an earlier generation of hospital administrators. Third, stable workers were desired and unions who would discipline their members, between contract times, might provide a more dependable pool of laborers. Fourth, government employees, as a consequence of President Kennedy's executive order in 1962, received the right to organize and join unions. Lower-level hospital workers in federal, state, and city hospitals joined these unions—especially the American Federation of State, County, and Municipal Employees—in large numbers. By the mid-sixties, major urban states had begun to pass laws relegalizing union activity in nongovernment hospitals; it was felt that this would make possible more rational planning to settle disuptes than the old wildcat or illegal walkouts and work stoppages. Finally, in 1974 Congress repealed the Taft-Hartley provisions in law which prohibited hospital workers from joining unions anywhere in the nation.

One of the most important unions to grow in the field of voluntary hospital workers has been Local 1199 or the Retail, Wholesale, and Department Store Union, AFL-CIO, or simply "1199". Foner and Davis observe that before unionization hospital workers were among the lowest paid workers in the nation, and had a hard-to-organize work force because of all the different parts of the hospital, and the federal laws governing them. A great majority were minority group members who tended to be suspicious of both unions and white organizers and generally passive with respect the power structure. Fighting for union recognition involves the additional problem of fighting the extremely powerful trustee structure of an American hospital. Godoff and Mitchell, two organizers working for 1199, finally broke through at one New York City hospital in 1958:

> Leaning heavily on the voluntary organizing efforts of pharmacists and other drug store workers and the funds they provided, 1199 broke through by winning a consent election at Montefiore Hospital. The victory electrified the city's long-despairing hospital workers. In a three-month period, 6,000 workers joined the union. Refusal by hospital managements of the union's request for representation elections released the pent-up anger of the cooks, dishwashers, nurses' aides, janitors, clerks, plumbers, and laundry workers who provided the needed services in the institutions. On May 8, 1959, 3,500 "forgotten workers" at seven New York hospitals commenced a bitter 46-day strike.[3]

The mass-media coverage given this startling new event was the beginning of a realization by the public that a problem existed. Although some gains were made at this time, the sixties were the primary period of growth for 1199, as well as for two other main unions: the Service Employees International Union (SEIU) and the American Federation of State, County, and Municipal Employees (AFSCME). By 1975, Union 1199 has become a national organization of 62,000 workers and has organized the majority of hospital workers in some of our largest cities, especially in New York City, their home office.[4] On the other hand, a beginning is still all that has been achieved by 1199 or any other union, in some areas. For example, only a minority of private voluntary hospitals has been organized as of 1975.

Each aspect of 1199 tends to illustrate both the advantages and dilemmas of the American labor union as an organization for reforming the health system, as contrasted with its more limited function of advancing the narrow economic interests of the union's members.

First, 1199 has an older elite of white, Thirties-style leftists who founded the union through organizing retail druggists. This elite, still in power, has had for many years a strict disciplinarian leader, Leon Davis. In the Sixties, the conditions referred to above made organizing the unskilled hospital workers a possibility. Out of this has grown a union composed primarily of a white middle class elite, a corps of black male organizers, and a mass of primarily black and Puerto Rican females. The historical origins of this internal class structure in the union (which has a separate subunit for nurses and other professional staff) does not require the *perpetuation* of the structure, of course. Yet the tokenism shown to blacks and women in the union elite is typical for American unions. For example, far fewer women join unions than men, and when they do, they seldom are promoted to leadership positions.

Langner, in two observational reports based on her experience in 1199, notes a second feature that characterizes unions—or any other bureaucracy, for that matter—but which she felt was extremely marked in 1199: the pressure toward conformity and the almost totalitarian control over the minds and information of 1199 rank and file. The union elite justified crushing divergent opinions on the grounds that dissent during the year could lead to a lack of unity at the critical contract time, when absolute unity was needed for the confrontation with management:

> During contract negotiation time all the chickens in a union's barnyard come home to roost. The union's history and character come together and are revealed as having a functional, not an arbitrary, source. This was certainly true of 1199. Patterns that seemed abstractly "authoritarian", rooted in power hunger, egotism, or sectarian conceptions of structure seemed, when the contract was at stake, to make perfect sense.[5]

At this time internal dissension, or a loss of focus on the goal of higher wages and better working conditions, could lead to a lower salary settlement, possibly involving real hardship for the members. So when militant community groups or health activists attempt to force unions to endorse their goals, the union responds with apathy or downright hostility. On the other hand, overdiscipline and over-control in this union (or any union) can lead to a second generation of passive, naive, and inexperienced leaders who have gained their positions not by fighting and making their own decisions but rather by favoritism and obedience—hardly virtues that would help the union in the long run.[6] Finally, since the bargaining situation usually narrows down to monetary issues, and neither the union's elite nor the hospital might want to consider structural reforms, career-ladder or on-the-job training proposals receive little or no union support. Again, the union leadership will not pay for the costs of the training, and neither will the hospitals, unless they can persuade the unions to take a lower settlement in other areas, which they are not likely to do. Thus, the union's relationship to management makes even internal reform of the job hierarchy almost impossible. On the other hand, 1199 can advance the narrow aims of its workers, and it has done so with marked success by tripling wages in many job categories since 1960.

Because of these successes, the loyalty of the mass of lower-echelon workers is unquestioned. But the history and style of the organization, the discipline of the bargaining-confrontation situation, and the unwillingness of either union or management to push hard for reform of the blocked career hierarchy, means that in this particular case the actions of the union constitute a confirmation and buttressing of the status quo in health work rather than a series of changes in the structural situation. But the leadership of American unions, since Gompers, has *always* held this position. Local 1199 may be symbolically more interesting to the public than are some other unions, because of the nature of the clientele, and may constitute to leftist intellectuals a kind of romantic rerun of the thirties. But the function of labor unions in the health field, as in any other field, is to preserve the overall structure of the present system, not to change the pattern of delivery of services to the community. In this general sense, the role of 1199 in the health field seems to mirror the role of American unions in general. In contrast to the primary political role of unions in most of the world—that of a group working for basic structural changes in the economy (e.g., for socialism instead of capitalism), unions in America are an *element* of the capitalist system. As such, they cannot be expected to basically challenge the system or its managers in specific fields such as health care.

PROFESSIONALIZATION AND UNIONIZATION: A COMPARISON

If an occupational group wants to act as a unit in advancing the interests of its members, it has two basic alternatives: professionalization and unionization. Although the philosophies, as well as the strategies, of these two approaches differ, they share one aim, that of advancing the interests of the occupational groups. The success or failure of either strategy (or some combination) depends on the actual skill leverage possessed by the acting occupational group, the degree of organization, and whether other groups in the society, from the citizenry and government to other affected occupational groups, are strong enough to advance or frustrate the aims of the striving group.

Professionalization is a process of seeking a wider community and occupational mandate for a group than is possessed, usually through a series of strategies intended to increase the prestige of the occupation. The typical sequence, as Wilensky points out, is to define the work as a full-time special task, establish a training school (preferably at a university), form a professional association, lobby for licensing status in the state legislature, and create a code of ethics—a type of community-directed ideology of "purity and service".[7] The title of Wilensky's article, "The Professionalization of Everyone?" points out that there are major limits on the extent to which such techniques can succeed; this is especially true in a field such as health, where one key group "got there first" and dominates the division of labor. In addition, the licensing process, being political in many of its aspects, is also subject to the superior power of the dominant group's influence over the legislature and its control over the service setting. Note that the aim here is the upward mobility and achievement of *individuals*. Group advancement is through increased prestige and acceptance by the top groups; it is achieved on an occupation-by-occupation basis.

In theory at least, *unionization* means combination of individuals and occupations, often in groups wider than that defined by one narrow occupational label, to *unite* and form a struggle group for collective defense of all the members, which aims to advance the interests of the group through the use of power. The ultimate weapon is the strike, an activity aimed at paralyzing a system through the group's withdrawal of services, without regard for the employer's opinion about the prestige or status of the strikers. While "professionalization" often appeals to those with status-seeking values, unionization appeals to more basic fears and realities of deprivation, frustration, and anger. In addition, there is a difference in the role of skill: in professionalization, the group is trying to sell the society and the others in the overall occupational field on the importance, value, and indispensability of its services; in unionization, skills are considered less important, and fewer people have the most advanced ones in the occupational field. Cross-occupational unity is the strategy, for in numbers there is strength. In general, professionalization appeals to a social consensus model; it aims to gain acceptance by all other occupational groups in the field and by the general public, of the new higher value of the striving occupation and the legitimacy of its request for more rewards, power, status, and so forth. Unionization, in contrast, is a conflict-based process:

the individuals and the occupations band together to *force* from the power structure and the society what it will not give up without such a struggle.

Two such different strategies and philosophies as unionization and professionalization would seem to be unmixable at first glance, yet the health field has seen them both separately and in combination, utilized by a variety of groups higher and lower on the occupational hierarchy. On the other hand, the higher the hierarchial level, the more likely *either* strategy, or *both taken together*, is to succeed. For example, unionization can take place when top-ranking professionals such as physicians find themselves threatened by the increasing power of the state: Israeli physicians unionized and struck in the fifties and Belgian and Canadian physicians organized and struck in the sixties, to prevent government control of the payment system beyond the point they were willing, as physicians, to tolerate. Most recently, physicians in America are using work stoppages—a form of strike—to protest higher rates for malpractice insurance, while interns and residents have stopped work for shorter periods.[8]

Groups intermediate on the status spectrum, such as nurses, have devised a strategy that can be called "unionization within professional organizations". Here the professional association—the American Nursing Association in this case—organizes itself nationally, state-by-state, and locally into collective bargaining units. These units increasingly use strike threats, as well as actual strikes, to get raises and improvements in working conditions. The unskilled and semiskilled occupations, of course, find unionization a more likely pathway than professionalization, for the needs are immediate and the education-prestige-consensus pathway of professionalization is too time-consuming in a situation where withdrawing the occupation's skills, such as they are, is not enough of a threat. A society can replace one laundry worker or orderly, but if all of them go out on strike, the bargaining power exists.

Even if professionalization and unionization are independent processes, the haves get further with either technique than the have-nots. More specifically, if doctors unionize and strike, the central nature of their skill seems to give them more bargaining power than if nurses or orderlies do. Israel is an example of a state which began somewhat socialized and in which different levels of occupations unionized. But the eventual hierarchy didn't come out even in terms of pay: doctors have more independence and power, as well as salary, than nurses or schoolteachers, in a situation where all are unionized.[9]

Where the individuals are on the occupational hierarchy (either inside or outside the union) will determine whether members of an occupational group will fight it, join it reluctantly, attempt to gain special privileges within it, or seize upon it fervently and desperately as the only way out of an otherwise impossible situation. On the other hand—and this is really the other side of the coin—if unions are a *part* of the present social power structure in American society, the desperate adherence to unions of those at the bottom of the system guarantees that they will be "organized into" the system instead of being a force for change from without. Although these processes and possibilities seem abstract, they are at work on a day-to-day basis in any labor union in the health field, as we have just seen in the daily dilemmas of health organizers in unions such as 1199.

IDEOLOGY AND CLASS POSITION: WHO RISKS WHAT?

In American society the ideology of an action group does not always coincide closely with its basic interests. Health activism in its relation to union struggles in the community gives a clear example of contrasts on this issue. The elite in the society at large—the college students from middle-class backgrounds and their counterparts in medical school—always seems to include a small group who espouse radical reform of community health systems, but this is often done in a way that involves little risk to their own long-term careers. Conversely, the poor are often politically conservative, especially if they have gained the first foothold on the ladder of respectability and security as members of a union of health workers. Clashes between "activists", either from the liberal-radical elite or from the community base on the one hand and the unions on the other, have tended to show, over a series of incidents, that the support of elite youth is often untrustworthy and the action of outside community members, although relevant to *them* and their needs, can actually be threatening to the interests of those poor community workers who are within a hospital union.

"Position effect" is a summary concept describing this phenomenon: the elite can afford to be radical because they do not risk much and can always opt out if the going gets too tough; those in the middle occupational ranks—nurses, technicians, and others—are often sources of internal controversy within unions or outside of them, acting some times in unity with the unskilled and at other times apart from them; the poor are either desperate outsiders supporting the idealistic and often unrealistic plans of militant community activists or passive, conformist union members thankful for whatever security they have.

Some examples from the history of the New York City branch of Local 1199, and from other hospital unions in other parts of the country, point out the implications of the position effect. First, in the late sixties there was an idealistic notion that student activists on college campuses might join with labor union workers to form a "student-worker alliance" similar to that seen in France in the events of May 1968, when that nation was on the brink of revolution. But Langner observed that she was misled by her own susceptibility to radical rhetoric to deny the fact that the student uprising was tame and ephemeral, that it produced no lasting organization with which the leaders on the union side could come to terms. The hard fact is that a year later the union still exists, following its own path toward incremental gains for the workers, and that the students, as students, are hardly in sight.[10]

In the 1970 hospital strike in San Francisco, Bodenheimer shows that the interns had two sets of demands, first for their own higher pay, and second, for greater community control of the hospitals. Medical schools connected to the striking hospitals threatened to refuse certification of their internship period as valid; however, it worked to get them their salary demands on the condition that they would call off the community control issue. The interns, given raises, called off *their* strike at the last minute; the union, which had not been interested in community control, got neither intern support nor a raise, and when they struck, they had to do it alone:

Though the interns' and workers' moves came together in time, they failed to merge in goals and content. Individual hospital workers and nurses could relate to the patient care issues, but the union leadership was strictly concerned with pay. The interns made one attempt to persuade union leadership to merge the interns' and workers' demands into a single package and were rejected outright, on the grounds that the union could not negotiate patient care issues. When it came right down to it, neither the bread-and-butter union chiefs nor the professionally oriented average intern was really interested in such a coalition.[11]

In the middle ranks of the occupational hierarchy, the nurses' and technicians' associations were beginning to act as labor unions. Handel's study of the "Economic Security Program" of the American Nursing Association shows that the Association is structured to use its state branches as collective bargaining units in the classic union sense, and has even lobbied in many states to pass legislation giving nurses the right to formally unionize, strike, and bargain with hospitals. He also notes that there is a "ripple effect": if only ten to fifteen percent of all nurses belong to the state branches of the ANA, they still set the salary standard for all other hospitals in a situation of shortage. So nurses who do not belong benefit from the "professional union" action of those who do.[12]

Even within unions, there is often a divergence between the attitude toward the union and the attitude toward some form of professional identity and action. This independence or set-apart status desire of professional and technical people in unions is often institutionalized. In Local 1199, for example, the "Guild" was the subdivision for nurses, social workers, and other professionals. Significantly, they were the source of most of the internal dissension in a situation where the unskilled union rank and file were loyal to the leaders of the overall union.[13] The *alternatives* available to middle-range workers may be a factor in their lack of total loyalty and discipline, in contrast to that of most lower-level workers. Nurses and technicians can look toward forming and using their own professional organization as a bargaining unit, or can take the option of not joining anything at all: in this case, as we noted, they can benefit from the ripple effect of union action.

At the lower ranks in the health-worker hierarchy, where neither professional elite position nor middle-range professional association-based bargaining exists, there are no realistic short-term alternatives to union loyalty. Thus, the actions of militant community groups calling on racial or ethnic loyalty fail: the poor workers of a hospital union, even if they live in the ghetto, do not see the community militant groups as people who will pay their grocery bills. The structure, in fact, pits one group of community residents (hospital workers) against the other, in a situation where national, state, and city priorities do not provide enough money for better pay for hospital workers as well as better programs in other areas, for the community. In addition, "community control" of the hospitals functioning threatens the union's control of its members every bit as much as the hospital's control of its work force.

Langner vividly recounts the result. In one contract bargaining session in New York's 1199 local, the Young Lords (a Puerto Rican militant group) disrupted a union strategy meeting. They argued that there were no plans for upgrading the workers' jobs, that the hospitals were affecting the local community through buying slum landlord property and becoming slum landlords themselves, and that the poor black and Puerto Rican rank-and-file women should have a greater role in union decision making. But the time of a strike was approaching:

> By that time, they were totally dependent on the union. It was the only instrument that existed through which they could get not just what they'd been told they needed but they needed in fact. The vision of the Lords seemed too general, and therefore, irrelevant. The Lords were taking what seemed like rhetoric. The members needed the machinery, the system, the preestablished processes through which gains, however small, could be realized. The Lords were thrown out.[14]

Unionization is thus a fateful choice for an occupational group, and one with many implications for the wider society. Although the majority of lower-level health workers are not unionized at present, there is a trend in this direction among voluntary and public hospitals in urban areas. The success of the unionization process depends on a combination of factors, especially: the skill level of the occupational group; the manner in which the group is organized; and the degree to which their opposition is strong and organized. In spite of the bitter fight needed to form a union in most settings, and the marked advantages union organization and action has for the members, it has not been a vehicle for changing the way in which health services are delivered. Attempts to reform the internal social processes of unions, as well as attempts to influence union action from outside, come up against the committed co-optation role which unions play, through collective bargaining and contract signing, as an integral part of the present power structure in the health field.

The Future of Unionization

Historical factors, the concrete patterns of hospital growth, the cycles of the economy, and the persistence of occupational ideologies have all had their effects on the degree to which hospital workers have unionized in the past; it is therefore not surprising to suggest that they will continue to have their effect in the future. We can conclude our brief presentation of unionization issues by taking a broader theoretical perspective.

Conditions in the work-place are a first consideration; the public sectors, and the larger hospitals in any sector, will be the places where cost-cutting pressures are most severe. In the public sector—where the hospitals deal with the poor—neither the capitalist class nor the employee classes wish to pay more tax money to improve conditions, but these poor conditions are precisely where people have to work day in and day out. This sector would thus be expected to produce the work conditions and pressures—of increasing productivity while keeping wages low in a time when staff is short—that would make unionization of workers a lot easier. Larger settings, regardless of the distinction between public and private hospitals, are more likely to have an impersonal management and an industrial or assembly-line attitude toward work and workers; this leads to alienation and the dissatisfaction organized in a union drive. The Ehrenreichs observe:

> To the extent that the modern hospital is not a "mission of mercy" but a business enterprise whose management structure and priorities are not dissimilar from those of an industrial corporation, the service ethic is a potentially subversive force. "If you have any feelings of responsibility for the patients, you can't stand it anymore", said one practical nurse. Another told us, "You have to see this place as a giant bureaucracy. I'm at the bottom of it, or maybe the patients are, and there's not a lot an individual can do".[15]

The response to alienation combined with low pay and hard work, especially after the legal restrictions against collective bargaining have been removed, has classically been unionization on the workplace. On the other hand, rural and smaller settings will be less likely to have the numbers available, or such impersonal conditions, to make the appeal to unionize as attractive as in the larger places. Thus, for example, as of 1970 (latest year for which complete records exist on this topic), the highly populated Pacific states had a 27.5 percent rate of hospitals with union contracts. This was followed by 21 percent of the hospitals in New England and 25 percent in the Middle Atlantic states—all centers of high population concentration having a tradition of labor organization. The rural, southern, and less "unionized" areas are in direct contrast, and the same facts are found in the health work area. For example, 1970 data indicate that 7.8 percent of southern, 5.6 percent of southeastern central, and 3.8 percent of southwestern central hospitals had contracts.[16] Historical factors play a role too, of course. By federal executive order in 1962, President Kennedy allowed collective bargaining in federal hospitals. Thus 52 percent of all federal hospitals had such contracts by 1970, whereas nonfederal hospitals had only 14 percent in that year. State and local *public* hospitals had a slightly higher percentage unionized (14.1) than did the voluntary sector (12.4).

Size is the clearest indicator of all concerning the conditions leading to unionization. As Table 2.1 shows, the percentage of hospitals with contracts doubled in three years—from 1967 to 1970.

Social trends of a broad nature evident both in the table figures and also in the demographic shifts of population, have implications here. The trend is toward *larger* hospitals, a greater role for public hospitals or state control of the private hospitals, and a shift of population toward the South, which will in coming years increase the size of hospitals in that region. This in turn can lead to a more modern economy, biracial unionism, and the specific conditions for a growth of unionization there. In other words, the existing trends in

83

TABLE 2.1

Extent of Collective Bargaining Contracts (Unionization) by Bed Count of Hospital, 1967 and 1970

BED COUNT	TOTAL # OF REGISTERED HOSPITALS		% WITH CONTRACTS	
	1967	1970	1967	1970
6–24	524	447	1.3	2.2
25–49	1,629	1,475	2.4	4.3
50–99	1,734	1,713	5.4	8.5
100–199	1,365	1,473	8.9	14.7
200–299	686	698	14.0	25.2
300–399	375	427	14.7	24.2
400–499	220	261	15.5	33.7
500+	621	629	17.4	38.6
Overall % with contracts			7.7	14.7

hospital size and population location, projected into the future, may well portend a rise in the rate of unionization. These same trends in hospital growth may also create work-place conditions that psychologically prepare workers for the message of the union organizer.

The trend in "professionalism" as an ideology is a second factor that will influence future trends, especially in the growing ranks of middle-level, technology-related and hospital-based occupations. It is considerably harder to assess, precisely because the middle-level occupational groups in the past—and to a degree even today—have had the choice of a unionization strategy or an organization-through-the-occupation strategy, either to form actual collective bargaining units or simply to push in the now traditional way for state licensure. This last strategy is almost impossible to accomplish without the medical profession getting into the act, since they have lobbyists watching for any attempt by an occupational group to push through an "independent" licensing bill. Nurses have been following the model of education, especially such organizations as the National Education Association, in using their own professional group (the ANA and the state groups) as an organization for collective bargaining with hospitals. But not all nurses like this idea; to many middle-level professionals in health care the status is still more important than the additional power and money. (Schoolteachers passed through this phase about a decade ago.) Thus one observer of the conservative groups within these occupations notes the reasoning and whom it primarily benefits.

> The advantages to the hospital are obvious: *Workers* are too quickly alienated by fragmented jobs; true *professionals* rejoice in the exercise of their craft. *Workers* identify with other workers in their institution, and can unite on the spot around common grievances; *professionals* identify with other members of their profession, and look to a distant professional society for long-term advancement. Finally, *workers* need discipline and close supervision; the true *professional* can be trusted to adhere to the ethics and standards of his profession in any situation.[18]

Furthermore, the status prejudice of the upwardly striving lower middle class individuals who often aspire to these new technical occupations is appealed to by professionalization, but not by unionization. An uninvestigated aspect of this, in need of far deeper investigation, is the experience these individuals have had at home before and during the years in school: many come from working-class homes whose fathers have had genuine reasons to be disillusioned with the American labor movement. For every honest and well-run union such as 1199 there have been many corrupt ones. Even within unions such as 1199 the status fears of the nursing and other advanced technical groups must be calmed by having a separate subsection for them.

But there are other factors at work today in the national and international economy which can be summarized by the concept of "the fiscal crisis of the state" in capitalist societies.[19] The processes this crisis has set into motion may not only bring the middle-rank occupations into the union fold, but the physicians' position may be so changed that even for them unionization may seem a possible strategy.

To begin with, the state's fiscal resources are not endless. If inflation pushes health-care costs up, with hospital expansion, drug costs, and even the success of previous labor organizing adding to overhead, then consumers must pay the new higher bill. Eventually corporations call the state in to try to regulate the costs; the state then pushes to raise the productivity and cut the costs. The traditional control of hospitals by physicians, and pleas by that group that too much cost cutting destroys the quality of service, fall increasingly on deaf ears—those of hospital administrator and the government. Costs are cut first among those with no power and those who are not needed at work, the poor and helpless. But soon the pressures are brought to bear on the middle-class settings and the middle-class workers. In other countries, as Badgely observes, the reaction to this is often to emigrate to the U.S.; but now the reaction has a new dimension since the U.S. is heading in the same direction.[20]

Defensive action (striking to protest challenges to their dominant position) is increasingly viewed by physicians as an alternative to the old-style AMA lobbying. The strike actions may confront the actions of the government in regulation and planning, against capitalist sectors such as malpractice health insurance companies, and so on. In fact, there is no reason to assume automatically that a physician strike must be anticonsumer in nature. In fact, the push against the insurance companies on the malpractice issue could work in their interests if the premiums were lowered or if physicians worked out another way of guarding their own quality of practice and their legal problems. The fact that hospitals, government, and the corporations are all pushing hard against the profession, in a situation where the old professional lobbying style is far less successful than before, may lead to stronger organization to avoid the scapegoat role. What could be happening, in other words, is the long-term "proletarianization" of the medical profession, to use a Marxian term: their being driven into lower-paid and less powerful positions under the direction of nonphysicians. We then can ask one final question: might someday *all* health professionals be in the same spot, and all be able to see the world similarly enough to be in one health workers' union?

But the past, and its attitudes, is still with us: while some physicians and nurses are in collective bargaining arrangements and view it as the wave of the future, the majority are not. Nor, for that matter, are the majority of ordinary hospital workers. The point we must make in summary is that unionization, as well as the actual functioning of unions themselves, does not constitute a panacea; unions may in fact freeze existing structures in the short run. Long-term trends might drive all health workers together, and as a unified group, they might change the nature of conditions at work. But this is neither the present situation nor that of the near future. In the observed relations the workers are in conflict, and their conflict directly affects the nature of service relationships. It is to these relations, within the service organization, that we now turn.

3

The Critique of Service

In the more standard approaches to the sociology of health, the subject matter of this chapter encompasses much of the text. We by no means intend to slight the action that occurs within the hospital setting, yet the purpose of this book is to show that the social context may have far more to do with what goes on inside the walls of a treatment setting, and with the relationships between the servers and the served, than just the activities inside. For those in health work itself, clinical teaching often deals with the "how-to" of relating to patients, and the traditional approach in sociology has been to emphasize the microsociology of the doctor-patient and nurse-patient relationship. But we wish to deal here with the way the world view of the health professions, the hierarchy of occupational power, and the dynamics of the world *outside* the walls of a treatment setting affect the intimate experience of being helped while ill, inside such places.

We can begin with the politics of diagnosis: who says who is sick or not sick, with what, and why. We will need to consider how the physician's view of this process compares with others' views. Two models of the doctor-patient relationship are inspected next: the traditional superior-inferior relationship and the newer, more egalitarian model. Prejudice in the relations between the servers and the served will be covered next, for this prejudice in health care simply reflects the personal and structural or institutional prejudices of the wider society. The setting as a bureaucracy is our next topic; the way people relate to one another in the service setting has been for almost two decades a major topic for research in medical sociology and the sociology of nursing service. We can conclude with the idea of cultural hegemony—the way that ideologies of legitimacy, as perceived by the service staff and the patients themselves, perpetuate existing orders and existing problems. In all our considerations of the relationships between practitioners and patients, we can here only touch on the vast literature, but will raise new points and issues from the critical perspective.

THE POLITICS OF DIAGNOSIS

When help is sought, the relationship to the health care practitioner assumes an emotional importance that makes the seeker very vulnerable to whatever happens, from minute to minute. The practitioner usually does the defining (how ill, what kind of illness) and important consequences follow from that. Who the patient is socially will critically affect the kind of treatment: racism, sexism, and cultural chauvinism distorts many relationships. Whether the patient is of a higher or a lower social status—rich or poor—will be critically important to the kind of courtesy (or lack of it) that patient will receive. Others outside the immediate eye-to-eye contact situation will influence what happens every step of the way. Each of these

89

issues involves power, participation, and control, and each is presently part of the controversy between the forces protecting the status quo and those working for change.

Defining the Relationship— Medicine, Psychiatry, and the Law

Traditionally, the doctor decided what the illness was, and how the patient would relate to the doctor. However, as the history of medicine reminds us, until quite recently the doctor had little in the way of expertise and the patient little in the way of real faith in his competence. Thus an important part of the clinician's job was establishing a *human* relationship of trust with the patient. The Greek word *klinikos*, from which the word "clinician" is derived, refers to the human side of the relationship. In modern times, the ideal has been that of the "impersonal, neutral, caring-but-not-too-much" medical scientist, one who could keep a patient's secrets but not get too involved in a patient's life.[1] Buttressing this interpretation has been the growing ideology of total expertise: the doctor as a universal expert. For every patient who can challenge this combination of professional-curer-expert, ask questions, or argue, there are many who do not dare. In spite of a growing public mistrust of the action of the organized medical profession, people who confront a doctor feel their self-confidence dissolve and their mistrust collapse. For people usually approach physicians and other health care workers when they are sick, and they are vulnerable because of the sickness.

Defining who is and is not a patient is becoming a major social issue. For example, Zola and Illich are both concerned that one main way the medical profession expands its power and control over the wider society is by defining problems formerly *not* thought to be medical (school misbehavior, prison uprisings) as "medical problems". Then the profession can get the wider society to set up processes and organizations to give them power and control over those they define as ill.[2] This "medical imperialism", while not extensive at present, is rapidly becoming an issue in fields such as the American prison or elementary school. Many school systems are using physicians as "rubber stamps" to agree to the administration of tranquilizers to children who are irritable in school, even though they may be manifesting a healthy reaction to poor teaching or harassment by the teacher and students. Another example of overextension of the illness-labelling activity occurs when a physician diagnoses someone as ill who might not be (such a possible appendicitis case) and then carries through a medical procedure for the money. In California, a study was done comparing the rate of operations for appendix removal of two groups of surgeons, those on salary as part of a group insurance plan, and those who gained money for each separate operation; the more the operations, the higher the income. The second group operated and took out appendixes at nearly twice the rate, while the two patient groups seemed similar in almost all respects.[3]

The issues of iatrogenesis (creating disease by definition) and the dominance problem (labelling as an exercise of power) have been quite common in the field of mental illness. Szasz, a psychiatrist, states the reasoning here:

Power is power. It does not really matter—especially to the victim—who wields it. Pope or prince, politician or physician, each can oppress, persecute, and kill those subject to his power. Politicians wage war against enemies, and in the process sacrifice their own people. Physicians wage war against diseases, and in the process often degrade, injure, and even kill persons who voluntarily surrender to them as patients or who, as in pediatrics and Institutional Psychiatry, are surrendered to them by their families and the state.[4]

He goes on to note that in the mental health area, with patients locked up and away from society, the excesses have been extreme, at least in part because no one was watching, or cared:

There is no significant difference between the former persecution of masturbators and the present persecution of homosexuals; nor is clitoridectomy as a treatment for masturbational insanity more "bizarre", "sadistic" or "insane" than is lobotomy for schizophrenia.[5]

Zola, Szasz, and the activist health worker organizations are also concerned about the ultimate *political* implications of using the medical definition of "illness" as an excuse for repression of deviants and dissenters of all sorts. The medical profession can and has used drugs and psychosurgery in many actions in the service of the state. In this latter area, psychosurgery, such as lobotomy, has already been used under federal grant funds as an experimental procedure for partially destroying the brains of inmates in the prison system, as a technique of "crime prevention". This activity, even more extreme than that seen in Burgess' novel, *Clockwork Orange*, could with only the slightest change be extended to political prisoners or to activists jailed for organizing work.[6]

In totalitarian societies, the use of the physician-patient relationship for political ends is already well advanced. For example, in the area of physical illness, the Soviet Union maintained in the Stalinist era a direct control over the diagnoses made by physicians in industrial plants. In periods of economic stress, government directives were given to physicians to be more strict with excuses from work because of illness. To give out too many certificates meant that the physician got in trouble with the state. Field concluded:

> Interviewed doctors reported that to limit the physician's discretion the medical bureaucracy had devised two norms or indices, readily available and understandable both to physicians and the medical bureaucracy. The first index is that of temperature: patients who claim they are sick must show a temperature above a certain minimum.[7]

Second, a physician had a quota, a limited number of certificates he could give out:

These norms, expressed in percentage of individuals on a physician's panel, may also be revised according to the situation. The doctor who consistently exceeds his norms will be called upon to explain his actions and may be admonished or punished unless he observes the quotas.[8]

In the Soviet Union, in Chile after the military coup that ousted Allende, and in regimes of all political coloration, medical diagnosis—especially psychiatric—is used as grounds both for *denying the validity of statements made before locking the subject up*, and *as an excuse for locking him up*. This is not to say that more than a minority of physicians in any nation are "diagnostic entrepreneurs", or conscious manipulators of their privileged role vis-a-vis patients. Rather, the issue that must be raised here is that the power relations between each of the three parties—the physician, the patient, and the state—are critically important in determining what happens to an individual after he has been described as "ill" with a given disease. The need for more patient power with respect to both the physician and the state is clear, to guard against abuse of power after the diagnosis is made.

The Type of Diagnosis:
From Physical to Social

Another way of looking at the definitions and the definers of illness and disability is to ask who benefits when a decision is made to call someone ill or disabled. It is necessary to do this kind of analysis for four different kinds of definitions: the narrowly medical, the psychiatric, the social, and the legal.

Taking strictly *medical* definitions of physical illness, we can see that, in the United States, physicians in private practice have a patient or can treat an illness only if they can define the patient as officially ill. The physician's economic advantage, in private fee-for-service practice, lies therefore in overdefining people as ill.

Conversely, if a group prepayment plan is set up, the reverse situation obtains, for each group plan member has already paid a sum into the pot for the year. Thus the more people defined as sick, the more work the doctor and the setting have to do for the same amount of money. Here, therefore, the economic advantage lies in *underestimating* illness. Most people, in addition, prefer to be told they are not sick, except for that minority who will persist in defining themselves as ill even when no medical evidence exists. On the other hand, a small minority actually prefer the dependency of the sick role, especially if supportive activity and help is given in a situation where being well means being returned to a stressful environment, such as a large office or a factory assembly line. These phenomena vary by social class, with far fewer poor people able for survival reasons to give in to the vagaries of psychosomatic illness unless it reaches the crippling stage. In studying definitions of illness, therefore, the motivations and interests of both the definer and the person being defined must be understood. Without some extensive investigation in each case it is unlikely that the subtleties will be uncovered.

Psychiatric definitions of illness depend on criteria that are not widely agreed upon, either by practitioners or by citizens. Aside from the extremes of autism and schizophrenia, and severe mental retardation, "diagnoses" of behavior and mental functioning are open to many biases and to the subjective social values of the definers. For example, Szasz suggests that psychiatry, in moving toward the area of "community" psychiatry, is *manufacturing madness*; that is, defining whole areas of normal community functioning, especially political conflict, as illness.[9] The motivation here is very possibly to find more work for themselves, or a more central role in the power structure. This potential overdefinition of the proportion of the community which is mentally ill can be contrasted with its reverse, again motivated by self-interest. The recent behavior of many state mental hospital systems has been to dump older chronic mental patients into community nursing homes, to shut down the

94

expensive large settings. This redefinition of the degree of illness is often far more economic than psychiatric in motivation, as is the decision of many nursing homes to send their more disturbed patients back to the mental hospital, if they take too much staff time and thus cost excess money to the nursing home management. Other examples of interests at work in psychological definition are the common use of psychological screening tests in corporations to eliminate dissenters from the ranks, or the use of mental hospitals in totalitarian states as a place for imprisoning social critics.

Social definitions of illness and disability can come from any group that bears a social relationship to the person being defined. In most cases, the argument is not over whether the person is different or not, but rather whether that difference is to be considered illness, deviance, neither, or both. To illustrate this, we can contrast being black or female—second-class statuses within medical service circles—with being homosexual. In the case of the female or the black, there may be social discrimination, but neither social category is considered an illness in itself. The homosexual, by contrast, faces a social definition both of deviance and of illness, and discrimination on medical settings as well. This group has recently politically organized and is pressuring to remove both the psychiatric label of illness and the legal penalties against sexual activities between consenting adults. In 1974 the American Psychiatric Association, under heavy political pressure by organized groups of homosexuals, finally decided that homosexuality would thereafter not be "officially" an illness as far as they were concerned. What shows the social nature of the definition is that any definition which can be *lobbied against* politically can hardly be considered illness in the narrow sense. Imagine cancer victims convincing the American Medical Association that cancer is not a disease.

The social consequences of social labels range from denial of needed health care (because of the prejudices of the service staff) to harassment and brutal treatment (all too common for open homosexuals). In the case of social labels of disability, as in the case of narrowly medical ones, the most important first step is to ask who benefits by calling the group disabled or ill. If the group itself organizes to fight against a label, or to change the connotation associated with it (black is beautiful, gay pride) the impartial observer owes it to the group at least to listen to their story as to why they resent the label and the consequences of having it attached to them.

Legal definitions of disability and illness come from laws made by legislators, politicians who will eventually be up for reelection. Thus social pressure to make or change laws includes pressure to make or change laws concerning the definition, treatment, rehabilitation, and support of the ill, disabled, and helpless. In addition, to the extent that an ill or disabled group is helped with public funds there will be laws on how the money is spent and for whom. Legal definitions of disability are thus directly political in their construction, although expert advice may be sought at some point in the writing of the laws. Some groups, such as disabled miners or ill ghetto residents, may want a law passed that would define their illness as legitimately requiring public support for the costs of treatment and rehabilitation. Other interest groups, such as the working class, might fight against any further spending that would increase its taxes. This is especially likely in a situation where assessing the extra costs from businesses isn't possible because of their superior political power over the legislature that will decide where the new money comes from. Here we have what some call a "zero sum" game, which means that until the basic ground rules are changed, helping one group means hurting another. In any case, the arguments over how a law will be written are political arguments, and the final result defines how strict the boundaries will be for who will be helped, with what aids.

Thus in our progression from medical, to psychiatric, to social, to legal definitions of disability, we go from scientific definitions to social or political definitions. But even most "medical" or "scientific" definitions have, in the real world as opposed to a neat scheme of categories, a mix of different influences. A physician working in a mine is influenced by whether laws exist to require companies to pay for cases of black lung disease, and by the conditions of his own employment by mine owners. The gravest error of all is to assume that most definitions and decisions about who is ill or who needs help are unbiased and unmotivated by factors directly related to the broader social context which surrounds the patient and the physician.

THE DOCTOR-PATIENT RELATIONSHIP: TWO MODELS

Central to the practice of medicine as it has evolved historically, and to the patient of the present day, is the doctor-patient relationship. At least two viewpoints are in conflict as to what the "ideal" doctor-patient relationship should be, and these viewpoints reflect the traditional and the antielitist perspectives which are in conflict in many other areas besides health care.

The Traditional View: The Patient as Inferior

Traditionally, the trust of the patient in the complete competence of the doctor, and the dependent desire to be "taken care of" by the doctor, have been considered essential aspects of the relationship. In psychiatry, this attachment of patient to therapist, called "transference" by Freud, was and still is considered the primary leverage the therapist can use to confront problems and work at getting the patient better.[10] Since almost all physical illnesses have a psychological component and a psychological effect, the psychiatric model has become quite popular in liberal academic medicine as the model for the nature and quality of the interpersonal relationship between physician and patient, in *all* fields of medical practice. In

97

effect, the general practitioner and the specialist are urged to educate themselves in psychiatric areas, or get mental health training, so that they may minister to the psychological as well as the medical needs of the patient.

Although this updating and broadening of the clinical role, and the professionalizing of the human relations aspect of it, has some common sense to it, there are real dangers of abuse. For in the traditional or modern model of medical authority with respect to the passive dependent patient, objections by the patient become filtered through the "clinical" or "psychiatric" screen which lies before the eyes of the doctor. Objections by the patient about the unequal power positions in the relationship, the problems associated with being ill, or the problem of paying the bill, come to be interpreted by the physician as manifestations of *illness*. That is, any aspect of the attitudes, emotions, and behaviors of the patient can become fair game under the new psychiatric model. One essential element of the relationship has not been changed in the transition from "father" to "psychiatrist": the unquestioned total authority of the physician to pronounce upon all aspects of the human existence of the patient. Most poor people, as well as most working-class and middle-class people, will at present agree with this authoritarian model and take it as normal and expected behavior on the part of physicians toward them. They may either *want* the physician to act this way, or, more probably, they could not conceive of a physician acting any other way.

The New Model: Patient as Equal

But there *is* another way. Characteristically, in societies with a radical "equality" goal, such as Mao's view in the Chinese cultural revolution, the relationship of service is literally meant as such: the server is to *serve* the served, on terms defined as much by the served as by the server. Joshua Horn, speaking about the relationship of physicians to patients in the People's Republic of China, observes:

The relationship between patients and doctors in China is based on equality and mutual respect. . . . There is no room for a superior or patronizing attitude on the part of the doctor and neither is there any room for the bluff heartiness, false familiarity, or any other of the devices which often masquerade as a "bedside manner". [11]

The patient's right includes the right to know what is wrong, why, and what is going to be done about it:

The doctor's job is unreservedly to serve the interests of his patients. Chinese patients, like patients all over the world, like to have things explained to them. They want to know what they are suffering from, how long it will take to get better, and what treatment they are having. It is part of the doctor's duty not only to explain this fully when asked, but to volunteer such information even when not asked. [12]

In the West, the relationship of the social elite to the Renaissance physician had some aspects of this equality: The physician was a hired hand, a craftsman, and when he lived in the household of a powerful prince, he could be discharged for cause, for whim, or for simple disrespect of his rich and powerful client. The *servant* role was meant literally, for almost all people were servants of the prince. The modern Chinese arrived at their "servant" role for the health practitioner by an obviously different route: Maoist communist ideology, where all experts are to "serve the people" and really do so, not as a figure of speech. Of couse, the health-care field in China itself is probably not without "backsliders" or elitists who do not enjoy this relationship to patients any more than a western physician might. But the model is a different one. *It grants expertise to the physician, but does not allow the expertise, or the psychological dependence of the ill on the practitioner, to become the justification for a dominant power relationship over the ill*. The model does not allow one party to feel, for whatever reason, that they may legitimately manipulate the other "for medical reasons", refuse to inform the other as to the reason for treatment, or to show any signs of simple disrespect.

A change toward a more democratic practitioner-patient relationship is not likely to occur unless power realignments in the social background of both change the nature of the present relationship. That is, either greater sanctions and controls over the way physicians relate to patients, more power in the hands of patients, or both, is necessary to guarantee any new relationship. If backsliding occurs even in such a nation of ideologically motivated individuals as China, consider how much more difficult the job is within the American social context. A small beginning has been made in legal challenges by law and health activist groups, who are demanding that hospitals let patients see their own records. "The right to know" is the catchphrase of these groups. But action takes place within the authoritarian structure of hospitals, and points up the need to change the whole social context, rather than to tinker with one relationship within an unchanged society. For example, could the new Chinese doctor-patient relationship have worked in pre-revolutionary China?

PREJUDICE: RACISM, SEXISM, AGEISM, AND CULTURAL CHAUVINISM

Prejudice is taught to children along with the very language they learn, often as part of that language. In adults it forms the basis for social arrangements which function in prejudiced ways, even if all the members of the organization are not prejudiced. Simply put, there is *individual* racism, sexism, ageism, and cultural chauvinism, and it affects many health workers in how they relate to those who need help. There is also *institutional* racism, ageism, sexism, and chauvinism on cultural grounds: patterns and ways of operating which naturally and normally treat in less satisfactory ways those who are different from the power holders. We will need to examine each of these forms of prejudice in both individual and interpersonal terms. First it is necessary to look at the way they affect the immediate relationship between health-care practitioners and patients. Then, for each form of prejudice, it is necessary to see what kind of social arrangements perpetuate and support the continuation of the "ism" under observation. At that point we may be led to an overall pattern common to all forms and to possible strategies for countering them.

Racism: Individual and Institutional

During the Watts riots in Los Angeles in 1965, the black employees of the only hospital in the area had to come to work by the back alleys, in order to avoid being shot by the police. *Racism* in health care is simply one aspect of the overall racism in American society, which at the present time is seen to be as strong or stronger in the North than in the South. Individual racism is unreasoning hatred and fear of those whose skin and other physical features are different, is learned early in life, and exists at many levels of the personality. Institutional racism—the pattern of inferior schools, nonexistent medical services, discrimination in employment—is motivated both by individual prejudices and by an economic system which no longer needs or wants to support the poor and the black, since technology and industry has passed into a phase that no longer has room for the unskilled. In health care, individual racism exists in the ways white health care workers relate to black patients in the emergency rooms and outpatient clinics of the ghetto hospitals which are usually the only source of service for the black poor. *Institutional* racism is manifested, for example, in the ways medical schools decide to build new hospitals and the rationale they give for cutting back on services to nonwhite groups. In New York, for example, Einstein-Montefiore Medical School chose to build a new large hospital not in the black and Spanish-speaking areas of Brooklyn, totally without such services but within their area of responsibility; rather it built on the border of the suburbs; Boston University took over Boston's only ghetto city hospital from Harvard and then cut back services in basic, elementary areas, as an "economy measure".

Institutional change in the form of community control of the health service settings dealing with blacks and other racial minority groups, is required, however, before real changes can be possible for the majority of racial minority patients in most health-care settings. For if the place ignores, harasses, or "refers elsewhere" the majority of blacks who come to the door, the typical member of the minority group will give up on the setting and not come, preferring to be ill or to die in dignity. One or two idealistic interns do not change the manner in which an elite-controlled public hospital or clinic operates in a ghetto area.

To sum up, separating individual and institutional racism is a useful intellectual operation, but it is an artificial one, since most minorities experience both simultaneously. To the black, Puerto Rican, Chicano, or oriental patient who is ignored, mistreated, or made the object of experiments and teaching exercises for medical students, the acceptance of care is forced upon the individual because of the total lack of options. At the same time, as we have seen in earlier chapters, the same system prevents people who might be in sympathy with his or her experience from getting into positions of power in the health occupations or the service setting.

Sexism: Individual and Institutional

Sexism is so much a part of American culture and American institutions that until recently only those who were its objects (women) were aware of its effects. And among women, only some were distinctly and clearly aware that "the way it is" need not necessarily be "the way it always will be". Sexism in general is the discounting of the validity of a human being because the being is female, or the treatment of the female as an inferior object—a child, a thing, a sex toy—rather than as an equal partner. "Professionalism", with its inherent elitist bias and (in health) its predominantly male power group of physicians, tends to buttress sexism and sexist behavior by practitioners toward patients. Sexism is found in the health care setting in four main ways: as direct behavior of one group toward another; as an institutional pattern of medical treatment behavior; as a form of information control over women relating to their special problems; and as an aspect of the profit-motivated behavior of the medical-industrial complex.

First, as Frankfort points out, direct sexual exploitation of women by male physicians is found in the physical health-care area especially among abortionists, and also in the mental health area. Here there is documentation for a rise in propositioning of and sexual exploitation of female psychiatric patients by male therapists.[13] In fact, some male psychotherapists openly advocate this kind of sex, which is, whatever else it is, not a relationship between equals. Many more conservative analysts of both sexes feel it is more endangering to health than physical abuse itself. In the area of abortion work, political opposition to the woman's right to decide what she does with her body leads to compromises, such as requiring women to sign fetal death certificates after the legal abortion is performed. But interpersonal sexism is not simply a case of deliberate cruelty; in some cases, it is an extreme of the impersonality accorded to all patients, less respectful in its impersonality because of the inferior social status of the woman patient. For example, the "gynecological ritual":

> The receptionist, the magazines, the waiting room, and then the examination itself—being told to undress, lying on your back with your feet in the stirrups, looking at a blank ceiling while waiting in an orderly air-conditioned room (the doctor isn't the one without clothes, after all) for him to enter—and no one thinking that meeting a doctor for the first time in this position is slightly odd.[14]

The direct response to this kind of situational sexism has been the demand by the women's health movement, a subgroup of both female liberation organizations and health activist organizations, for more women in health, as well as a demand for drastic revision of the education which physicians and others receive.

Institutional sexism varies all the way from the way health-care activities dealing with women are set up, to more systemwide problems. These include the lack of basic research funds for study of the mild but chronic female illnesses and problems, and the organized opposition of the Catholic Church and political right-wing organizations to the woman's right to an abortion.

Concerning abortion: medicine, the church, and the state often have viewed the woman as having no choice; no reassessment was made until a case was taken all the way to the Supreme Court. Sexism stands strongly behind the motivation for this fight, for the issue involves the right of a woman to control her own body in whatever way she chooses. For example,

> If a woman is free to end an unwanted pregnancy, she might choose not to have children, to remain unmarried, or to love someone of her own sex. In fact, she might destroy all the traditional role expectations that have enabled her to be a pawn in games designed by men for their own convenience. The right of a woman to control her own sexual organs *in whatever way she chooses* is probably the real reason abortion is such a controversial issue, although fears of women's independence are often cloaked in old theological robes.[15]

Another consequence of institutional sexism, affecting the relationship between women and the health-care setting, lies in the control over the information available to women on the alternatives they have for treatment, or the impact of female-specific drugs such as birth control pills. This is directly tied in with the profit motivation of the medical profession and the medical-industrial complex. If we take two topics—potentially unnecessarily extreme breast surgery and the effect of chemicals on the female body—we can see the ways in which information control and profit motivation go together. In the surgical area, American fee-for-service medicine supports extreme over limited surgery, for more can be charged.

104

Surgeons sometimes prefer the more radical removal of the chest wall along with the breast, radical mastectomy, over the less mutilating operation, which takes out part of the breast and follows up with chemotherapy and radiotherapy. We are aware that this is an unclear area even today, and the controversy is far from over on scientific, much less ideological grounds.[16] But the "play-it-safe" rationalization also means higher charges. One practitioner told me confidentially that in his area—known for high-quality medicine and not a backwater—surgeons commonly use a "bait-and-switch" technique with women patients. They promise a limited mastectomy and then, as planned, perform a radical while the patient is anesthetized. In the area of chemicals and drugs, a similar disregard for women operates, as for example the thalidomide case and the long-term side effects of many birth control pills are beginning to show.[17]

The battle against institutional sexism in health care is inevitably one part of the overall battle against institutional sexism in the overall society. An idea gaining popularity in the women's movement is the informal course, by women, and for women, on women's bodies. This is accompanied by the growth of a counterliterature in such paperback, self-help manuals as *Our Bodies, Ourselves*.[18] To say that the school system and the society, not to mention the medical profession, *should* provide females with information about their bodies and control over the factors affecting their health, is to state an empty moralism. The power still lies elsewhere, and it is used to protect the profits available from women if the system remains as it is. Only by a more thorough-going political organization of women can the action probably be taken, in the short run, to remove the greatest abuses of sexism in health-relevant activities in health care itself.

Ageism: Individual and Institutional

Ageism is the systematic discrimination against the elderly that is widely prevalent in American society. In contrast to societies of other types, and to our own in an earlier era, the elderly do not gain a position of respect with increasing age, but rather one of social superfluity. With forced retirement, high costs of living on fixed pensions, and family breakdown as well as family mobility, the old are most often poor, isolated, fearful, and dependent. Their illnesses are often chronic, which makes them unattractive to health-service settings, as they in many cases cannot really be "cured", nor can they pay for all of the treatment expenses themselves.[19]

In interpersonal terms, the general hostility against the older patient is often summarized by words such as "crock" to refer to the demanding, elderly patient who insists on dignified treatment and the right to complain if service is not up to his or her standards.[20] As with racism and sexism, the individual older patient is often ignored and the body simply placed, by looks, into the negative category. The frustration of health service personnel enters into the picture as well, for many old people live alone, in conditions which will almost immediately undo the efforts of service workers on the health care setting itself. Already frustrated, they respond with hostility to any additional influx of older people because this further reminds them of their helplessness.

Institutionally, the treatment of the elderly reflects their position in the wider society. Roth and Eddy studied the rehabilitation process in a hospital for the chronically ill elderly, and concluded that the main function of such settings was segregation of patients from the mainstream rather than curing at all.[21] Furthermore, the institutional mistreatment of the aged is big business: a recent extensive national study of nursing homes inspected the profits available for large chains and large individual facilities, and noted a pattern of exploitation of the elderly in the nursing-home setting including exhorbitant charges for nonexistent services, unskilled or absent staff, inhuman living conditions, and bribery of health department inspectors, as well as other forms of political corruption used regularly to protect the profits of the nursing home system while preventing any understanding of the true state of affairs on the setting itself.[22]

Action has only recently begun in the area of ageism, and it has significantly been in large part by the elderly themselves. Although it is difficult to change the interpersonal behavior of health care workers, the political organizations of the elderly have already begun to make their mark in some areas. Medicare, according to Richard Harris's study of the passage of the legislation, succeeds at least in part because of the political pressure of senior citizen organizations.[23] But there is a long way to go. For the majority of old people at present, directly hostile treatment is an everyday experience on the health-care setting, and old institutional patterns have remained essentially the same in the last two decades. The nursing homes that run at a profit often do so on the basis of Medicare funds, which are regular and come in for patients who are kept at barely tolerable conditions of crowding and poor food. The conditions and food are carefully calculated to be less expensive than the federal funds coming in, but since these are so meager, the experience on the setting for these older people is so intolerable that many try to leave the only way they can—through deliberate attempts to die.

Cultural Chauvinism: On Having a "Better" Culture

Cultural chauvinism, or being ethnocentric, means believing that one's own culture is better than any other. For health-care workers, this means believing that the western, modern American white upper middle-class bureaucratic hospital is the only way a good health-care setting can be set up, and that the only good (i.e., desirable or scientifically effective) relationship between practitioner and patient is that which occurs on such a setting. What really happens when people from two different cultures, with different expectations about general behavior and health care, confront each other?

> Ethnocentrism is likely to operate from two directions. Unless they are careful, medical personnel may find themselves making invidious judgements about people who impress them as being dirty, lazy, unambitious, promiscuous, ignorant, superstitious, and backward, while those being served by the program have occasion to talk among themselves about the crazy foreigners who make a fetish of time, wear outlandish clothes, are compulsive about bathing, and know nothing of the real causes of illness and disease.[24]

In the above description the "medical missionary" model is being used, yet even *here* there is not a little cultural chauvinism. For not until very recently did the health field understand the importance of social and psychological supports for ill people, while most of the world's cultures were very strong and knowledgeable in this area. Nor were such traditional Chinese medical techniques as acupuncture viewed with anything but scorn in the West until the evidence began to mount that they worked; in China they were immediately tried out and refined for regular use by modern medicine.

Zborowski noted that people from different ethnic backgrounds respond differently to pain and illness.[25] For example, Italians and Jews who are deeply into their older cultures are more vocal and expressive than New England yankee WASPs, in talking about pain and symptoms, just as they are in talking about almost everything else that is personal. Yet personal information is basic for diagnosis on a treatment setting, so one question immediately arises. Perhaps the behavior of the close-mouthed WASPs is preferred by health care workers for two reasons: it may be the behavior of people with higher status in the wider society—higher than most health-care workers—and also it may mean less work for them, for it is easier to ignore the wheel that isn't squeaking all the time. But segregation always risks dangers, as in the case of the black hospital. Those deliberately set up by black physicians, as well as those which are "de facto" black by being public and being located in ghettos, often suffer from the racism of the overall society. Community support, city services, and the attitudes of staff, especially in the public ghetto hospital, remain virulently racist and the "separatism" has all the disadvantages of this approach and none of the advantages.

Another case illustrating the importance of cultural group organization has been the struggle of the Spanish-speaking community of New York City as compared with that of the Spanish-speaking community of Cuban emigrés in Miami, over the past two decades. In the first case, a group of extremely poor emigrés, predominantly from the lower class of Puerto Rico, has been limited in resources and education as well as community skills, and dependent on the public services of New York City. Their attempts to succeed were consistently defeated; a turn toward more militant strategies, through the Young Lords and other paramilitary organizations, has brought attention to the cultural discrimination against the group in New York City. But attention is not institutional change: compare their progress to that of the Cubans of Miami. Here, by contrast, was an educated, predominantly middle-class and working-class population, with many of its own physicians, which set up its own system of services and almost immediately brought health levels up to those of the white community.

Institutionally thus far, the most successful solutions to the problem of ethnic and cultural discrimination appear to be separatist ones, with their success dependent on the degree to which the ethnic or language group has power or resources in its own community. This is itself a comment which does not reflect well on the wider community. In the Third World this problem is even clearer. Fanon, in a series of essays written from the point of view of the racially and culturally different Algerian rebels, viewed French colonial medicine as part of the oppressing institution. It was literally oppressing in the case of refusal to treat the Algerian natives before and during the rebellion period, and in the case of the

French psychiatrists who acted as consultants and participants in the torture of rebel leaders. Fanon's advocacy of rejection of the western model was based jointly on political and cultural grounds: it was dangerous for the rebels to depend on French doctors, who would then have leverage over them; conversely, the French seemed to have little idea of what the deeper feelings of the natives were, and how these affected the state of their health and the ways of helping them.[26]

In America, the geographical segregation of the cities early led to ethnic, racial, and religious hospitals: the Catholic, Jewish, WASP, and ethnic hospitals in many large cities. Here staff, especially physicians, at least spoke the same "language" as patients and shared some group memberships.

An overview of individual and institutional prejudice indicates that in every case it works toward preserving the status quo, or toward adaptation which allows the prejudiced individuals and institutions a way out. That is, by setting up special counterinstitutions for blacks, women, chicanos, etc., a short-run improvement in care is achieved, but at the expense of the removal of pressure for permanent *structural* change. In other words, the fact that institutions and individuals are prejudiced must be attacked. But to those presently suffering from neglect and discrimination, the truth in the long run is hard to take. This is precisely the tragedy of it: by acting to help themselves in the short run, as isolated individual groups, each removes the pressure which all could simultaneously bring to bear to compel the staff of the original institution to do their job, to serve all regardless of color, creed, sex, sexual preference, age, or cultural origin.

BUREAUCRACY: HEALTH CARE
IN THE IRON CAGE

Since the Middle Ages, the predominant form of social organization used for integrating the activities of different health-care workers has been the bureaucracy. Church bureaucracy, in the form of the cathedral-attached hospitals, had been copied from the rationally organized field hospitals of the Roman army. In the medieval and Renaissance community, solo practice had its place as well. And at present, we have a whole spectrum of health-care settings, running from the highly bureaucratic teaching hospital affiliated with the medical school (the descendant of the medieval hospice) to the deliberately informal and more democratically run community-controlled neighborhood health centers. In order to understand what does and what does not happen to people on the health-service setting, it is necessary to review the nature and problems of all bureaucracies, and then inspect a series of typical bureaucratic pathologies, to see what they portend for the hospital and office.

The Nature of Bureaucracy—
An Industrial Ideal

Bensman and Rosenberg, discussing Max Weber's ideal bureaucracy, summarize what its (ideal) advantages are supposed to be, as a social form: that it is efficient, predictable, impersonal, and fast.[27] This ideal must be matched against the usual bureaucratic realities: inefficient, unpredictable, full of personal prejudice, and slow. It is, furthermore, an *industrial* ideal, for the processing of people as if they were so many widgets takes an industrial mentality.

The ideals of bureaucracy, then, must be compared against its excesses. Efficiency *is* a virtue in health care, but as a religion it can be run roughshod over personal needs. Predictability is what science aims for, and scientific medicine is no exception; but people have unpredictable reactions to "predictable" drugs and medical procedures. And there is always the question of human uniqueness: even "routine" cases may differ slightly in many ways. Impersonality, in the sense of a lack of bias and prejudice, is a desirable trait in a bureaucracy, but one which quickly turns to a harmful way of relating to people in crisis. Speed of treatment is desirable in medical emergencies, but no patient enjoys getting the "bum's rush". In sum, the ideals of bureaucracy might work better for industrial production than for health care, though even here, in production itself, the pressures created have costs in terms of stress-induced disability. But, since most health-care settings are in fact bureaucratic, it is important to investigate the central problems of bureaucracy, and then inspect these against a spectrum of health-care settings, ranged from the most bureaucratic to the least.

Qui bono? Who benefits? This is the most important question to ask about any organization that announces a purpose relevant to the needs of people. Marx believed that in capitalist nations the state bureaucracy—and private capitalist bureaucracies intertwined with it—existed to serve one main end, the perpetuation of the power of the capitalist ruling class. On the other hand, the history of the Soviet revolution teaches that a socialist ruling elite can seize power and, in the name of the people, begin to use the bureaucratic machinery of government to exploit people as effectively as any capitalist society. The most pessimistic statement of all on the behavior of governments is perhaps that of Michels; he believed that any political organization would assume bureaucratic form, with the tight disciplined leadership perpetuating itself while in power.[28] Both Marx and Michels agree with Weber that one of the most dangerous aspects of bureaucratic forms of social organization is that they combine authoritarian structure and efficiency, and make it possible for whoever gains control to do more damage with this human machine than would be possible without it.[29] We will have a

chance to see the close way that ownership or control relates to resulting experience of patients. Evidence to date indicates that the
majority of settings place the priorities of the owners or managers
ahead of the patient.

A second set of problems involve the internal dynamics of
bureaucratic settings. Blau, in his *Dynamics of Bureaucracy*, noted
the many ways in which informal relationships on bureaucratic
settings are necessary to make the organization really function. But
these arrangements may deviate from those on the formal chart of the
organization, the way it is intended to function.[30] Cohen goes
further, in a book whose title (*The Demonics of Bureaucracy*) is an
intended critical play on the title of Blau's book: he suggests that
external pressures, private prejudices, and impossible work demands on lower-level bureaucrats lead to many situations where the
ideology of the setting goes one way, the reality another:

> Where there is a conflict between demands of formal procedure and
> exigencies or conceptions of work on the operating level, operating-
> level bureaucrats meet the constraint by fabricating or manipulating
> information on records and forms, and by acting as if they follow
> procedure when they do not.[31]

Crozier, in his study of several French bureaucracies, noted that
in a *skilled* bureaucratic setting—a place where people with real
expertise work—the expertise itself can be used as a bargaining tool
to preserve the independence of the lower-level workers from
upper-level supervision and control. They can threaten to withdraw
needed services, or slacken the pace of work, if they get too many
unwelcome messages from the top.[32] This corresponds exactly to the
observations made on a hospital setting by Strauss and his group in
their article on "the hospital as a negotiated order".[33] The informal
agreements that are necessary to keep a health-care setting going
involve negotiation, compromise, and more negotiation. The problem which these compromises cause for advocates of basic change

113

on a health-care setting follow from this. Strong ideological positions ("total respect for skid-row alcoholics"; "no sexism in treating women") come up against the day-to-day acceptance by the top administration of the setting workers' prejudices, in order to keep the peace. In effect, the internal dynamics of many bureaucratic settings require the kind of delicate and accommodating attitudes which often sacrifice basic change for order and predictability, and which force most workers into immediate opposition to any radically new way of doing things. The new way usually threatens short-term chaos and the destruction of all these carefully built-up ways of doing things.

A third set of problems involving all bureaucratic settings lies in the fact that ultimately all are made up of people who have feelings, prejudices, attitudes, and personal goals which may or may not coincide with the place where they are working. We have just considered these prejudices. On hiring day everyone, if asked, gives a patriotic statement of support for the organization and its official goals; yet hidden agendas for choosing a particular line of work may be extremely deviant by the standards of the wider society. Individuals may even have twisted and inhumane motives, as in the cases of sadism and rape reported on all kinds of medical settings, but especially mental hospitals and schools for the retarded. At best, only a segment of bureaucratic workers can be expected to continue with the enthusiasm that they might have originally brought to their job. The majority may, after a period of activism, retreat into what Merton called "ritualism": going through the motions while no longer really caring about the goals and purpose of the organization.[34]

A fourth problem characterizing the bureaucratic setting is the *social separation of the patients from their social context*. Service bureaucracies attempt to increase their "efficiency" by separation of the person they deal with from his or her family and friends. In most cases, the separation is not so complete as the virtual solitary confinement of patients in some public mental hospitals. But in many cases the blockade which the organization sets up against interaction of the patient with family and friends creates as many problems for the patient as it solves for the setting. Of course, if the setting were *really* doing its job, the sacrifice of patient comfort or even patient progress for administrative convenience would not be considered an acceptable cost of operation.

It is apparent that many settings *do* accept these costs of operation, and expect patients to cope with separation. Of course, few places short of an isolation hospital dealing with dangerous contagious diseases make a deliberate policy of totally separating the patient bodily from friends and relations. Rather, the complex operation of the health center assigns a place for the patient and then considers time spent accommodating the patients' social network as an "extra", to be weighed against time spent on direct patient care or running the place. In addition, many hospitals prefer to socialize the patient to the rules of the place upon entry, in order to maximize cooperativeness with the sometimes strange and seemingly irrational demands which will be made on the new patient. Such training is most easily accomplished away from the potentially conflicting influences of the family. As a consequence, most health-care settings with "total institution" (24-hour-a-day) status try to interrupt relations with outsiders during the entry phase and then to control relations with outsiders after this time. The rules for the degree and kind of interaction with outsiders are made and supervised by the institution, to serve its ends and purposes, regardless of the consequences for the patient.

Information control is a fifth bureaucratic pathology, one which is part and parcel of the industrial model. Any illness is a crisis situation to the individual who is ill, but the crisis is usually intensified rather than lessened by the way the typical setting explains his or her illness and treatment to the person upon arrival for treatment. Crozier, for example, observes that lower-level groups in many organizations often attempt to gain greater independence from those above them by keeping them ignorant of their activities while keeping their own skills a private preserve and not sharing their insights with others. What is of importance in all this is the effect on patient care. Coser suggests that the *observability* of a group in a health-care setting—how closely they can practically be watched by their colleagues and superiors in the chain of command—is a delicate and explosive issue. Too tight a ship, too much inspection over shoulders, and colleagues get angry or underlings revolt; too little, and they may go their own way at the expense of organized patient care.[35] Neither extreme helps the patient.

Information control is a problem for patients even when an institution is functionally operating in a "normal" manner. There are usually policies deliberately chosen by health-care workers, which confuse and misinform patients, for the convenience of the setting and the comfort of the workers. Each of these is presently under attack by the "patient rights" movement, which has progressed to the stage where civil liberties–style lawyers are writing popular paperback handbooks on how to get the rights that one is entitled to in these areas.[36] Yet the process continues because it is so deeply embedded in the normal scheme of things. For example, professionalism is an inherently elitist ideology: expertise is assumed to be possessed by one group, and conversely, the patient is not presumed to be better off with a technical knowledge of his problem. Also, since it takes time to inform and educate patients and answer their questions, other tasks may have to be cut short. Furthermore, since uncertainty is always a problem in medical diagnosis and prediction, there is the fear by "open" workers that they may be proven wrong by events, leading to anything from embarrassment to a malpractice suit; far easier not to tell the patient anything unless forced to do so.

But of course, patients keep on trying to find out the information which is denied to them. For example, Roth studied information seeking by tuberculosis patients in a sanatorium. He showed the inventiveness of the typical patient, when presented with stonewall policy on information.[37] Patients compare their progress with one another, argue with physicians about the validity of the information they have been given, threaten to leave the institution against medical advice, and in other ways bargain not only over the information available but even over the timetable of treatment itself. This in turn leads to compromises between the ideal treatment for the patient and the political solution that is reached in the "closed information" situation. Still more complexities are created by health-care workers trying to guess whether the patient is telling them the truth, and vice versa, or whether either of the partners knows that one or the other is deliberately lying. These problems are created by a policy of "no information" and they more than equal the additional smoothness of administration that is the supposed reason for such a policy. This not only engenders a climate of mutual mistrust between patients and staff, but it leads to the noncommunication of vital information on all sides. In such a socially-disintegrated situation, all suffer, but the patient is the primary victim.

Summing up, the bureaucratic form is inherently a flawed one for the treatment of the ill, and is presently under revision by those who wish to improve upon it. Yet other, deeper revisions may be necessary in our way of looking at the role of service in a modern society. The critique of modern man's dependence on the curer is a source of trouble in its own right, according to some critics. We can conclude our review of the issues with this topic.

MEDICAL HEGEMONY AND
THE CRITIQUE OF SERVICE

Medical hegemony, or what Illich calls the medicalization of the lifespan, is an aspect of the present-day technological medical ideology which is found as strongly in some socialist nations as in the capitalist West. The phenomenon arises from two sources: the growth of technology in medicine and the continuing power, status, and profit motives of physicians. Medical hegemony is found in its consequences: a way of looking at oneself and at the organization of health-care institutions that legitimates the present position of the profession. One of these methods of self-perception is the mechanical self-image, the person viewing himself as a machine. Illich comments: "People are strengthened in their belief that they are machines whose durability depends on visits to the maintenance shop."[38] This leads in turn, quite naturally, to permanent doctor dependence, because of the need for annual checkups:

> The medicalization of early diagnosis not only hampers and discourages preventative health-care but it also trains the patient-to-be to function in the meantime as an acolyte to his doctor. He learns to depend on the physician in sickness and in health. He turns into a life-long patient.[39]

Other issues are arising because of the new developments in technology. Prolonging of life (the Karen Quinlan case, for example) has begun to make a mockery of the meaning of "service" in the service relationship. As the courts and the society finally begin the long-overdue debate on this issue, technological change does not wait—it develops into an instrument of torture. The ancient Greeks had a term—*hubris*—for the overbearing pride and conceit of mortals who wished to eliminate the boundaries (such as death) that made them mortal. Yet "modern cosmopolitan medical civilization denies the need for man's acceptance of pain, sickness, and death. These are new goals, and goals which have never before been guidelines for social life".[40]

Institutional change involves challenging not only the existing institutional structures but also the values held by the individuals, which uphold the institutions in the first place. For example, if Illich's proposals for a radical detechnologization of medicine, combined with a major assault on medical professional hegemony over health decisions, were submitted to the average voter in

America, he or she would vote it down resoundingly. For every "advance" is trumpeted in the mass media by modern medical science, along with every new wonder drug, and every scheme of checkup-urging is played in the media through the use of anxiety: "How do you *know* you don't have cancer, heart disease, high blood pressure, unless you have a checkup—now, and regularly"? In addition, the expanding occupational structure of health services and the proliferating health bureaucracies need patients—well ones if sick ones can't be found. Unions have a stake in the industrial model and the present structure, as we have noted; a new approach to self-care could be as threatening to them as automation in other areas of work. Certainly community control of medical bureaucracies and the special category clinics for minorities have made some progress toward the goals of eliminating interpersonal prejudice and the impersonality of bureaucratic service. Yet the hope for a cure for death and the propaganda of the disease lobbies work on people's minds to prevent their even considering another model and another set of assumptions.

Challenging cultural hegemony of any kind—such as the way people look at their bodies, their health, the service system, and life itself—is a time-consuming process. What will need to be critiqued is the basic idea that people can be processed, that people are machines, that they need *maintenance* rather than care. When we look at the definition of disability, the models for relating the server to the served, the prejudices in interpersonal relations, and the pathologies of bureaucracy, we see that this basic issue underlies all. Once we forget that health care is a human relationship, anything becomes possible; our problem is that we seldom if ever consider the idea in the first place.

But there is another dimension to this problem, and we cannot leave the issue without stressing it. The Illich argument about medical dependency can be taken too far, and Illich does wish one to do just this. That is, the argument can be used as a rationale for demolishing existing supports and services without providing a less bureaucratic, less mechanical, and more humane alternative, or for that matter any alternative at all. We have been sensitized to this danger by Navarro, who warns that antitechnology and antidependency can often be a useful ideology for those who wish to cut back on services anyway, especially to the working class and the poor, and who find in Illich a philosophical justification for their position.[41] For ideologies and systems of service always go together, one supporting or cutting under the other, as the next section of the book will illustrate.

PART TWO

Patterns: The Systems of Care and Neglect

4

The American System:
Ideology and Fact

Imagine a jigsaw puzzle made of living pieces, with every piece
jealous of the position of every other. Imagine further a set of
coaches, urging the pieces on from the sidelines, urging conflict
rather than cooperation. And further imagine someone ill, who
needs to put the pieces together in order to get help. This is a
metaphor for the American health-service system. The metaphor is
limited because underlying the differences and the conflicts there is
a rationale: to provide one kind of care for the individuals and
families of productive workers, another kind for those not needed by
the corporate productive system. How deliberate that distinction is
will be the subject of one chapter in this section. But first we will
need to look at the shape of the system, in simple descriptive terms;
for this we will need the concept of a "program".

A program can be either a formal or an informal set of activities
directed toward a goal. What characterizes the American health

service system is that it is not just one, but rather many programs. We can begin by looking at the programs of each major interest group, that is, each piece in the puzzle. Then we can introduce the idea of the two-class system, one part of which is for the "haves" and another for the "have-nots". Three kinds of theoretical model can then aid us in understanding the ways the system operates: the approaches of exchange theory, the demographic or ecological approach, and the Marxian approach. This first chapter on the American system ends with a reinspection of the phrase "organized chaos".

THE NATURE OF PROGRAMS:
IDEOLOGY PLUS ACTIVITY

Patterns of service, such as the precise way a community's doctors' offices, hospitals, and patients are arranged with respect to one another, are ultimately the consequence of an operating political philosophy, which is then translated into the way power and control is exerted in the system. The transformation of a philosophy into action can be called a program: a plan for action with priorities; statements about who should be served in what way. To change the patterns of service, therefore, is to deal with three different but related levels. The first is change in the overall governing philosophy of the wider society as it affects the health-care system. This is the broadest or most philosophical level: the change, for example, from a laissez-faire capitalist to a welfare-state or socialist philosophy, by the majority of citizens. At a second, more detailed level, changing a program means changing its structure: the formal ways the parts of the system are spread out over the map, the ways in which "who does what to whom" is set up. Finally, there is the issue of change within an existing program: the priorities in terms of who is seen first, or most respectfully treated. One basic question we will need to address about the nature of programs, is whether a change in operating priorities, on a day-to-day basis, can really be made effectively without a change in the overall structure, patterns, architecture, or arrangement of services. In turn, it is important always to ask whether this *pattern* is the way it is because it directly acts out, in reality, a particular political philosophy about who the important people are in a society, and how money and power inequalities should be handled. To sum up, philosophy justifies programs and the priorities within them; change at any of the three levels, to be successful, necessarily involves change at the other two.

A program can either be an official, clear and stated plan of action, with a name (OEO Neighborhood Health Centers Program), or it can be a general thrust in a certain direction, such as the continuing push of most private physicians toward independent or small group fee-for-service practice arrangements out in the community. That is, we need to contrast a *formal* or stated program with the informal kind, and look at the spectrum in between. This problem must not be glossed over, for programs have underlying philosophies, and thus goals, which may differ. The more limited and more "publicly visible" programs, often sponsored by some type of governmental or private foundation grant, usually get more of our attention. Thus we tend to forget the more important, informal background programs, such as fee-for-service private practice in the community setting, which is still the primary program for delivering health care in the United States. The fact that it is not as well laid out and is hardly ever studied in any detail, does not mean it is not the most important program to understand, if we care about operating priorities in terms of who is to be served in what way.

Priorities are judgements on the relative importance or unimportance of certain goals of a health service system. In inspecting any system it is important to ask several questions about these priorities. First, who sets them? Is it the practitioners, the community, the ill themselves? Is it the corporations that sell materials to the practitioners, such as drug companies and medical supply firms? How are the priorities of the practitioners and their settings acted out as a particular pattern of services in a community? Once priorities are set, the groups that set them and the groups that benefit by them often may turn to an explanation or justification for their way of acting, a way of telling everyone why the program must look the way it does. We can call such justifications *ideologies*, or underlying philosophies. Different ideologies will justify different arrangements of health-care services and different priorities for serving people; for example, serving one group more thoroughly than another, using a different (and perhaps less complete) kind of service machinery, in a different part of town.

Ideologies are *emotional* as well as intellectual in content; they are quick to justify action. To question a health-care practitioner's ideology, or an organization's, is very similar to questioning a person's religion. If it is justifying their way of life, it is not up for rational discussion. Arguments between groups who have different ideologies can only be expected to be rational in part, for in truth they interpret and justify very different worlds which may be only partly compatible at best. Since ideologies or underlying philosophies justify the specific patterns of service set up in the community or the nation, and the priorities as to who should get the best care, arguments between the groups sometimes approach the heat of religious wars—prolonged and bitter, with the winner getting to reconstruct the world and its organization in terms of the new dominant ideology.

Four Ideologies and What They Support

Although there are many disagreements about where the lines should be drawn, one way of dividing up the ideologies is as a fourfold set: the *entrepreneurial*, the *technocratic*, the *radical populist*, and the *pragmatist*. We can briefly discuss each in turn, as to what the ideology states, who pushes for it, and what the consequences are for the pattern of services when those holding it are in power and directing the day-to-day activity of the health system.

126

The *entrepreneurial* or "pluralist" philosophy is a descendant, in our present society, of the old capitalist philosophy of laissez-faire. Here an official form of "free competition" is considered to be the best way of organizing a society; in terms of human welfare, the historically related philosophy was Social Darwinism, or "survival of the fittest". This provided a justification for not providing food or sanitation for starving factory workers, as "the strongest would make the best workers, and death would weed out the poorer producers and the weak."[1] While modern health-service "pluralist" philosophy is not as extreme, it nevertheless advises free competition between large and small settings, between the employee class and the poor, and between the powerful and the weak in their struggle for health care. Different types of providers, some wealthy and well-organized, some poor and dealing with the poor, are to compete with one another. Pluralism, according to Ginzberg, is "the division of position, power, responsibility, or obligation among groups or institutions; it implies both sharing and competition, frequently conflict, although it does not imply hostility".[2] The consequences for change:

> The high order of pluralism which has been built into the health services complex may mean that there is a strong tendency toward the maintenance of the status quo. . . . With many interest groups built into almost every decision system each one tends to have a veto over any changes. These vetoes are likely to be exercised by any group which fears that a new departure may undermine or be adverse to its interests. . . . One can reasonably conclude that it is almost impossible for a single individual, institution, or group to effect any independent action.[3]

The second ideology, the *technocratic*, grew up over the years in many fields, especially in economics, in part as a reaction to the entrepreneurial ideology. Here the central idea is the desirability of expert control of the system through rational planning from a central position of power, in a situation where the expert planner actually has direct (or close indirect) power over the social situation for which he is planning. This is an ideology that is closer to an operational fact in eastern Europe, even though here there is a struggle with political bureaucrats in the Communist Party. But the centralization and the power and the reality of planning exist in socialist nations, whereas in the capitalist world few planners have any power at all in their own right. In Meynaud's extensive study of France, or in Benveniste's study of what he calls "the politics of expertise" in America, the ways are shown by which a "plan" is often the justification for a particular interest group's attempt to gain political support from those who believe that the planners and the planned are truly neutral. [4] In health care, the elite medical schools have many professors who publish books such as Rutstein's *Blueprint for Medical Care*. Here a blueprint is presented in detail and without much argument or apology—a method for centralizing all power and control over the health-care system in the university/ medical school–related teaching hospital, a setting in which medical school planning professors such as Rutstein play an important role. [5]

The realism of an ideology has to do with its potential; in this case, the degree to which other power groups are motivated by the ideology and use it as a plan for action. As a consequence of the manifest unreality of many of these plans, which tend to underestimate or ignore the goals and power of the nonmedical school members of the medical profession, and other groups "out there", they seldom get enacted into reality except in an experimental form, under government fundings as a "demonstration". The technocratic ideology makes a virtue of scientific planning and neat plans, without the messy participation of the community; it is nourished by some planners within the federal government and within the medical school, and occasionally espoused by a liberal politician or two. But it is effective only within the backyard of the university, and even here is increasingly meeting with opposition.

A third major ideology active in the health-care field is what can be called *radical populism*. Here the emphasis is on the power of the health-care consumer over the health-care system. The central content of the ideology is that total power and control over the system is preferable to anything which falls short of it, as a method for improving the quality and quantity of health services delivered to the consumer. How and in what way citizen control will be exerted differs from group to group, but all share the belief that the technical experts in health care do not necessarily work in their interests. A mild version of this ideology inspired the Community Action Program of OEO and the citizen participation rules for the planning and operation of neighborhood health centers.

Health care practitioners motivated by this ideology have initated some real (if limited) political action in organizing consumers, especially the poor, to demand some improvement in the services delivered to them. But this is far from a revolt of the client, to use Haug's and Sussman's term.[6] For the ultimate power and leverage over the consumer, possessed by a health care system tired of being pushed around, is the withholding of services, a threat far more effective against the poor than against the middle class, who often have a wide range of settings to choose from. Also, ideologies in health care either resonate with or clash with the overall spirit of the times: the radical populist ideology in health care which met societal understanding, if not broad support, in the sixties, seems a lot more idealistic and pathetic in the seventies. The forces which work against citizen control in the wider society gain strength in more conservative times, when they are not actively opposed.

Fourth, there is pragmatism, the usual operating philosophy of the people on the front lines in health care. They confront the pluralists, technocrats, and radical populists with a simple but hard to answer question: "That's all very well, but what am I supposed to do today?" Though it probably falls short of a formal ideology, the pragmatist has a simple guide to action: doing what will get him, or the setting, through the day and the immediate crisis. The pragmatists may, depending on the situation, be a pluralist before lunch, a technocrat that afternoon with a friend who is a professor at a medical school department of community planning, and a populist that evening at a meeting of a neighborhood health center of which he is a board member. Nor is this always done out of cynicism, either, for there may very well be aspects of the philosophy and recommendations for action which will seem relevant to the individual with operating responsibility for a setting, with decisions to make immediately, in the here and now, and operating with the constraints and pressures that always press in on those with sick people to be seen, in the waiting room or the hospital ward. This operating philosophy is probably the most prevalent of all, though because of vagueness and lack of open advocates, it is the least visible to the researcher, the consumer, or even to those in health-care work themselves.

In general, the radical populist ideology is the only major one that even considers the interests of the consumer, but its problem has been that it has not been successful as a guide to action. For it advocates control of the local level without change in the wider political-economic system within which the local setting is simply an insignificant and powerless piece. Still, as far as the interests of the consumer are concerned, it is probably an advance over the others. The pluralist ideology allows a legitimation of the two-class system, with health settings for the poor as an element. The technocrats will plan a new system which might include the poor, but not provide the political strategies to get them equal treatment; in addition, the spiderweb plan that is typical of this group—gathering all facilities around the teaching hospital spider—features the greatest control over services for the poor by the one group in medicine that has probably exploited them the most in the past. The pragmatist can also be considered a pluralist without a stated philosophy, but usually sharing the same overall acceptance of the existing structure of the health-care system. But ideologies by themselves are only the first step in understanding. The actual groups that compose the system must be understood as users of these guides to action, in the patterns of care (and its absence) that characterize the American system. It is to this system that we now turn.

THE AMERICAN HEALTH-CARE SYSTEM: ELEMENTS AND RELATIONSHIPS

In describing the actual structure and function of the American system, we will need to begin with the consideration of the *overall* structures in the wider society—government, corporations, and communities—which are the immediate context for the health system. Then each major interest group active in the health field must be considered to review the role they play as a system element, as a piece in the jigsaw puzzle. Then the pattern itself, as a two-class system, can be inspected, service by service (emergency care, outpatient care, inpatient care, etc.) and several alternative explanations can be considered.

Three major societywide structures affect the pattern of health services in major ways. Their shape is the system's shape, and in some ways they are elements of the system in their own right. First, there is government, with its three main levels of federal, state, and local along with levels between each major level, and a complex of regulatory bureaucracies. Second, there is the private corporate power structure, as it affects the political life of the nation and the functioning of government. Third, there is the arrangement of power and control of resources at the community level, the community power structure. All actual health service settings are located on the ground, somewhere, in a community. Thus the general arrangement of power in communities directly affects the pattern of services delivered.

The Role of Federal, State, and Local Government

Federal health and welfare activities, in their modern sense, are a recent creation in our history. For example, HEW in its present form dates only from 1955, though the elements of it were scattered through government before this time. Historians of the public role in health care point, for example, to the Marine Maritime Service, which has provided health care for sailors since 1789. Rosenkrantz documents for Massachusetts the long struggle to establish state-level Departments of Public Health, against the wishes of both private medicine and private industry, which in each case felt threatened. During the period 1914 to 1936 in Massachusetts, a compromise eventually was reached that was characteristic for most American states: the public sector would concern itself with contagious disease and general public sanitation, plus a small amount of research on communicable disease prevention and industrial hygiene.[7] It would be the recordkeeper and remain away from the areas of practice, except in areas where the community physician did not want to go; for instance, chronic mental disease would become a state function, through a state mental hospital system. The federal government's role would remain minimal except for health care for military personnel. It was not until the post–World War II era that governmental functions in *health* began to expand the way they had by the thirties in social security, unemployment compensation, and other human services. With the passage of new laws and the expansion of previous bureaus in the sixties, the federal government became directly involved in two new ways: the financing (and administering) of health care in the private sector and the large-scale funding of medical research.

In the federal governmental system, several smaller service bureaus provide medical care directly, but by far the most important is the Veterans Administration, with a network of 170 hospitals in

1976 and a responsibility for medical care for all those with "service-connected" disabilities. The expanding role of medical research funded by government in the fifties and sixties led to a powerful national role for the National Institutes of Health, the primary research funding agency for academic medicine, and also the location for much government-based in-house research. But research money, while it supports the flow of information as well as the research labs of the medical schools, is not the main influence on health care. This is ,rather, HEW itself, especially the branches directly concerned with the provision of health care for the poor: the Medicare and Medicaid administrations, the Health Services Administration, the Health Resources Administration, and all the other regulatory and supervisory agencies which are concerned with the planning, organization, and evaluation of health services which involve federal money. Many, not all, of these program are presently grouped together in a giant HEW building in Rockville, Maryland, the Parklawn complex. The federal system in general and HEW in particular also has a set of *regional* offices, such as one for the West in San Francisco and one for New England in Boston, where attempts have been made in recent years to "bring the federal government closer to the people". In effect, each of the federal operating programs has at least one representative at the regional level; in this way, federal agencies play a part in the immediate community context of health services, at the local level. New laws passed by Congress, or new programs initiated by the federal bureaucrats themselves, may result eventually in new requirements and rearrangements in the pattern of services delivered in a community.

Present-day functions of *state government* cover a wide range of areas within the health field. But with the major exception of the mental hospital systems, these functions are primarily regulatory in nature, either that of a go-between in handing federal money for services down the line to local settings and patients, or a *regulator* of the activity in the health field. In this latter area, licensing boards for health occupations, agencies to regulate the building of hospitals and the planning of delivery systems, bureaus for the control of health-care costs, and the operating agencies for regulating occupational health and safety, are some of the examples of existing state functions. Usually, these are *not* well organized and integrated any more than the federal programs are.

At the local level, *city government* usually operates public general hospitals, clinics, and special service settings, such as alcoholic treatment programs and drug addict rehabilitation settings, as well as having small regulatory agencies of a type similar to those of the state.

Each level of government has a set of functions and responsibilities that has an impact on the ways health services are delivered, and to whom. Furthermore, this role is growing yearly, both in terms of funds for paying for the care and of regulating the ways in which the care is delivered. But there are "growing pains." Obvious to those within government, and to those who deal with government on a daily basis (such as many health practitioners and settings), are the problems each level of government has in dealing with every other level. In fact, a whole field has now developed, called "intergovernmental relations", to deal with the complex hassles that occur when "the feds" want something, the state wants something different, and the mayor wants to go his own way quite independently of Washington and the state government, regarding a particular topic. In other words, conflicts of interest between the players exist within government, between the levels. Wright charts a series of "eras" in intergovernmental relations: from the sparring for position when federal agencies were first formed, to cooperation under the pressure of war, to the complex experimentation and by-pass strategies of the Johnson era (when federal action agencies, for example, totally by-passed not only states but also cities to give funds to citizen groups directly), to the present struggles for diminishing funds under the Nixon-Ford administrations.[8] For the health field, these influences have been cumulative. The present relations between the levels in health have echoes of all the eras, and these create problems. Ultimately, the problems come with the programs down to the community level. This remark about the urban problem is just as relevant to health:

> Speaking in the late 1960s, the director of a local model cities program contended that "our city is a battleground among federal cabinet agencies". Similar sentiments came from mayors and city managers whose limited control and coordination powers over federal programs caused them to feel like spectators of the governmental process in their own cities.[9]

The Capitalist Class

A second critically important part of the overall national power structure, which affects the possibilities for change in the existing pattern of health services and works to preserve the present system, lies in the coordinated political power of the 400 largest American corporations, with their influence on Congress and the executive branch. In general all major corporations share a similar philosophy of limiting the role of government when it negatively affects their interests, and an interest in using governmental regulating agencies for their own ends by co-opting them to serve business or profit-making ends rather than those of the consumers. In addition, lobbying efforts are constantly directed against legislation which will either narrow profit margins or decrease the leverage and control of the private sector over government. Close working relationships between the corporate elite and the national economic planning bureaus in the executive branch often mean that long-term economic planning is carried out in the interests of corporations rather than in the public interest. This overall power group strongly influences executive priorities and legislative action, perhaps even more in bad economic times than in good. In times of economic difficulty for the nation, corporations can plead the national interest in their role as *employers*, thereby directing the attention of many away from their role as profit makers.

Corporate influence on government policy and the direction of new legislation has both direct and indirect effects on the delivery of health services. By preserving the present economic system with its distribution of wealth and poverty, the overall societal inequities are preserved, along with the disease rates which characterize both work and home environments within this system. Furthermore, corporations *outside* of health will work with health-area industries against major action in Washington to reduce the power of such industries. For example, they would fight together against a plan to nationalize a sector of industry involved in health care. General Motors would certainly lend its lobbyists to the Merck and Squibb drug corporations if there were a concrete threat. The "foot-in-the-door" concept brings the corporations together in situations like this, which they would certainly consider a *general* threat to the corporate political order. Thus we must add corporate power to governmental complexity and self-interest as additional factors working to preserve the status quo.

Community Power Structure: The Local Struggle

All health-care settings, and all patterns of relationship between such settings, occur in particular places at particular points in history. The study of community power structure, especially the process by which important decisions are made in a community, is helpful in understanding how and why a particular pattern of health services is set up. For example, the early community study of Hunter on a one-industry city (the tobacco industry in Raleigh, North Carolina) led him to conclude that the important power bloc in town made its decisions behind the closed doors of a private businessmen's club. After the main decision was made, they informed the absent mayor. Such decisions could and did involve public projects proposed by citizens or professional groups, such as a new hospital. Roadblocks could be quickly removed by a group if they were in favor; but if a new arrangement of services, or a plan for a new element in an existing pattern of services, threatened their interests, the plan could not get off the ground.[10] Dahl modified this simple pyramid-of-power model in his study of power and decision making in a larger city (New Haven, Connecticut), where he found competing elites: segments of the community such as organized business, the ethnic groups, the Catholic Church. These elites combined on some issues and competed on others, especially concerning plans for changes in services to the community. Which elite sponsored a plan for new services, or a change in the existing pattern, was critically important to its fate.[11] In addition, the role of power brokers has been singled out by Banfield and Wilson. Power brokers are individuals in either the private or the public sector who have bargaining and manipulative skills, and who are key elements of the "favor" network. They gather up indebtedness from different small power groups, especially in a complex metropolis, through doing favors; then they call the "debtors" in to gain support for a pet project of their own. Plans to develop new health-care settings, or to rearrange old elements, are always someone's or some group's pet project. How these individuals relate to the community's power brokers will often determine the fate of their plans. In these ways, the community social and political context is always a direct influence on the shape and structure of a health-care system, as is the power of corporate business and the governmental structure itself.[12]

INTEREST GROUPS IN HEALTH CARE:
A SURVEY

Directly within the health care field, there are a series of *interest groups* that are at one and the same time the main actors and the main elements in the system. They are the active, alive pieces of the jigsaw puzzle metaphor mentioned earlier. We can consider each as an interest group, and the way their interests affect their behavior as a system element.

First, there are the *practicing physicians*. We must make several distinctions here in their role as an element of the system. Distinctions are necessary concerning their degree and type of specialization, the nature of their economic relationship to patients, and the degree to which they are involved in organized political and planning activity as well as in the practice of medicine. By definition, single specialists are helpless, as they must exist in a medical milieu with other specialists, as well as with general practitioners who refer them patients. The degree of specialization is dependent on the location, for superspecialization can only occur in large centers where there is enough of a clientele to support it. Thus a highly specialized group of physicians implies a complex network of referrals. But the most prominent fact about the practitioner group in America at present is the scarcity of general practitioners. This means that a few physicians are responsible for overall patient care. As a consequence, those present are overburdened with work, and many patients must seek out their own specialists.

A second important dimension of the practitioner element is their economic relationship to patients. Three main relations exist: private practice of a fee-for-service sort; group practice in a prepaid plan; and public employee status (Army physicians, VA physicians, state hospital staff, city hospital staff, etc.). The precise political action which these groups take is at least as importantly related to their economic interests and "arrangement" as it is to their degree and type of specialization. This is in turn related to a third dimension: their degree of participation in professional organizations, such as the local and state medical society, the AMA, and specialty associations such as the American College of Radiology. Those who are high participators in professional associations may be so as scientists (going primarily to the scientific sessions at national meetings), as social arbiters (combining gossip and golf with a little information gathering), or, most importantly for our purposes, as that minority of private practitioners who often are suspected by their colleagues of "power hunger", but who devote much of their time to political action work. This group usually works to preserve the existing pattern of services and their existing opportunities to earn a living in a manner to which they have become accustomed.

The *academic medical elite* is a second group within the health-care system having interests in many cases quite different from the private practitioner's, especially the specialist or general practitioner in fee-for-service medicine. To begin with, medical professors, researchers, or administrators within a medical school or an academic teaching hospital are often on full-time salary, with a career that has two goals: the advancement of "medical knowledge" and the practice of medicine, with the status and prestige to be found in the former area. Characteristically, in recent years, knowledge is being defined by the academic medical elite to include expertise concerning the planning of the pattern of health services in the future, and their role becomes that of critic of existing systems and proposer of new ones.

Hospitals, since the Middle Ages, have been the workshops of medicine, and they remain today a key organizational element of the health-care system. To begin with, the interests and priorities of hospitals depend on their type. Three main divisions are the public (a part of government itself), the voluntary private nonprofit, and the private profit-making (proprietary). Most teaching hospitals are in the private nonprofit category, with the public ghetto hospitals also used as teaching settings on the medical school's terms. Location is a critical factor in understanding interests and place in the system, for the public hospitals tend to be both poorer in resources and staff than the others, and more likely to be located in the poverty areas of urban communities, while the voluntary nonprofit and profit-making or proprietary hospitals are more frequently found in suburban areas. Associations of hospitals, such as the American Hospital Association, act politically to influence the role of hospitals in the community. In addition, private accrediting associations such as the Joint Commission on the Accreditation of Hospitals "join" such groups as the American College of Physicians, the American College of Surgeons, the American Hospital Association, and the American Nursing Association. They direct their influence toward quality control of hospital functioning, but do not necessarily direct their attention to pushing for new forms of health care. On the other hand, once a new form of health care, such as a series of neighborhood centers, becomes established, the Joint Commission is willing to develop a program to accredit them.[13]

In general, hospitals are of such different types that they cannot be considered to be acting as a unified group, unless some action threatens all their interests together, in which case the different subtypes of hospitals can work together to counter the threat. But regardless of the type of hospital, as key elements of any community health-care system, they have a natural clientele. The social and political relationships between the clientele and the hospital will tell much about the persistence in a particular pattern of service, or about a change over time to another form.

Profit-making corporations supply the bulk of the drugs, hospital and office medical supplies, and the technology used in health care. As such, they have an enormous interest in maintaining the political and economic status quo. Supply networks include, in the case of drugs, a task force of "detail men" who go from office to office peddling drugs to practitioners, and a complex system of financial support of medical journals through drug advertising, which often in the past has been used as an influence on these when they have considered publishing editorials against the use of brand-name drugs. Medical technology companies have fostered a competitive situation where many health-care settings engage in status races to have the latest in medical equipment ("a heart-lung machine in every operating room"), even when the costs of this are borne by consumers. Blood is bought and sold in this nation as well as other things, sold for profit, leading to situations we will investigate in a later chapter. Profit-making corporations have relationships to the medical profession and the provider organizations which become formalized and intertwined to form what we will call a "medical-industrial complex": an interest group of several elements, whose main aim is to divert resources away from consumer aid. This too we will look at in detail later.

Those insurers who pay for a majority of present-day health care, as organizations, constitute another important element in the health-care system. Often called *third-party payers*, because they are neither the patient nor the doctor but go-betweens that handle many of the financial details, they have assumed an increasingly powerful role in determining the way the system is designed, or the ways in which the pattern of services might be changed in the future. Three main types of insurance organizations are of major importance here: the government itself (such as the Medicare-Medicaid programs), the private "nonprofit" Blue Cross/Blue Shield plans, and the private profit-making insurance companies. They relate to different segments of the health-care system, although all to some degree pay for practically every type of service. The governmental programs deal usually with settings specializing in the poor and elderly, such as public hospitals and public clinics and nursing homes with a strong welfare-profit orientation. The Blue Cross/Blue Shield system deals primarily with the working and middle class in the high-rent parts of cities and the suburban areas, as do the private insurance companies, though in a more scattered way. Government's role is expanding, as more legislation writes a "regulating" role for government into new medical service programs. The Blue Cross/Blue Shield plans, which began as creatures of hospitals and medical societies, are becoming more independent as a power force lobbying for administrative control over the whole system of insurance, in anticipation of the creation of a national insurance system. Much criticism has been directed at them for not working in the consumers' interest but rather for the hospitals and the physicians—an issue we will return to later. Private profit-making insurance companies are simply one segment of the overall corporate elite. Thus there is no *single* third-party payer group, but rather three main competitors for power and control over the collection and distribution of insurance funds for health care.

Government is both an interest group and an important element of the system itself. We have already addressed the context of the "State" or of general government, that is, the federal-state-local structure of human service bureaucracies and regulatory agencies. Even though they usually do not provide direct service, they have planning, funding, and regulating responsibility for the elements of the system that do. In addition, Veterans Administration hospitals are a major federal service element, as are the state mental hospital system and the city-owned and city-run hospitals and clinics throughout the nation. The complexity of our system is evident when we try to categorize the elements in list fashion, as attempted here. Were do we put public hospitals? Under "government"? Under "hospitals"? Under both? Do the publicly-owned and -operated sectors act as a force independent of *general* government? No, but they act *within* government as an interest group. Do their interests as service settings sometimes conflict with their role as elements of government? Yes, when overall cost cutting imposed on government gets down to their level and staff must be dismissed. Can we separate "government" and "hospitals", therefore, into two separate elements of the health-care system in America? Obviously not, to the extent that this element, like others, wears two hats, as the metaphor has it. But if they are wearing two hats, this means they are connected to other elements in two ways, and changing their role in the pattern of services means challenging both government and a given hospital. Finally, the overlaps between general government administration, general government regulation and planning, government funding programs, and specific government-owned and -operated settings make clear distinctions difficult. For example, are the Medicare and Medicaid programs part of the insurance element (government subdivision), are they a service (money support) for the providers, or are they a regulatory program (he who pays the piper calls the tune)? They are all of these, of course, depending on which dimension of the program is being considered. Perhaps talking of a public subsystem would be more satisfying, but there are arguments against merging—in conceptual terms—the public and private parts of a function such as insurance or hospital service. In addition, each piece of governmental activity may be more closely connected to, and involved with, its equivalent private segment than with the rest of government in health. At the federal level, this means that people on different floors of a government health building at HEW may work more closely with the groups out in the society—their "clientele" groups—than with the people on another floor, who are dealing with a different element of the health-care system.

Unions are becoming an important element of the health-care system in at least three ways: as the organizers of most blue-collar and some professional manpower in health care, as an insurer in the health field, and as an innovator and planner of new approaches to the organizing and financing of health care. Historically, unions were prevented from organizing the health-care worker until the Taft-Hartley Law against this was nullified, which wasn't until well after World War II. Since then, their role has become more important in the case of professions such as nursing, where union organizing strategies are being used to advance changes in the way nurses operate on the setting, such as striking for greater independence. Union insurance plans are an innovative force for change in the way services are delivered, with many in recent years favoring the prepaid group practice of medicine, through the signing of large contracts between a union and a service-provider group, or even setting up their own separate health-care subsystems.[14]

Finally, the *consumer* is an element of the system. In official ideology, no matter which one of the four ideologies we considered

143

above, the health-care system exists "to benefit the consumer". Yet the consumers' lack of organization at present—in terms of direct organization of a sort effective enough to change the chaotic field of elements and forces we have just sketched out—means that they are one of the weakest elements of all. Such consumer-oriented groups as Nader's Health Research Group can be considered to have "organized consumer expertise", but to date their action has been to educate consumers to pressure Congress rather than to organize at the local level.[15] We need, therefore, to make a distinction between these legislation-oriented groups and the groups which organize the poor and others to fight locally for changes in the health-care system. Here one can point to organizations such as the Medical Committee for Human Rights, and Science for the People, both of which do some work of the "research-for-legislative-action" type, but which also work more directly in communities, doing political organizing work to influence the pattern of health services. In general, however, few consumers are involved in this work; and in terms of present power, ordinary consumers are a trivial force. It's *their* health or illness, but not their system.

THE PATTERN ITSELF: A TWO-CLASS SYSTEM

A brief outline of the pattern of services as it exists at present must begin with the observation that we are an urban society, with a concentration of people living in standard metropolitan areas, twice as many people living this way in 1970 as did in 1950.[16] Second, the concentration of physicians has increased in the urban areas faster than the concentration of all occupational groups. For example, the number of rural counties with zero physician manpower has *increased* during this time period even though the numbers and per capita rates have remained even or gained slightly.[17] *Hospitals* are primarily an urban phenomenon, as are medical schools. Consequently, the rural areas having less, are not generally in a power position, nor do they possess the overall resources to even the balance. Rushing and Wade remind us that physician and hospital differences between urban and rural areas are simply one element of *overall* differences between urban and rural areas. For example, large populations are attractive to all kinds of industries and service providers: more buyers, more suppliers, more research parks, support institutions, support manpower are there. The greater community income means possibilities of higher salaries for the professionals and better schools for their children:

> The distribution of physicians, therefore, is intertwined with a complex of demographic, social, and economic factors. These factors work in the direction of keeping rich communities rich and poor communities poor. Community social and economic advantages (or disadvantages) are cumulative, and physician manpower is just one part of this cumulative pattern.[18]

A second part of this pattern is the location of hospitals by type of hospital, and also of doctors' offices, the two main places where health care is presently delivered. Here we have an overall pattern, in which a minority (usually less than a fifth) of all the settings are publicly-run hospitals, with the Veterans Administration (federal) and mental hospitals (state) in rural or suburban locations for the most part, and the public general hospitals (city-run) in the poverty and ghetto areas of our major metropolises. In most areas of the nation the private, voluntary nonprofit hospitals are the majority setting, making up from 50 to 80 percent of the hospitals in most metropolitan regions—primarily serving the working, middle, and upper-class patient and located either near medical schools or in the suburbs. Private profit-making hospitals tend to be either a *major* element of the system, in the newer and fast-growing population areas such as Houston (44 percent of all hospitals) and Los Angeles (41 percent), or as in the East and Middle West, they make up a small minority, about the same proportion as that held by the public institutions. We exempt nursing homes, and "extended care" homes here, of course, for they are overwhelmingly private and most (85 percent) are profit-making.[19] Doctors' offices follow the pattern of the voluntary nonprofit hospitals, especially as they are concentrated in elegant high-rent downtown areas or in the suburbs.

Oversimplifying, but not excessively, we have, combining the doctors and the office and hospital settings, a two-class medical care system. On the one hand, few practitioners and a few public settings for the poor in either the ghetto or rural areas; on the other hand, many practitioners and voluntary nonprofit hospitals for the middle class and the upper class in the suburbs. Medical schools affiliate with both the nonprofit and the public institutions far more than with the private profit-making hospitals. We have already inspected the contrast in the experience of the poor and the middle class in the settings which routinely deal with them, in the previous chapter on the health-care-setting. It may now be helpful to inspect the pattern of services by *types of services* to get a clearer idea of how the two-class system operates. Thus emergency room, outpatient, inpatient, and chronic care services all need to be reviewed to see whether there is one way in which each of these services is delivered for the poor and another for the middle class.

Types of Service: Two-Class Care in Action

Emergency services are provided by hospitals for those in crisis and also for those with no alternatives. The overall absence of private general practitioners and community clinics in many poverty areas has meant the rising use of the public city hospital emergency room as a kind of general practitioner for all complaints and problems, major or minor. New York City is typical here:

> Lower-income patients using emergency rooms do not have private physicians, and look to the emergency room as their basic source of medical attention. They view the emergency room not merely as a place to obtain treatment for minor illness, but as an entree, when needed, to

146

the hospital's more intricate services. Thus, the emergency room has become the primary source of medical care for a significant portion of New York City's population.[20]

For the middle class as well as the poor, the shortage of general practitioners, and the possibility of good cost coverage in emergency rooms through their Blue Cross/Blue Shield insurance, has meant a growth in the use of suburban hospital emergency room as well. But the power relations are different here, for the middle-class patient may *have* a doctor who can check on the emergency-room care, or meet the patient at the emergency room, or in some other way sponsor the patient, watching over the shoulder of the on-duty staff that night. Poverty patients have no such sponsors, nor any social standing with respect to the hospital. They are very dissatisfied with their emergency room care, especially since they are asking that it fill all medical functions. The pressure on staff plus the need to see the real emergencies first often combine long waiting with rapid, impersonal care at the end of the line. In addition, in some local areas the private practitioners fight against the expansion of services in the emergency room, since they view such services as potential competition for their own private offices in the community. As a consequence, when the Medicaid program first became operational, some poor patients fled the public city hospital emergency rooms for private physicians' offices on the fringe of the city, where for a while they could pay for the care with a Medicaid "charge account". But funds for the Medicaid program were quickly cut back and enough restrictions placed on the poor so that they soon were redirected back to the emergency room.

Outpatient or *ambulatory* services clearly take different forms for the poor and for the rest of the society. Poor people, when they do not have an acute problem but rather a chronic one, are usually referred to one of the hospital's *outpatient clinics*. The pattern, and the problem involved in the pattern, has been described by Robertson and his group. For the poor:

147

Most of the facilities available to them reflected medical specialization or governmental interest in certain health problems. The large hospitals operated, in addition to emergency clinics, a plethora of outpatient clinics, each of them usually established for teaching the diagnosis and treatment of a particular disease. Thus, five members of the same family, each with a different set of symptoms, could be seen in five separate clinics of the same hospital. This situation was aggravated by a lack of coordination among the independent facilities; a given clinic was not necessarily cognizant of all the problems and of its patients, let alone the problems of other family members.[21]

Of course the lack of general practitioners, and the need for patients to find their way among the forest of specialists, is common for the middle class as well. But what makes the major difference at present is the power relationship in economic and in social class terms, between patient and system. A middle-class patient can choose among eight ophthalmologists if one angers him or gives poor service, whereas the poverty-level patient must take potluck at the only eye clinic for the poor in town. Again, as with emergency care, the poor prefer more individual care if for some special reason it has ever been provided them. But it seldom is.

Services *inside the hospital* were reviewed in the previous chapter. Bureaucratic pathologies were seen to operate for all patients, but were especially severe for the poor. Communication breakdown, impersonality, exploitation of patients for research, were all seen to matter less to hospital staffs when they affected the poor. Mumford in particular singled out the key political dynamic behind the difference between the treatment of the two groups in one hospital, or the difference between the quality of personal experience in a city hospital and a community suburban one. In the suburban hospital or the small community, the medical staff and the patient may have social ties and networks on the *outside* of the hospital; the experience of the patient may matter to the physician and the health-care setting for this reason.[22] By contrast, the poor are effectively unrelated socially to staff and powerless vis-a-vis the health-care settings they use, unless it is that rare entity, a truly community-controlled neighborhood center for the poor. They may complain about the quality of care received within the walls, but they are not in a power position to do anything to try to change it.

Finally, *chronic care* in this country is an impoverishing experience, given present levels of financial support for the ill and their families, and a de-humanizing one, given the disrespect for the old found in the typical nursing home. Because of the costs, the two-class treatment system here finds a lot more old, middle-class people in it on the bottom layer, lumped with the poor and contrasted with the few "country clubs" in each city that deal with the really wealthy families and their aged relatives. The bottom rung contains perhaps the most morally repulsive health-care settings in the nation: the profit-making nursing-home chains specializing in profiting from the old on public support. In these settings, the combination of cost cutting (especially in food), understaffing, overmedication, and actual patient abuse has led Mendelson, after an extensive national review of the situation, to conclude:

> Nursing homes are a very lucrative business. Despite the pleas of poverty from operators caught cutting corners in the care of their patients, despite the chorus demanding higher government payments, despite the many variations on the theme of . . . . give us a dime and we'll give you a dime's worth of service—it became abundantly clear to me that nursing home operators are getting rich at the expense of their patients and the taxpayer.[23]

For chronic mental illness and for the retarded who are institutionalized, the same two-class system exists, and the studies that appear every year seem to have no effect on the situation. This is not an accident, because strong influences are brought to bear against change. There is money to be made in the bottom rung of a two-class system, especially in the area of chronic care. Even organized crime seems to have taken an interest in the field.

THE TWO-CLASS SYSTEM:
SOME INTERPRETATIONS

There are overlaps in the two-class system, of course, depending on which area of care is being considered. An example of this was just given; where the line is drawn for chronic care is different from where it is drawn for emergency services, yet all of these services are elements of an overall pattern of services. Generally, however, the pattern holds, and is obvious enough for those with very different analytical approaches to agree on its existence before giving different interpretations as to *why* it exists. It is important for us to consider briefly at least some of the main reasons—interpretative frameworks—which are given as explanations for its existence as a phenomenon. Three are clearly relevant: the *exchange* or *referral* approach; the *social geography* approach, and the Marxian *political-economic* approach. Each can be related to the pattern, overall and in detail, in order to see what explanations the different approaches give, as to why the system looks the way it does.

Exchange Theory: The Patient as
Gold or Wooden Nickel

An exchange theory approach considers the patients as tokens or valuables being exchanged by the elements of the care system. In anthropology, Levi-Strauss observed the kinship systems, especially systems of marriage and intermarriage in nonwestern societies, could be viewed as a set of rules for the exchange of people from one subgroup to the next. These were rules governing which group could give who to whom.[24] Health care organizations can be seen as having "turf" or domains which they own, and special functions for which they need patients. This can and does lead to fights over patients. Levine and White observe:

150

Intense competition may occur between two agencies offering similar services, especially when other agencies have no clear criteria for referring patients to one rather than the other. In some cases, the conflict situation may be resolved by having the two agencies involved handle the same category of patients but at consecutive stages. For example, one agency may assume responsibility for patients when they are bedridden and the other when they become ambulatory. Another means of removing conflict and achieving consensus is to divide the population segments among the agencies in question.[25]

Notice, in this approach, the image of the patient treated as a passive thing passed from hand to hand—an accurate reflection of reality unless the patients object.

Certain parts of the system have informal rules governing the direction of referrals. For example, less prestigious practitioners, and general practitioners, usually refer patients to more prestigious practitioners, and the general practitioner refers to the specialist.[26] Complaints are beginning to arise in America by practitioners who refer patients and then "lose" them, as the patients transfer allegiance (and fees) to the other physician or health-care setting. Another way of using the approach is to view the patients as having different degrees of value, depending on what the exchanging partners want. For most suburban specialists, a rich patient referred to them by a colleague is worth several poor ones. Yet in a research-oriented city hospital with a medical-school affiliation, to a research worker interested in cirrhosis of the liver, a bunch of skid-row alcoholics referred to them by the emergency department is considered a favor—one that has to be repaid.

The exchange model is definitely useful; yet it has some drawbacks. First, the two-class nature of the system is often glossed over by those who have used this approach, although it is certainly possible to consider such a class difference and still use the exchange model. Second, the attitudes of the patient are not really considered by the model; they are not a problem to be explained.

This essentially passive role of the patient in the model is unfortunately an accurate picture of the patient's true passivity: the lack of information and lack of real choice when entering many referral systems. Few patients would even think to ask why they are being sent to doctor X instead of doctor Y, to hospital A instead of hospital B. In essence, the entire model is elitist in orientation, aimed at explaining the present system for those who run it and not focusing on the needs of the patients within the system. Often the goal of the analysis is to understand how and why the present exchange system operates, rather than analyzing how and why such a system needs to be changed to treat patients as active, perceiving, feeling human beings, rather than as wooden nickels and silver dollars.

The Road-Map Approach: Charting the Patterns

Ecological or *geographical* approaches are useful in organizing the data on health-care systems. We noted at the beginning of this section that the pattern of services cannot be understood—especially as to its trends and directions—except against the growth of urbanization and concentration of the population into metropolitan areas. All of social ecology's and demography's research tools and approaches are available to those who make an ecological or geographical model of our existing health-care system. It is certainly the quickest way to highlight some of its weaknesses: one look at a map with no dots representing private practitioners either in the ghetto or in the rural area, is worth a thousand words. The ecological/geographical approach also gives us an idea of possible *rearrangements* of system elements, as when we note that four hospitals in one part of the city do radium therapy, none in any other part of the city, and a fifth in the therapy-crowded area wants to build a new unit. As an areawide planning tool, this approach is invaluable, but it has one major drawback: it tends to leave the power relationships between the groups on the drawingboard unde-scribed and unanalyzed. This is not due to the lack of *knowledge* of communitywide power structures, or to specific struggles between neighboring hospitals or competing clinics. Rather, the statistical methods and quantitative approaches used by those in advanced ecological research often are inapplicable to the complex and fluid network of power relationships that actually determines the pattern of services at a given point in time. To sum up, as a first-run analysis of the existing pattern of services, an ecological/geographical ap-proach is essential, but as an analysis of the dynamics of the system, it has problems as a tool.

The Marxian Political-Economic Approach

A third approach is more historical, dealing as it does with the development of capitalism itself, the role of technological change within it, and the nature of state activity in support the capitalist class at the expense of the employee class (those who work for the corporations, excepting upper management, and the poor). The stress is on the role of ownership, power, and money as controlling agencies of the past, present, and future of the health service system. This political-economic analysis first requires a description of the elements of the system, then of the pattern of exchange of goods and services, and the geographical spread of services and people on the map. Then the basic question is asked: how does the pattern of services relate to the role of the capitalist class and the state, in preserving the status quo? Who benefits by this situation, and why? Who will therefore fight to protect the situation, and what strategies will they use to maintain power and control?

Second, it is necessary to ask a series of questions about the nonowners and noncontrollers of the system, as to their degree of consciousness of the existing situation and their degree of willing-ness to combine with one another *to change the wider political-*

economic system within which the health-care system is set. For it is the basic observation of this kind of theory that health care is simply one type of housekeeping function which a capitalist state needs to keep the wheels of industry rolling, and that no understanding of the health-service system is possible without looking outside of it to the wider political economy. For example, if there is a two-class system of care, how does this benefit the capitalist class? If there is poor enforcement of the occupational health and safety laws, how is this achieved, by collusion between the state and the capitalist class, in a situation where the state *must* keep things happy for business, since "the business of the state is business"? How might the politics of the wider society lead to a redistribution of power and wealth, which could then impact on the service system? Or can the service system be used as an example in other areas, as a way of showing what can work if the profit motive is eliminated? Marxian approaches are not monolithic, and analysts using these approaches may differ with one another. But it is clear that the stress is on the ownership of the means of health-care production, and the functions of the service system in supporting the capitalist economy.

For an activist, none of these approaches can stand alone. A plan for action must be preceded by the analysis of the exchange situation, of the geographic pattern of service, and of the relationship between the system and the wider economic power structure. For this reason we will use all three points of view, depending on whether our goal is listing the parts, looking at small-scale interaction, or understanding the way the system fits into our capitalist economy.

The American System: Organized Chaos?

To those who say that we have a nonsystem of health care, a response is easy: try to change it. If someone does try, many of the somewhat esoterically connected pieces will spring into action, and will usually shoot the would-be changer down in flames. They will then return to the chaos of business as usual. We began with the observation that there is not just one guiding ideology in our system, but at least four: laissez-faire entrepreneurialism, technocratic elitism, radical populism, and pragmatism. Then three sets of overlapping background elements were considered: government, the corporations, and the community power structure. After this, each of the actual pieces of the puzzle were presented and discussed as they are in reality, interest groups alive and fighting for greater power and control over the whole system. The pattern is, in spite of its complexity, clearly two-class in nature, with one system for the upper and middle class, another for the poor. Three types of interpretations helped us with the *why* of this system-exchange theory, geographical and demographic models, and the Marxian political-economic method. All were found helpful in presenting some of the reasons for its present shape as a system.

Yet we have just begun. We must continue by looking at the relationships between attempts at changing the two-class system and the basic reason for its existence in the first place, a reason not touched by the attempts at change. Of particular interest is the way the entire system reacts when attempts are made to eliminate inferior care for the poor. We may now turn to this problem, one which illustrates in detail that our patterns of service and nonservice in health care are primarily our overall patterns of discrimination and economic oppression viewed in the mirror of health service.

5

The American System:
Haves and Have-Nots

In a historical perspective, we find that the existing two-class nature
of the American health care system is part of a long tradition, in
which societies deliver one kind of care to the poor, another to the
rest of the people. Several strategies have been tried in recent years
to alter this situation, to change the degree, quality, and type of
organization of services. Yet they have all fallen short. We need to
know why. We can begin with the attitudes which poor people often
have toward the existing system. Then we can turn to four strategies
that were tried for changing the system: the OEO Neighborhood
Health Centers program, the "comprehensive demonstration"
strategy, the Medicaid program, and the attempt by medical school
teaching hospitals to build networks of service settings in poverty
areas.

THE ATTITUDE TOWARD CARE:
FEAR OF THE "SERVERS"

Some poor people make as many visits to health facilities as the middle class, perhaps even more for complicated cases, because they often must go from place to place. Others are chronically ill because of the conditions in which they live and must haunt emergency rooms to stay alive. Still others, less persistent, give up and hope they will get better. The main issue here is the organization of the care they receive. Even if on balance the poor have as many *visits* for care, this does not mean they are visiting the same type of system, or getting enough care to help them recover. Robertson and his colleagues speak in the past tense here, but only because they tried to change things in a small demonstration project, a project now over:

> The health care of the poor was uncoordinated, fragmented, and episodic; and, at the same time, it was impersonal and degrading. Where closely linked to welfare administration, it could seldom free itself from political and budgetary considerations of the local welfare department. The latter often specified the facility that welfare recipients could visit; at other times it attempted to regulate the extent or cost of the services received. As a result of location in "unsafe" neighborhoods, long waiting times, lack of attractive facilities, means tests, and perhaps the stigma attached to public clinics, facilities became more and more segregated. The clinics with many indigent patients, no matter how competent, tended not to treat the paying middle class patients[1]

They go on to note that these are simply one type of segregated facility, and that equality of services are seldom if ever possible under such conditions. Just as in segregated schools, the physical plants of segregated health facilities are poor, staff are overworked, harassed, underpaid, and, to some extent, hostile to the clientele.

One of the most common reactions of the poor to such settings has been to stay away from them—and thus get sicker and sicker at home until they arrive at the emergency room in the last stages of incurable illness. One cause of mortality in infants, for example, is dehydration as a consequence of intestinal colic and diarrhea. The infants scream and scream, but the mother is afraid of the reaction of the emergency room staff to a screaming baby, who is finally brought in in a coma. Research for more than two decades on the reasons why health-care settings are used by some people and not by others has led to the overall conclusion that poor people stay away from health-care settings for a variety of reasons.[2] There are, for example, money reasons, which have for most time periods prevented the poor from using private doctors' offices. The distance of the health-care setting from the poor has been found to play an important role, especially since the poor do not have the income to reach the few settings by taxis (which often will not pick up fares in the ghetto at night) or by buses (which don't run later in the evening). Where there are not close-by neighborhood centers, the care of the poor suffers. An extensive series of studies have been done on the social, psychological, and cultural factors that affect the way poor people perceive illness, and the way they do or do not perceive situations as medical emergencies. The nature of family dynamics and family behavior in coping with illness have been found to vary among ethnic groups. In addition, recent immigrants have often a competing folk medicine culture to which they turn first for solutions to problems; these practices may be more satisfying as a source of comfort, and sometimes of care, than the more impersonal technological medicine of the city hospital. In any case, the ways of coping with illness—in all groups, but especially among the poor, will definitely affect when, if ever, they approach a health-care setting. If we add the social and cultural values to their rather accurate and detailed knowledge of the bureaucratic hassles they know they will meet when they seek help, it is surprising that as many poor people come to the lower-class system as actually do.

Liberal health-service planners, observing the symptoms above, have developed strategies for delivering increased services to the poor. The basic outline of four strategies, along with what happened to them when they ran up against the field of forces described in the previous chapter, is our next topic. After each has been considered, we can return to the question of changing political economic systems through limited "experiments" and "demonstrations".

THE RISE AND FALL OF THE OEO NEIGHBORHOOD HEALTH CENTER

From the beginning of the Office of Economic Opportunity, there was a debate among health and welfare professionals, government bureaucrats, politicians, community people, and activists as to what the phrase "maximum feasible participation of the poor" would mean in the design and operation of local community action programs (CAPs). This early debate had implications not only for OEO in general, but, as a constituent member of the agency family, for the OEO Neighborhood Health Centers program in particular. According to the original diagnosis, existing settings did not really "belong" to the poor and were not actually accessible to them, so the settings should be brought to them and put at least partly under their supervision. The War on Poverty seemed a natural home for a new program to return medical care to the poverty neighborhoods, rural and urban. Why it didn't work out that way is an important story.

Early in the operation of the Head Start program for preschool children, many poor children had been identified as having uncured illness and tremendous dental problems, yet OEO had not set up a health program as part of their overall community effort. Furthermore, since the poor were bound to have so many medical problems, only a comprehensive program could be considered if the goal was to be taken seriously. Since health care is expensive and OEO's budget was limited, those within OEO who wanted a health program began it in the most strategic fashion: a set of demonstration projects on what could be done in a poverty area neighborhood.[3] Using the OEO/CAP model of "citizen participation" in the planning and running of such a center, Dr. Geiger and Dr. Gibson of Tufts Medical School received the first grants to set up an urban center— in Columbia Point, a welfare housing project in Boston—and in a rural poverty area in the Mississippi delta—Mound Bayou. Levitan, one of the main historians of the War on Poverty, summarized the working rules for neighborhood health centers, which were developed out of these initial efforts by Geiger, Gibson, and a few others, in the first year and a half of work by the Community Action Program division of OEO:

> Out of the negotiations over funding these centers, CAP developed a four-point model for comprehensive health centers: (1) a full range of ambulatory health services; (2) close liaison with other community services, which implied referrals and exchanges of services; (3) close working relationships with a hospital, preferably one with a medical school affiliation; and (4) participation of the indigenous population in decision-making that affected the center and, whenever feasible, their employment in subprofessional and other positions.[4]

Senator Edward Kennedy became the primary sponsor of the special program within OEO, beginning in 1966. By August 1968 there were thirty-two neighborhood health centers in operation around the nation; seventy-five percent were in urban poverty areas, with rural centers including special settings for migrant laborers (in California) and Indians (in Minnesota). But—and it is a very strong but—the OEO program never intended to set up a network to serve *all* poor people. In 1968, for example, only one out of twenty-five poor people who needed such services were to receive them from an OEO Neighborhood Health Center. Rather, the strategy was *to sell the idea* of comprehensive neighborhood-centered, neighborhood-run health centers for the poor. Levitan comments:

Granted the soundness of the neighborhood health center approach, OEO could hardly have been expected to bring about major changes in the delivery of health services to the poor; and the agency's officials recognized that OEO could not compete with the billions of dollars available for that purpose to the Department of Health, Education, and Welfare. OEO hoped rather to serve as a catalytic agent in bringing about changes in the health care delivery system and in pooling the funds received from scattered sources. Thus it has used its resources to fund a few demonstration projects.[5]

HEW and the Social Security Administration's Medicare program were responsible for most of the medical care for the poor at the usual places: public city hospitals and outpatient clinics. OEO was to be the innovator, and eventually if the approach worked it was to be "adopted" by HEW. This led to conflict within the government, with the OEO activists fearing that HEW, under far more political influence by organized medicine, and inherently more "professional" and conservative, would destroy or bureaucratize the Neighborhood Health Center Program if they eventually took it over. But other factors inherent in the way the Program was set up would do a large part of the destruction of the strategy as a new idea, long before it became more formally absorbed within the HEW structure.

The Escalation of Conflict

It was fateful that Geiger, Gibson, and other "academic elite/ new-wave planners" were asked to set up the first few centers, and then were asked for guidelines for the Neighborhood Health Center Program. There would eventually be a conflict between the guideline calling for close working relationships with a university medical center teaching hospital, and the guideline requiring participation of the poor in decision making; this conflict would create the greatest problems for the new program. To begin with, medical-care administration, and the high-pressure, high-speed grantsmanship strategy needed to keep the dollars coming from OEO from year to year, required a kind of technical expertise few poor people possessed. As a consequence, as Hollister found in his intensive case studies of two neighborhood health centers, the poor on the community advisory board either became a rubber stamp for the administration of the place, or a source of major conflict and turmoil as the staff fought against the board.[6] Furthermore, the academic medical elite was interested from the beginning in the training possibilities of such settings for their medical students: a chance to have an experience in "new-wave community medicine". Soon struggles began to develop between town and gown over the management of the center, who would hire whom with whose permission and approval, and who would have real power and control over the setting. These battlegrounds most definitely included the original urban and rural prototype settings: Columbia Point and Mound Bayou. The future was the primary concern: would the neighborhood centers simply become just another training center for white middle-class medical students, just as the emergency rooms and outpatient clinics were already? Or would the community have the right to make real policy decisions, and have the opportunity to screen students who might work there, or even refuse to have students at all if they didn't want them? On the other hand, for the major years of the program, the medical schools had the ultimate weapon: the grants either went directly to them, or their approval (affiliation) was necessary to make the neighborhood center legitimate and grantworthy in the eyes of OEO. Too much community opposition, too much struggle, and the medical school could threaten to withdraw: to take its money elsewhere, or pull back its sponsorship. The battles soon consumed much valuable time of staff, administrators, community members, bureaucrats, and activists. As the controversy escalated, it began to call into question the whole possibility of real community control of a project funded by government and supervised by a medical school in the area of the center.[7]

By June of 1970 OEO itself was on the way out as a major influence on social policy, and the Nixon administration had other ideas on national priorities than had the previous administration, at least in domestic areas. In 1970, there were only forty-nine OEO comprehensive neighborhood health centers in the entire nation. Thus the fights over power, money, and the administration of the centers must be assessed against the wider picture which indicated that they were, and are, only a minor element of the health-care system for the poor.

As a demonstration, neighborhood health centers did catch the imagination of many in the health field. Ordinary hospitals now routinely hire a Spanish-speaking aide for the emergency room, and, OEO-fashion, make at least a token effort at getting community input into policy making. Many newer health-care planning program laws structured community participation onto the ordinary process of administration. Furthermore, a national evaluation of the Neighborhood Health Center Program by Langston and colleagues found that where the centers did exist, they did reach about two-thirds of the eligible individuals, though they were not that much more popular than other settings in terms of patient attitudes.[8]

But many centers remained torn by conflict between medical school and community. When the money from Washington began to dwindle, or when the community insisted on controlling the money, or both, the medical schools began to back out of the scene (as, for example, Tufts did in Columbia Point). The conflict continued even when the center became totally community run, with one segment of the community berating another. The results, as elements of a service system, are a scattered set of neighborhood health centers, in an otherwise second-class system of services to the poor.

COMPREHENSIVE CARE FOR THE POOR:
DEMONSTRATIONS VERSUS REALITY

Among liberal and well-meaning health professionals, and especially in government during the sixties and early seventies, the idea
of the "demonstration project" held a major place. The OEO program was a demonstration project, but it was only one of many
concerned with "comprehensive care". Key elements in the strategy
were the stress on *comprehensiveness of service*, the attempt to
localize services in one place, and the stress on *continuity of care*,
both in the sense of forming an enduring social bond to the individual or family in need, and in the sense of "keeping tabs" on the
person or family in a preventive, future-regarding way as well as
dealing with present crises and problems. The demonstration was
proposed as the solution to the problem that services to the poor were
disorganized and inaccessible; it would provide *organized* and
accessible care. Three main projects of this type deserve some
inspection.

The first project, while not focussed on the poor, was nevertheless
dealing with many of the same problems the poor had, and also was
historically one of the first of its type. We refer to the *family health
maintenance demonstration*, organized by Silver with Health Insurance Plan (HIP) members in New York City between 1951 and
1959. The second was the *welfare medical care* demonstration by
Goodrich, Olendski, and Reader at Cornell University/New York
Hospital between 1960 and 1965, and the third was the *comprehensive family medical care demonstration* at Harvard Medical School/
Children's Hospital Medical Center in Boston between 1964 and
1968. After each is briefly presented, the community's strategies
and findings can be compared and then assessed as a strategy for
changing the two-class nature of our medical-care system.

Silver's project, the family health maintenance demonstration,

164

was funded by private foundation sources and based at Columbia University. The demonstration dealt with members of a prepaid medical-care plan in New York City, primarily middle class and working class in background. They were to receive "comprehensive family medical care" and a control group would continue to use the Plan's physicians (scattered across the map) and the large numbers of settings where they could "cash in" their Plan membership for services. The control group, in effect, would continue to partly organize their own pattern of services. The experiment was to maintain a family's health as a family unit, rather than treat each person in isolation. As such it was an attempt to take social and psychological factors into account, and carefully relate the organization of the service providers to the organization of the family unit. It aimed at motivating families to be more "health conscious", and recorded many general observations on family psychosocial functioning, to relate to health levels. It also recorded differences in health levels over time, between the experimental and the control group. "Comprehensive" here meant social work and mental health as well as regular medical help, for all project members, with the servers working in an integrated fashion as a team. Results appeared positive to the project staff and the patients. Both the experimental group and the practitioners preferred being a patient or a practitioner within this integrated comprehensive system, and fewer experimental group members quit the Health Insurance Plan than did control group members, over the decade or so that the project continued. Evidence indicated the experimental group (given comprehensive family care) as healthier at the end of the study than at the beginning, and slightly healthier than were their fellow plan members who were not in the project. The experimental group used about twice as many services, *at about double the cost*, of the control group's care. But careful investigation indicated that this was not a result of hypochondria by the experimental group but rather their willingness to tell "their" doctors about real illness and thus be helped with them.[9]

The second demonstration, of *welfare medical care*, essentially repeated most of the Silver group's strategy with one key difference: the target group was the poor, the welfare clients of New York City. Here the experimental group of welfare clients received a full range of integrated, personalized, localized (at Cornell/New York Hospital) comprehensive health care, while a control group would seek out their services on the usual catch-as-catch-can basis common to welfare patients going from place to place, from clinic to clinic, bureaucracy to bureaucracy. The experimenters concluded:

> The relative success of the undertaking depended on a number of innovations in customary outpatient practice. The most important of these were (1) providing a clinical team within the hospital that could come to know the patients over a span of years and that would provide the continuity such care requires; (2) taking responsibility for the care of people in the community before they presented themselves for treatment (taking the initiative in beginning care, with an appointment for a physical examination, proved even more successful than leaving the patient to establish contact himself); (3) guaranteeing availability of services to patients so that they did not face repeated screening for eligibility.[10]

In a sense, this was an experiment in replacing the usual delivery system of care for the poor with a quality, integrated kind of treatment, in fact more integrated than that which many middle-class patients have. Not surprisingly, the welfare patients liked it. They used it more than the welfare patient controls used (or were able to demand) care from the usual welfare medicine sources. It cost far more per patient than the control group's care, because all the real illness—much higher in the welfare group than in the middle class—was identified and then treated. The overall quality of care delivered did seem to be superior to that of the regular system.

The third major demonstration, that of *comprehensive family medical care*, chronologically followed the second, just as the second followed the first, and was yet another demonstration of the possibilities of "comprehensive integrated care". It combined the family focus of the first study (with a special stress on children) and the target group of the second. Both foundation and government support were given to the Robertson group at Harvard's Children's Hospital. Both the experimental and the control group came from low-income (welfare and unskilled) people who showed up with their children at the emergency room of the Children's Hospital Medical Center in Boston. The project staff wished to provide "a practical representation of the comprehensive philosophy", focused mainly on the *children* of the families in the program. They wanted to prove that it was possible to provide "continuity of care", to "minimize fractionation of care", to maximize interstaff and staff-patient communication, and to provide "preventive and curative care".[11] And, to a reasonable extent, they did so, for the children in the experimental group had a lower rate of hospitalization for illness, got more treatment for their diseases, and seemed more satisfied. But parents did not trust the *overall* medical-care system any more at the conclusion of the study. In addition, the black subsample broke off relations with the project more frequently than did the whites—at least in part because they were ordered to do so in some cases by their welfare caseworkers. Cost? Of course it cost more, but as with the first and the second demonstration, they *needed* the extra care. Also, the foundations and the government were paying.[12]

What did these demonstrations prove, then, and what did they *not* prove? First, they proved that with extensive support from foundations and government, university-based health-care teams can temporarily provide intensive quality care to those who badly need it, and ordinarily don't get it. Second, they prove that the poor and the working class usually appreciate the extra attention and service, and from the project personnel's point of view, it can be an enjoyable experience to provide it and study it. What these demonstrations did *not* do was change the medical-care system for the poor. At the completion of the action phase—in 1959, 1965, and

167

1968 respectively—the demonstrations folded their tents and stole away. Then *all* the participants, including the previously coddled "experimental" groups, had to return to an essentially unmodified system, one that in the case of the last of the three demonstrations was, if anything, getting even worse than at the beginning of this "demonstration era". For no major structural changes had been made in the overall society, in the area of power over the medical-care system, and over the inherently two-class nature of the system. To create a temporary first-class island for the poor, in a second-class sea of care, is not to change the sea. The "demonstration approach" in human service is, in other words, an exploration of the possible rather than the creation of the probable. Surely the cost is the ultimate political problem. The foundations and special bureaus within government that fund the demonstrations disappear when the time comes to fund these innovations as permanent changes. Demonstrations are one thing, structural change quite another.

THE MEDICAID PROGRAM:
A VOUCHER STRATEGY

A third major strategy for changing the delivery of services to the poor was a "voucher" strategy: specifically the Medicaid program. The *problem*, as diagnosed by those who advocated the voucher strategy, was that the poor are *poor*, that is, without the money or the insurance coverage to buy services in the top level of the two-class medical system. Given the money to buy care anywhere (the ticket or the voucher) the poor would go away from the undersystem and it would wither away, as they cashed the vouchers in at nonprofit voluntary hospitals and doctor's offices.

When the Medicare/Medicaid legislation was passed during the Johnson era, in 1965, it was a three-part law, the first two parts of which created a medical insurance system for the middle-class elderly, administered through the Social Security Administration;

and the third part of which—Medicaid—was to be administered in Washington by the *welfare* divisions of HEW. In theory, the "vouchers" would be payments both for those on welfare and those *not* on welfare but too poor to pay for their own care in the top-level system. They were to be called the "medically indigent". With the new Medicaid money, they could theoretically go anywhere, and say, as if they had Mastercharge or BankAmericard, "Take me, too, Medicaid will pay for it". The private physician, or voluntary hospital, would then get paid by the local welfare department or the state government for the services they gave. This was the strategy—and it didn't work. The reasons are our present subject.

To begin with, when the original Medicaid law was passed, no strong central administration was set up at HEW to run the program, so each state could and did decide for themselves who would be eligible to use the new vouchers. Wealthier and more progressive states such as New York and California were more generous here to their poor, and also were able to demand and get more federal "matching funds" (money to match what they put up as states) than states which had not moved so fast. Soon the demands for money just from these states alone in the first year and a half of the program, outran the lawmakers' estimated cost of the program for the whole nation.[13] Then there was the critical issue of whether this was really a "voucher" system, or whether it was simply to be another element in the existing welfare system. Did the poor have a *right* to this money, or would it be up to each welfare department, in each state, to decide who the "deserving poor" would be? *The decision to run the program through the Federal Welfare Bureau, and then in each state through the welfare departments, which was a decision made at the beginning of the Medicaid program, doomed it from the start as a strategy for change.* For the program was to be run by the low-prestige welfare system, which had already been under fire for years, and which itself was a major element in harassing the poor in many poverty areas. One year after the program began, Stevens and Stevens concluded that

HEW itself inevitably gave priority, insofar as there were clear priorities, to run Medicare, which as a prestige operation run by the powerful Social Security Administration as part of the Social Security program was the darling of the politicians and the electorate. Without real power within the Department and without a clearly-defined political constituency, MSA and Medicaid found themselve the whipping boys for rising medical costs and rising "welfare" expenditures for which they were, at most, only partially responsible.[14]

As the costs of the program shot up, the screams of antiwelfare politicians bounced off the walls in Congress and quickly led to cutbacks in the overall program. Campaigns to sign the poor up in the program were followed a year or so later by the disqualifications of many of the "medically indigent" who no longer qualified as the maximum income level for qualification in the program began to *drop*. Power struggles began: the new Welfare Rights organizations were campaigning for higher rates for welfare clients in general, and for more people being allowed on Medicaid, while at the same time the politicians and the American middle class, motivated in part by racist considerations, fought against what they called "welfare cheating". Soon it became evident that hospitals and private physicians were in some cases getting rich on Medicaid payments, that profit-making nursing homes were springing up everywhere to take advantage of the federal money (in 1969, 14,470 out of the nation's 18,910 nursing homes were private profit-making ones),[15] and that fraud levels by physicians were approaching five to seven percent of the cases in New York City. An investigation found the practice of "mass visits"—a physician walking past a line of forty patients and charging for a visit to each one. Unnecessary medication and tests were often prescribed—sometimes to a drugstore or lab that gave a kick-back to the physician.[16]

The beginning year of the Medicaid program was a time of expansion. The second period, from 1967 to 1969, was a time of cutback in payments and restriction of the program down to those on welfare, in many places. By 1970, there was also a stronger focus on the fraud of providers. Neither the escalation of costs nor the fraud made the program popular with the voter, and unpopularity in political terms does not mean a bright future for any program. But regardless of the politics which were determining the program's fate from year to year, the most essential aspect of the experiment in the first place was to have been that the poor would be treated the same as anyone else in the society; that they could get the same care that others could. But to be poor in America is to be a hostage of the welfare system, and to have to beg for health-care vouchers just as one has to beg for a bed or an extra few dollars for children's clothes. There was no due process of law for several years, and a welfare worker could and did sometimes decide to deny Medicaid support to a particular client as a way of punishing him or her. Even today, it is hard to get the "hearing" that is the right of the client without a storefront lawyer at one's side in the welfare office. Stevens and Stevens present this from the welfare client's point of view:

> As welfare or near–welfare recipients, Medicaid patients were often treated as social dependents rather than "consumers", even in the thick of the consumer movement. Not only did recipients frequently find it humiliating trying to get on Medicaid, they often faced humiliation when they had a complaint about the program, or there was some doubt about their continued eligibility. . . . Regulation of recipients has thus largely been repressive rather than protective.[17]

But what of the ability to buy out of the bottom system? Several limitations on this have been important, and they relate directly to the overall patterns of service and the strength of the elements of the existing two-class system. First, since costs far outran predictions, many states got far behind on their bill paying. Since the private physician and the voluntary hospital have control over who they want to take, and since after a while the Medicaid voucher system began to look very much like a $3 bill, the signs began to go up over all the metropolitan areas: "Medicaid cards not honored here". Others, who *specialized* in Medicaid patients, did so for money and not for service, cutting corners to the point where their "private" care was, if anything, worse than that which the poor were getting in the public hospitals. The poor could not afford the trip to the suburbs and its hospitals, and doctors' offices; many soon became suspicious of the new "Medicaid factories". So they took their vouchers to the only place left—the city hospital. Because of bureaucratic politics in Washington, for many years they couldn't even cash them in at neighborhood health centers of the OEO type. And welfare workers, holding power over the poor, could and did tell them where to get medical care. Few people could argue with them, because they did not know their rights. In the Harvard comprehensive care project we discussed above, some poor patients would not join even when urged by the project staff because, they said, "Their welfare worker wouldn't allow them to". Robertson and his group, with all the resources of a major medical center and a special project, could not win the battle against the local welfare department:

> It is also known that long after the Medicare-Medicaid legislation, which allowed welfare families to use whatever facilities they wished, some welfare workers had not conveyed this information to their clients and were continuing to urge them to use City Hospital. Since the families in our sample used many facilities, these admonitions were not always effective but some may have been confused by being told different things regarding their rights.[18]

The final chapter in the Medicaid story is the fiscal crisis of the state in the mid-seventies. Here the working class is set against the poor by the refusal of the capitalist class to pay more in taxes to support social service, in a situation where they are under pressure from world competition from socialist and Third-World activity. Since the white- and blue-collar workers will not pay the bill either—for they cannot and still have money left for consumption—massive cutbacks become necessary to the service for the poor. In 1975 Massachusetts, a generally liberal state, removed all general relief recipients from the Medicaid program. They were officially made charity cases and from the time of the action on, have had to beg their medical care wherever they can find it, with no reimbursement for those giving it to them.

To sum up, the voucher strategy shared with the comprehensive service demonstration strategy and the OEO Neighborhood Health Center strategy certain assumptions and certain fates. As ideas, by well-meaning liberal theorists, they were attempts to rearrange the pattern of services delivered to the poor and increase the quality of these services; that is, to deal with the two-class system. But the existing interest groups, and the overall structural pressures bearing on the capitalist class, went to work on Medicaid even more quickly and thoroughly than in the other two main areas we have discussed (OEO and demonstrations of comprehensive care). The money in the other two areas was trivial in comparison to that involved in the Medicaid program. Political opposition to the creation of genuine equal opportunity in health care for the poor, and an alignment of the main system elements causing the trouble in the first place, plus the profit motivation of the private system, led to the quick deflection of the program from its original goal. Thousands of poor people have had greater support through Medicaid, even more than were helped with the OEO Neighborhood Health Centers and the "comprehensive care" demonstrations. But the program simply channeled money into one existing element in the lower class of the medical system. If anything, the hand of the agencies dealing with the poor was strengthened by the program, as was the two-class system itself. And eventually, by the mid-seventies, the fiscal crisis of the capitalist state—especially in the cities—sounded the death knell of the program, even as a *support* system for the lower class.

AFFILIATION CONTRACTS: GEOGRAPHIC POLITICS AND THE DELIVERY OF SERVICES

Few health-care settings stand alone, without a relationship to others. For any clinic or hospital to survive, it must have a continual stream of patients who either walk in the door on their own, or come referred by health-care workers elsewhere. In addition to these informal ties within communities, between health workers and institutions, there are many formal ties. One of the most important for our present purposes is that between medical schools and hospitals. The varieties of possible relationship between the two institutions are summed up by Yohalem's and Brecher's description of "academic medical centers":

> In academic centers a hospital's relations to a medical school may take one of three forms: It may be a major unit in the medical school's teaching programs; a unit that provides limited support for undergraduate clinical education; or one that provides only graduate training programs. In some cases certain hospitals are owned by the medical school, or else both hospital and medical school are owned by the same organization, usually the state or a university; in instances where there is no common ownership or control relations generally take the form of an "affiliation".[19]

Affiliation contracts are formal agreements between a community hospital and a medical school, where the two are essentially separate organizations, where there is "no common ownership or control". To begin with, this means that at the time the contract was first established, each saw something to be gained from the relationship. Usually the community hospital believes it will gain better training and teaching, plus consulting help and access to technology possessed by the medical school. Most important, benefits are expected to follow from the presence of the skilled and research-oriented physicians in whatever part of the program the hospital has set up as an "affiliated" program. By the affiliation route, the medical school administrators gain a setting for training medical students, or they gain an element in some type of citywide delivery system of which they envision themselves as the architects and eventual administrators. But the relationships in existence, as studied by several different investigative teams, seem to be burdened by several types of problems: structural (the fairness or unfairness of the exchange between the medical school and the community hospital); geographic (the extent to which the relationships—on a map of the community—form anything like a rational delivery system involving the two main elements of medical schools and community hospitals); and the political-economic (the extent to which one partner uses political power and expertise as ways of exploiting the other to the detriment of the patients served by that other partner). After looking at these pathologies in the most extensively studied area—New York City—we can assess the extent to which these problems are specific to New York City or are general, and what is being attempted to deal with the problems.

New York City—Typical or Exceptional Case?

In New York City, the experiment carried on in the sixties was a radical departure from simple "arrangements" between part of a medical school and part of a hospital. A citywide arrangement was created whereby *every* participating public city hospital would be staffed and run by one of the seven medical schools, and city money would go directly to the medical schools while the city would continue to keep up the physical plants of the setting.[20] This approach was an attempt to fight a trend toward the presence of poorly-trained foreign physicians as the only staff in the public system, which in general was understaffed in all worker roles. A decade of dissatisfaction with the new arrangement followed. The medical schools complained about the city's lack of maintenance of

175

the public hospitals, and the city complained that taxpayers' dollars were being used for expensive research equipment that the medical school wanted, rather than for the staff that the medical schools had promised in return for the money. If the staff *were* there, they were not necessarily accessible to the nurses and others who needed advice; the professors and technology of the medical school often turned out to be completely beyond reach, even though they were supposed to be more "accessible" in return for the city's money. The exchange was not equal, in other words; the medical schools were placed in a position of power to manage the terms of the exchange.[21] In geographical terms, since the private hospitals and the nonmedical-school–affiliated hospitals were not part of the affiliation agreement, this citywide experiment did not provide an organizing tool for the total range of health-care settings. Attempts at regional planning of a network of settings across the map, had to involve both the medical-school/public sector arrangement and hundreds of smaller, private settings. In one area of the city, this was the result:

> We have pointed out that the integration in health care in the Bronx has not been an outgrowth of a conscious effort to implement a regional plan. Interhospital relations have been explained by a unique combination of chance, personal drive, financial considerations, and a variety of other institutional and interest group concerns.[22]

In the late sixties a new organization, the Health and Hospitals Commission, was founded as a way of trying to develop some order out of the chaos. In political-economic terms, attempts to organize a citywide system had been sabotaged by the private nonprofit hospitals' refusal to be a part of the other medical-school/public subsystem. They didn't join the Commission, and in addition the unions successfully fought against allowing community participation in the planning of the new corporation's activities, while the city took back some of the money control which it had handed to the medical schools in the previous decade. Politicians refused to exempt many of the nonprofessional jobs from straight patronage. Because of all of these factors, Ostow concluded that the new organization "is not likely to result in any essential change in the present dual system of health care".[23]

Two major questions can be asked about this affiliation process. First, is New York unique in either its strategy or its problems in having a two-class system managed by the medical schools? Second, what new strategies are being tried, and by whom, to improve the development of services through the "affiliation" route, and do these constitute a basic change in the two-class system of health-care delivery? In answer to the first question, we can observe that New York City and Los Angeles are often found to have, in a more *intense* form, the same types of general urban problems found in all metropolitan centers. In the health field, the rise in public funds from federal sources in the sixties, followed by their sharp cutback in the present decade, led every city first to attempt new methods of funding programs and new ways of administering the public sector. The academic medical elite in many American cities, especially professors of health-care administration and health economics, were especially interested in these problems from an intellectual's point of view. They often encouraged the medical schools to take a greater role in running the public system.

But not all medical schools have kept their enthusiasm into the decade of the seventies. As the urban problems have escalated, and costs with them, some of the medical schools have pulled back. In communities where the medical schools' role was especially exploitative (such as in New York City) consumer activists early began to call attention to the problem, and pressure was brought to bear on schools to define their role more clearly.[24] Costs have forced as much of the withdrawal as has the pressure of activists, however, along with tighter federal controls over such items as overhead costs on grants to community programs.

The Future: Affiliation and
the Academic Medical Elite

Is the future simply to be a repetition of the past, with minor cosmetic changes? In a recent Macy Foundation conference on "The University Medical Center and the Metropolis", the following were some of the presented papers:

"Models for Health System Linkages"
"A Network for Health Care: The Case of Rochester, New York"
"Five Communities: The University of Chicago Medical Center"
"The Detroit Medical Center: A New Concept"
"Innovative Health Care Delivery: The Third Leg of the Stool"
"The Insurance Company and the Medical Center: Partners in Innovation"

Here we had the academic medical elite at its most inventive and creative, with many new plans for arranging or rearranging services under the general supervision of the medical school, without sharing power or administrative control with the community. The planners at the conference recognized the growth in political pressure by communities on medical schools and presented a series of minor reforms in the architecture of medical school-public hospital relationships. But they were primarily variations of the basic spiderweb design, with the storefront clinics all grouped around the central spider: the medical school teaching hospital. The role of the federal government as a potential external control—of much money for most services—was recognized in the conference's summary statements. The poverty-level community's "unrealistic expectations" for quality care—which the medical schools admitted they could not meet at the same level as for other areas of the city and with the middle class—were also noted and sadly accepted as "facts of life". There was no overall commitment to abolish the two-class system. In this mid-seventies conference, the discussion indicated that among the conference participants "there was a difference of opinion about whether patient care should serve the needs of education and research only, or whether it should be designed to serve the needs of the community".[25]

IN SUMMARY: THE USES OF
THE BOTTOM SYSTEM

In Beckett's play, *Waiting for Godot*, the central two characters sit in their twin trash cans, and wait. They are expecting the arrival of Godot. But Godot never comes. Neither does quality health care for the poor. They are deeply suspicious of the promises that have been made to them over the years, and wary of the bottom system of health service, because of years of direct experience. And they are cynical about the special programs which the nation constructs from time to time to deal with its guilt, cheaply, without changing the system that continues to produce the conditions from which they suffer. In the meantime, they will take what they can from a neighborhood health center, a special medical school project in comprehensive care, a program to help pay some of their medical bills.

But the poor do not get overly enthusiastic about these programs, for they have seen them come and go, or as in the case of Medicaid, turn sour before their eyes in the space of a year or two. The poor are not needed by the economic ruling class of the society, except as a reserve army of possible laborers, desperate for any type of job, and they know this. As the unemployment rolls grow, more and more Americans begin to have direct experience with this bottom system. Their initial puzzlement turns to rage, but the rage soon turns to despair, for they quickly become aware that the kind of political, structural change in the society which would guarantee them a job and a quality health-care system could only come with major rearrangements in the present societywide system of power and privilege. Money can be made from action programs, demonstration

179

projects, and Medicaid. Also, money can be lost by corporations and the upper class, if it is given to the poor. They know that they, the poor, do not have the kind of strength to make this possible, nor can they count as yet on the working and middle class as allies. Thus, strategies for gaining and holding money and power, in general and in the health field, are of special importance to them. But they are important to everyone: they will be our next area for inspection.

6

The American System: Political Economy

A classic response to the plans or ideas of an innovator or activist meant to deflate the proposer and to suggest that the critic is a solid citizen while the other is a dreamer, is to ask "Who'll pay for it?" Yet this is *not* an unfair or irrelevant question. It may instead be the most important question of all, if our goal is to understand the existing patterns of health service and the opposition to changing them. Nor can we leave the issue to another book—one, for example, specializing in the economics of health care. For money and power go together in our society, and money is used to keep power, while power is used to maintain the existing social and political arrangements to keep those who are benefitting happy, to control the climate and the context, to protect investments. The health field is no exception: struggles to change and to preserve the status quo are in large part money motivated. If our goal is to understand the picture "out there", we will need to address this issue directly, for there are no dotted lines on the world labelled "health economics", "health system sociology", and "health politics".

To begin with, a description is needed of the major *money games* that are played by the existing groups in the American health-care system: the complex money-related strategies that we will need to be familiar with at an elementary level, at least, in order to see how profit-motivation preserves the existing pattern of American services. But we will need to see that the world is always in flux, even in America, that power balances shift if groups successfully organize and force them to change, and that these changes have immediate consequences for the flow of cash and the degree to which specific groups gain or lose in a particular situation on a particular topic. After presenting the strategies, we can inspect them in a series of specific cases: the control of the supply and demand of health manpower: the politics of blood; the cost of malpractice insurance; the health maintenance organization (HMO) debate; and the medical-industrial complex as a production/profit mechanism. We can conclude the consideration of the American case by summarizing at a more general level, and using a more general theoretical approach, as it explains the iron constraints preventing any significant change in the present system while this form of economic organization remains unchanged.

GETTING MONEY AND USING IT: THE MAJOR STRATEGIES

If the system as we have described it can be viewed as a series of intertwined potted plants, each needing soil and water to survive, then an analogy can be drawn which will get to the heart of our present concern with money. Suppose the water and soil were gradually stolen from the pot of one plant, and given to another. The deprived plant, and its branches, might eventually wither and die;

its branches would fall out of the thicket and be replaced by the now larger and more complex branches of the plant to which the extra earth and water were given. By studying the way that interest groups control the flow of money, and the ways in which they use the money they have as a weapon to advance their interests, we are studying the use of "soil and water" in terms of its effect on *the overall pattern of services*. The assumption—to be reinspected at the end of this chapter—is that the amount of soil and water is *limited* and those within the health field are not the main determiners of these limits.

It may be helpful if we begin by considering the major strategies which are used to gain more control over money and to use what one has to advance one's power position. We may briefly call these strategies *the carrot-and-stick approach, monopoly creation, budgetary infighting, cost shifting,* and *politics through expertise*. Each can be related to the social and political dimensions of money in the shaping of the system of health services.

The first strategy, the *carrot-and-stick*, depends on the possession of significant funds to begin with, and the use of these funds to buy the opposition, in a situation where the group using the strategy has some power and control over at least part of the pattern of services. The "carrot" here is the reward of increased money support for going along with changes in the organization and delivery of services which the provider wishes. The "stick" is the threat of cutoff of money if the target of the strategy persists in doing what the provider of money doesn't want. Two kinds of "sticks", for example, are consumer boycotts and government cutoff of funds from federal or state projects, in health or in any other field. How *big* the carrot is, in comparison to the size of the stick, will be critically important in the way this strategy is perceived by the ones for whom it is intended. For example, a large money reward offered along with a mild penalty for going along seems like co-optation or bribery to the target group, whereas the threat of force or loss of funds coupled with only a minor money reward is perceived as coercion. In specific cases, dealing with rearrangements in the pattern of services, the federal government is becoming an increasingly influential user of the carrot-and-stick strategy. The carrots here are the federal funds for supplying health care, the sticks the new laws which penalize behavior and activity of a certain type, or which set deadlines before which time the health-care professionals must rearrange some pattern of services or perform some kind of activity in order to continue to receive support. Consumers who have enough resources in the health area to boycott a service they do not like and which is dependent on them for funds, would be an example of the stick in action. Their offer to retreat with their money or their insurance coverage might be another.

Attempts to control new health-care legislation through the funding of congressional and presidential campaigns are an even older form of the carrot-and-stick techniques. For example, money has traditionally been provided by organized medicine with the understanding that those elected would check with the AMA to get their opinion before voting on a new law. The stick was the withdrawal of support the next time around if the legislator did not vote the way the AMA desired. In general, in order to play this game at the national level, far more resources are needed than most consumers have, hence the need for organizations such as Common Cause, which combine public educational activity with carrot-and-stick politics.

Second, there is a strategy of *monopoly creation*, or cornering the market. The world's most recent general example of this has been in the actions of the Arab oil-producing nations' OPEC (Organization of Petroleum Exporting Countries). By "cornering the market" on a large segment of the world's oil, and pushing up the price to nations that have no alternative, the end of enriching the monopolists is reached. But the Arab oil ministers learned this technique as graduate students at Harvard Business School or at other similar American or European capitalist training programs. Control of the market supply, while the demand remains unchecked, is a classic capitalist technique.[1] It demands enough political power to make free competition a myth, power which not all corporations or other political organizations always achieve. But it is a clear strategy which can be inspected in the health field. For example, licensed professions *legally* constitute monopolies "in the public interest", in that the license is the only legal qualification which allows one to carry out the activities. The abuse of the privileged position can occur through controlling the supply of people who qualify for the license (decreasing the number of graduates from a training program or keeping them the same as the numbers of people in need rises). This allows the "scarce" professionals to charge more for their services. Or to use another example, existing hospitals can gain control of a community hospital planning process and defeat attempts by weaker groups, such as a local neighborhood health center, to expand and compete with them for patients. Another word for monopoly is *cartel*; a social arrangement of providers which aims to control the amount produced, the price of the needed goods or services, and the political power balance between the providers and the consumers. Every planning and service-delivery process should be inspected to see whether the monopoly-building game is being attempted.[2]

A third strategy is that of *budgetary infighting*, or *the politics of the budgetary process*, to use Wildavsky's phrase.[3] Political strategies here are focused on getting final approval for a large slice of the overall pie, as a formal item in the budget, or, failing this, to informally beg, borrow, or steal more than one was allotted, using whatever power, connections, and persuasive skills one's group possesses. Budgets are documents drawn up by both private and public organizations, indicating where the resources will go in the next time period. If a new law is passed, for example, it may require the creation of a new program of health services. Those pushing for the new program will attempt to get a maximum share of the overall budget for their program. Opponents will fight to have the program funded at a low level of support, to take water and soil away from the new plant even at the start. At the community level, the overall resources available to a city also become a battlefield. At any level, the *priorities* for spending—health versus education, new programs versus old ones, private versus public—ultimately decide the size of each slice of the pie, or the size of the pie itself. These priorities are determined by political processes which are never fixed, are always open to new techniques of influence:

> Committee meetings, lobbying, politicking—it's all part of the budget allocation process, and at the core of this process lies the question, How do you go about dividing the funds? In our society there are more claimants and more goods that need to be fulfilled than there are resources to fill them. This is true at the local, state, and national level. Establishing priorities is of course one method for determining allocation of funds. But who will fix the priorities? Can clear priorities be established when the issues involved concern health and education, among other areas?[4]

Budgetary politics can be viewed as a game in which all the players *do not* start out with similar resources, or as a race with the runners placed at different distances from the goal, before the starting gun goes off. To the extent that a group already has power and money, it can use both to threaten the budgetmakers or buy them (carrot-and-stick), concerning their share for next year. The process assumes no major change in the authority of the budgetmakers, whoever they may be. Within this constraint, however, almost anything goes in many situations. The result can often be described by the biblical phrase, "To him who hath, to him it shall be given; to him who hath not shall be taken away that which he hath".

A fourth technique can be called *cost shifting*. A series of exchanges are made, when pressure is put on those with power, money, and control over the system, which ultimately result in the costs being shifted to the consumer. For example, when an industry is under pressure to reform itself—to put antipollution devices on factory smokestacks, to install safety devices in automobiles—the industry falls back on the strategy of obeying the direct order and then shifting the costs to the consumer in terms of higher prices for the product. Even intermediate players along the line can become part of the process: for example, unions in recent years have forced hospitals to raise wages for the blue-collar workers, who in turn raised their charges for service to Blue Cross (the insurer of many patients), who then in turn raised the cost of insurance paid by the consumer.[5]

Finally there are *the politics of expertise*.[6] Technical skill in health care includes expert knowledge in such fields as economics, planning, sociology, political science, engineering, and other areas. In areas such as regulation, which we will consider in the last section of the book, lawyers form another expert group. The political process here consists in having the money to hire the experts, and then using them as a "neutral" technique for advancing one's interests in a controversial area. Experts come in all shades of political opinion, and both the AMA and the neighborhood health center can find economists to produce sophisticated arguments as to why their particular plan for the future health system makes the best sense. The catch is that the AMA can and does hire a whole army of such experts, whereas the poor must usually make do with volunteers, often graduate students with other things to do as well. Legislative battles, again to be considered as a direct political process in the final section, are a key area for the politics of expertise.

Each of these strategies is used at some time by almost every actor in the field of health services. But, as we noted in describing them, those with the most in the way of resources often can use them more effectively in gaining their ends. Five case studies can now be taken up, to illustrate the ways in which these strategies for gaining or keeping control of money and the money-flow process work out at the present time. These are the cases of manpower supply and demand, the buying and selling of blood, the malpractice insurance costs problem, the debate over the value of HMOs, and the social role of the medical-industrial complex.

MANPOWER: CONTROLLING SUPPLY AND DEMAND

Defining "supply" and "demand" of medical services is not a simple matter. Fein, in a study of "the doctor shortage", observed that having a doctor in the neighborhood is of no use to a patient who doesn't have the money to buy the services. This, he said, is an issue of supply versus demand every bit as important as the *number* of doctors trained each year:

> Estimating the number of physicians required to offer sufficient services to the total population can be merely a statistical exercise. If it is to be more, programs are needed to enable persons to purchase the services (and programs to reallocate physicians). The shortage that causes parts of the population to consume insufficient care is as much a shortage of purchasing power as a shortage of supply.[7]

Fein also notes that the *way* health care is organized may determine how productive it is, in providing more service for more people for less money. The number of patients that can be seen by a given number of health workers, and the costs, will depend at least in part on the *arrangement* of the workers; solo practitioners spread out over the map with a nurse or two can be contrasted with a group of physicians, nurses, and auxiliary health practitioners working as part of a team. In addition, the size of the health-care team (or organization) may have advantages in itself, in terms of lowering costs:

> It is often found that larger organizational units are able to achieve economies that are denied to those of smaller size. These "economies of scale" result from the fact that certain divisions of labor and specialization are made possible and justified when the number of units produced—or services rendered—is sufficiently large. Furthermore,

various types of equipment and kinds of personnel are often available in "lumpy" units—one can't buy half a machine or readily hire half a person.[8]

In addition, the strategy of "monopoly creation" restricts the supply in order to raise the price. Historically, the AMA made a decision during the Great Depression of the thirties, for a policy which lasted until the mid-sixties, to keep the number of medical graduates constant, even though the population was growing rapidly. "Professional birth control" consists in part of taking only the *most* qualified of the qualified, not even a majority of them. Fein comments:

> An artificially limited number of spaces in medical school obviously restricts the number of physicians ultimately available. The restriction on available spaces in medical schools would, of course, seldom be defended on the basis of limiting new entrants. The arguments put forth instead appeal to scientific standards and to quality considerations. Yet, if the standards are artificial and unnecessary, if the definition of "qualified" applicants is arbitrary, if the tests to measure qualifications are inappropriate, the consequences are the same.[9]

Years of analysis of this sort (beginning in the thirties) were met by years of stalling by organized medicine. In addition to fears of lowered income if there were a higher ratio of physicians to patients, there were other objections. These especially included opposition to federal scholarships for qualified poverty-level and working-class medical students, or extra money from government to expand the number of places in each school. The profession wanted to avoid a "carrot-and-stick" situation, fearing that government subsidy of direct educational costs would soon lead to government direction of the curriculum, and demands that the students spend the first few years after graduation out in the rural areas, because the government had paid their education and had a right to a direct "return" for the money spent. This practice is of course routine in socialist systems. The ideology of organized medicine fought against it as long as possible.

But after the mid-sixties, the places in medical school began to multiply, at least in part because the federal government had enough leverage to force this to happen because of its increasing degree of subsidization of medical education, and some change had occurred in the leadership of the AMA, in a slightly more liberal direction. In addition to an upswing of new physicians, many new governmental programs began to train auxiliary manpower, to increase the number of helpers available for the new "teams". Such sixties programs as the Manpower Development and Training Act, the Allied Health Professionals Training Act, the Nurse Training Act, and the Health Manpower Training Act were examples of expanding federal support for training new health workers. In addition to the federal programs, forces working at present to expand the number of health workers include, in the case of the allied fields, the growth of community college training programs and the increasing interest of unions in getting "upgrading" training programs for their workers, at the places where they hold their jobs.

On the other hand, there are forces at work to *restrict* the supply. Two are specially important: the pressure by existing groups to increase the number of years of training required to get a certificate in their occupation; and the more general goal of "professionalizing" the existing occupation, by fighting against community training and open entry of new workers combined with on-the-job training. Goldstein has found that much of this status-directed training doesn't mean necessarily that the trained do work that is much different from the barely qualified. Nurses, LPNs, and aides, for example, had a great overlap in responsibility, from one level to the next, in terms of who actually did what precise task at work, in a series of on-site studies done by his research team.[10]

Reality has only a marginal relationship to status seeking, however. If a group can successfully lobby in a state legislature to raise the number of years of training legally required for a particular credential, they can raise the cost of the training by so doing, regardless who will actually do what on the work setting at a later point in time. One especially important example is the nursing profession's campaign to abolish three-year, hospital-based schools of nursing, and instead to demand that all nurses be trained in four- or five-year nursing programs based in universities.[11] This drastically increases the cost of the education and the time it takes new nurses to train. In addition, since the poor cannot afford college programs (hospital schools are usually tuition free, with work-study arrangements taking the place of tuition), the nursing field increasingly stratifies itself socially, causing a racial- and class-tracking system to develop while manpower supply is restricted and the cost of training is increased. It seems a heavy price to pay for status; and it is paid by the consumer, rather than the nursing profession.

An increasing supply of health manpower does not necessarily guarantee greater health service to those who need it; rather, the *pattern* of service is the determining factor. For example, even "teams" of doctors, nurses, and paraprofessionals can operate only where the physician is willing to go, and since he is usually unwilling to go to rural areas or ghettos, the new paraprofessionals are not able to go there either, except under special "demonstration project" conditions, in experimental programs. In this sense, then, increasing the numbers of health workers alone, without changing the structure or pattern of services, will not solve the problem, even with an increase in allied or auxiliary helpers. Since primary-care physicians (general practitioners) are the really important element in the physician-nurse system, and since the leverage of physician assistants and nurse practitioners might seem to be the greatest for patient care—were they really given freedom—the near absence of this element in the present community delivery system makes it very difficult to build up a solution which is based on a physician-centered system of auxiliaries.[12] In other words, suburban pediatricians using helpers such as pediatric nurse associates *will* deliver more care in the suburbs (and add to their income), but this won't change the rural or ghetto picture to any marked degree.

Another important example of the way the supply-and-demand manipulation strategy has been used is the status of foreign medical graduates, since this has varied depending on the availability of American-trained physicians. In 1967, for example, more foreign medical graduates entered the United States than the number graduated from American medical schools during this year.[13] Foreign medical graduates have traditionally filled gaps in the present system, such as in public city hospitals and state mental hospitals, where the salaries and working conditions are too unattractive for American physicians. But in the last few years, as the numbers of American graduates have risen in relation to population, this has begun to change. Two points of leverage have been found useful by the American medical profession here: state-level licensing boards and immigration laws. At the state level, depending on the degree of manpower shortage or surplus, licensing boards have raised or lowered the passing scores on a special qualifying exam which the immigrant physician must take in order to practice.

At the national level, the game is played through lobbying with respect to the immigration laws. There are complexities here: for example, during the past decade, before the upswing in the production of American physicians, there was a conflict between organized medicine and the academic medical elite. The AMA wanted freer immigration for foreign physicians (taking pressure off American medicine to produce more graduates and thus forcing them to fill the dirty jobs in medicine), while the academic side of the profession pushed for higher standards for all physicians, especially the foreign graduate.

In 1965 the immigration laws were loosened and a flood of foreign physicians began to enter, effectively robbing many developing nations, and some in Europe, of badly needed health manpower.[14] The results were tragic for them, and for us. During the years of the war in Vietnam, for example, typical scenes in city hospitals included Vietnamese physicians, struggling with English and with a poor Chicano patient, while halfway around the world there were almost no native physicians in the South Vietnamese regime to take care of the wounded and dying children and adults. In perhaps the most extreme example of this kind, the United States not only took a large hand in producing the human destruction but also allowed the native, who could have helped, to help us instead, and all of this in part ultimately motivated by salary and petty profit considerations on the part of the medical profession.

In general, it is necessary to speak of *the politics of manpower supply and demand*. To a great degree, this process continues away from the public eye, and is fought out in abstract statistical terms, in journals on health care economics, and in high-level governmental and private foundation conferences on "the manpower crisis". Certainly it is a complex field, and not all the solutions are obvious. But self-interest activity of the crudest sort still plays a major role in the way these issues are handled. As usual, the needs of the consumer are pushed aside. This goes especially for the poor, who have a difficult time benefitting from the existing type of manpower innovation, which does not change the overall structure of services in the slightest.

BLOOD, PROFIT, AND SOCIAL POLICY

Human blood is a precious fluid. This is especially true for those caught in disaster, or undergoing one of the new forms of extensive surgery growing more common at major medical centers. Where this blood comes from, where it goes, and whether it becomes part of the profit-making sector, will determine not only who may have it and who may not, but whether it may give disease instead of health when it is transfused into the patient. The political sociology of blood is thus a topic of great usefulness as an illustration of strategies and problems related to profit in health care.

193

Society surrounds the donors and sellers of blood (as well as the buyers and receivers) and affects the blood donation process in important ways. Titmuss asks the relevant questions at the beginning of his comparative case study of blood gathering and distribution in England and the United States:

What are the consequences, national and international, of treating human blood as a commercial commodity? If blood is morally sanctioned as something to be bought and sold, what ultimately is the justification for not promoting individualistic private markets in other component areas of medical care, and in education, social security, welfare services, child foster care, social work skills, the use of patients for professional training, and other "social service" institutions and processes?[15]

Titmuss compares the almost totally voluntary donor system of England with that of the United States. Our is a two-class system, with primarily middle-class donors giving to voluntary agencies such as the Red Cross while the poor, the alcoholic, and the drug addict, *sell* their blood to profit-making blood banks and even to some hospitals. The major public health problem which arises is the spread of hepatitis, a blood-carried disease, which is far more common in the veins of the poor and addicted than in the veins of the middle class. Since the profit-making blood banks—and *any* user of their services, including even the teaching hospitals of the medical elite in some areas—have a stake in the existing system, organized consumer pressure is necessary to change the situation. Eventually the aim would probably be the total outlawing of the buying and selling of blood. In Illinois, a step in this direction was taken by the Blood Labelling Act of 1972, which did not *outlaw* profit-making firms buying blood but required each bag of blood to be labelled either "commercial" or "donated" in addition to the blood-type information. According to Allen, in the first year after passage of the act, the rate of intravenously induced, posttranfusion hepatitis dropped forty percent.[16] The blood case, therefore, is a good example of the way in which a primarily profit-motivated activity—buying blood from skid-row alcoholics and then selling it with a markup—can sacrifice the health of all.

Even famous nonprofit, university-based medical centers have entered the blood-buying market. Their rationale is that their superior medical staffs can identify potentially ill donors and refuse to accept their blood. While in some cases this is true, and while it is also true that some hospitals have built up a group of regular donors instead of using the wandering junkies and alcoholics, they cannot yet identify ahead of time the hepatitis that, in general, appears more frequently among the poor—whom they *do* accept into the donor pool. Furthermore, when the medical center exhausts its supply, it may be driven to buy from commercial sources. Medical centers are especially "blood thirsty" because of the number of blood-consuming operations they carry on regularly, such as heart transplants, or more commonly, open-heart surgery and hysterectomies or other "organ-removal" operations. At the same time, it is only fair to say that some faculty at medical schools have been in the forefront of attempts to pass such laws as the Illinois Blood Labelling Act.

Battling over Blood: Interest Groups in Conflict

We need to ask what the present attitudes are concerning a change to a totally voluntary system, within the following five groups: the federal government (HEW); the major drug corporations; the organized practitioners (the AMA in particular); the voluntary nonprofit blood-collecting agencies; and the profit-making blood banks. The field of forces, and the struggles involved, will give yet another example of the costs which the consumer ultimately pays as a consequence of our present system. To begin

195

with, the federal government has in general, been essentially passive in regulatory effort in health, and until the recent past such organizations as the Food and Drug Administration were not willing to make life difficult for the food industries. In the field of blood regulation, the first announced national policy on blood appeared in 1971, as a result of a national commission to investigate the problem. HEW recommended more research, more accurate record-keeping, the creation of *one system* integrated on the English model, where information on blood as well as blood itself would be widely and cooperatively shared and exchanged for "credits". First of all, HEW stated, their policy would be:

> To *encourage, foster,* and *support* efforts designed to bring into being an all-voluntary blood donation system and to eliminate commercialism in the acquisition of whole blood and blood components for transfusion purposes.[17]

But note here that they—the government—were not going to fight *themselves* to abolish profit-making blood centers, and the buying and selling of blood. Rather, they were going to urge others to do so.[18] The policy, in other words, was not to be a "hard-line" one.

Only months after the government announced this policy, there was a counterattack by the blood banks and the drug companies.[19] This activity led Surgenor, a student of the politics of blood, to observe, concerning the first point in the government policy, that the government was beginning to weaken in its support of its own idea.[20]

A second interest group is composed of the profit-making drug corporations. Some specialize in collecting blood (in interstate chains of collecting units in some parts of the Southwest). The drug corporations buy the extra blood—that which has passed the three-week margin of safey for infusion as whole blood. They break the blood down into usable fractions for plasma and other products. For such corporations, it should be noted, the excess, untransfused whole blood which is usually the result of a disorganized collection and distribution system is an *advantage*, since the expired blood is cheaper than fresh and the corporations are spared the expense of gathering the material themselves.

A third interest group, the AMA, has recently come out in favor of voluntary donor systems, and against commercial blood banks. But their strongest opposition is to government controls, and to a strong, clearly-organized centrally-operated blood system run by the federal government, from Washington. Private practitioners usually share the views of their association, at least on clear issues of this sort.

Problems that lie in the way of a solution in this field involve at least two other interest groups, both opposed to each other and both strongly entrenched. "Pluralism" in action and the strategy of "cornering the market" are seen in the arguments between the *American Association of Blood Banks* (AABB) and the American Red Cross (ARC). Surgenor comments:

> The prospect of an ARC system covering the country with free blood constituted such a threat to the economic basis of blood-banking practice in hospitals that blood bankers formed AABB to resist this movement. Thus, the raison d'être of AABB from its very inception has been to oppose the Red Cross. The resulting struggle between AABB and ARC was fought in community after community across the United States. The stakes were the same then as they are now—control of blood collection.[21]

Since the American Red Cross *charges* the hospitals for its voluntarily contributed blood (to pay for its staff and overhead costs, and some of its other programs), as does the AABB as a group of blood-storing organizations, both have a direct money interest in the present system. In addition, each group naturally wants to expand its role. A change to a government system, or any other major change, would be a direct economic threat. They have acted in the past to protect their interests; there is little reason to expect significant changes in the future. Thus the ultimate result of the blood situation in America today is cost shifting. We, as consumers, pay both the increased costs due to the inefficiency of the present system, and the price of disease from the transfused blood itself.

THE MEDICAL MALPRACTICE CRISIS

A third case illustrating the intricate ways in which the flow of money, the control of money, the profit motive, and the pattern of services intertwine is medical malpractice insurance. When a patient sues a physician or a hospital for malpractice, a whole chain of events is set in motion. The more patients suing, the greater the consequences.

In earlier years, the doctor-patient relationship was not primarily a legal battleground. Yet in the present era, in a brief period, the number of malpractice cases has almost doubled (from, for example, 1.7 cases per 100 patients in 1966 to 3 per 100 in 1972).[22] Several factors are considered responsible for the rise. First, the increased educational level of the average patient, and the higher expectations they put on providers such as physicians and hospitals. When these are not met, or when things don't turn out well, more and more patients are inclined to sue, even though many medical procedures simply do not always work. Second, the money-directed political action of the medical profession in such legislative battles as the fight against Medicare, as well as the rising cost of health care itself, may have led more patients to view their relationship to providers as a commercial transaction or a contract. Viewed in this light, a mistake in treatment is the violation of a contract, and grounds for a damage suit. Third, and critically important for the costs aspect, the size of the awards given to those suing doctors and hospitals has been rising, to million-dollar award levels in some cases. Finally, the special laws governing malpractice favor plaintiffs (the ones who sue) over doctor and hospital defendants, an attractive state of affairs for lawyers who specialize in such work.

Increased numbers of law suits and the rising size of the awards made by juries have led to two kinds of consequences for the consumer—both of which increase the costs of medical care. To begin with, far more physicians practice what they call "defensive medicine", ordering extra tests to protect themselves against malpractice suits. At the congressional hearings on the subject one of Nader's research groups estimated that approximately 30 percent of the diagnostic x-rays taken each year (1.4 billion dollars worth) were defensive rather than medically necessary.[23] The AMA's poll of its doctors 70 percent admitting that they prescribed extra and "probably unnecessary" tests, while the American College of Surgeons gave a figure of 63 percent. These tests are billed to public, nonprofit, or private insurers, who must raise their premium rates to the consumer to cover the extra expense. Secondly, the escalation in the size of awards means that the costs of insurance to providers— the cost of the doctors' or the hospitals' policy payments—is rising so fast that it is threatening even *their* financial ability to pay. Here too the present alternatives are either closing the doors of the office (which has already happened to a few physicians who practice privately only part time) or more common, charging the consumer more. For example, a recent estimate by the American Hospital Association is that from one to two dollars per day of the present hospital bill is simply to pay the costs of the hospitals' malpractice insurance.[25] We may look into this complex problem further by considering the role of the each of the interest groups involved: the provider of care; the insurance company; the legal profession; and the patients who sue. Then a set of remedies presently under consideration can be examined, both for what they recommend and for what they *don't* recommend.

Malpractice Cases—Who Gets What

Providers are not all equally likely to be sued. Both insurance companies and research evaluations separate physicians into five main risk classes. The lowest-risk class is that for physicians who do no surgery at all. The next two classes are for those who do some surgery, and the two highest classes are for general surgeons and for specialists, such as orthopedic surgeons and neurosurgeons, who not only do high-risk work but who specialize in it. In general, providers complain that the laws are stacked against them, in terms of the body of decisions made by judges over the years. "Customs" or previous decisions have the force of law in terms of how judges and juries are allowed to interpret new cases in court. For example:

(1) The doctrine of *res ipsa loquitur* which shifts the burden of proof in negligence claims from the plaintiff to the defendant; (2) the doctrine of informed consent, in which the physician can be held liable if a patient can show he was not adequately informed of all risks of consequences; (3) the oral guarantee of good results in which the patient does not have to prove the physician was negligent, bu. simply that he did not fulfill a claimed oral guarantee of successful outcome of treatment even though a physician denies giving such a claim; (4) the discovery rule which allows for an extension of the statute of limitations in malpractice cases.[26]

The last principle allows patients to "discover" a problem years later, and then to sue a physician immediately. This means that insurance companies cannot predict when and how many new cases will be presented each year against providers. As a consequence, the insurance premium rates are up 100 percent or more from 1974 to 1975. One medical professor, who did some private practice in orthopedic surgery for children in New York City, paid $480 for her insurance in 1958, $4,800 in 1968, $8,000 in 1974, and if she had remained in private work for another year, would have paid $14,000 for the same coverage. No one had ever filed a suit against her.[27]

Insurance companies respond that they are not primarily motivated by profit in this particular field, and several major companies, including Liberty Mutual and Wausau, have either stopped covering physicians or are threatening to do so. One of their statistical specialists explains why:

The risk is not insurable as the situation exists today. . . . No company has the vaguest perception of pricing when there is a 20–22% annualized inflation in the medical malpractice market. Most of us would like out if we could. We don't want to make unconscionable profits but we certainly want to stop unconscionable losses.[28]

On the other hand, the huge escalation in rates may simply indicate a decision by insurance companies that if they *do* stay in the field, and guess wrong, they'd rather *overestimate* the costs and make a large profit than underestimate and take a loss. As long as the present arrangement continues, the costs are shifted to the consumer, through additional charges which the providers make to help them pay their new higher premiums.

All of the other interested parties point out the important role of the legal profession in the cost-escalation problem. The term angry physicians often use for those lawyers who specialize in the work and who encourage many clients to sue doctors is "ambulance chaser". They are referring to some of the approximately fifty-four percent of all suits that are eventually judged to be without sufficient grounds even for a case, according to a recently national study.[29] If we remember that the laws do seem to be weighted in favor of the patient suing, and that in American cases the lawyer gets a percentage of all the money awarded, then the incentive is for the lawyer to sue frequently and to ask for as high a price in damages as he dares. A private physician notes than even if a case is unfair or is thrown out of court, the physician's track record is worse as far as the insurance company is concerned, for they have had to put out some money to prepare the case to defend the doctor, and his rates will still go up the following year as a penalty—even when he did nothing and was innocent. As for the attorney, however:

The attorney, then, stands to win most of the time—ah, there is the rub! This is indeed the case. The defendant's attorney always wins, no matter what—guilty, no guilt, or draw. The plaintiff's attorney wins if settled out of court, if settled for nuisance value, if the defendant is found guilty. Only in one instance, when the plaintiff loses in court, does the attorney also lose. The odds for the attorney, then, are stacked high; the odds for the physician, zero. [30]

Some Proposals for a Solution: Who Benefits?

One possible solution to the malpractice problems might be a "no-fault" system which eliminates lawyers on either side, similar to no-fault auto insurance reform. But regardless of technical problems with this idea (the degree to which one can use the system in another field) there are two other problems, one political concerning the responses of lawyers and one concerning patient rights. The opposition of the legal profession to reforms that threaten their interests can be made through the lawmaking process itself, as many legislators are lawyers and at the state level may also work in private practice. Since auto accident income has just been taken away by the no-fault auto insurance laws, lawyers can be expected to fight even harder here, through such organizations as the American Trial Lawyers Association. And, they would argue, there is a patient rights issue. In the absence of the medical profession's willingness to police itself efficiently, damage suits are the only pressure the consumer can direct against the profession to improve its standards and discipline unskilled practitioners.

But the patient who sues is not necessarily gaining from the adversary process; it is more like gambling. A recent estimate is that only sixteen cents out of every dollar awarded ever get back to the patient, if he wins. The rest is consumed by court costs, lawyer's fees, and other expenses. And there is no guarantee of winning:

The individual patient who brings suit might—in a rare instance— receive an award of a million dollars—or he might receive nothing. Whether he wins all—or nothing—depends on a number of variable factors such as how good his lawyer is, what state he is suing in and what the going concept of informed consent happens to be at the

202

moment, and finally what mood the jury is in at the time it gets the case. All of this could be years after the injury has been received. In the interim, he has received nothing on one roll of the dice.[31]

Several remedies have been suggested, and then objections of the other interested parties noted. In each case, basic assumptions are made by the interest groups proposing the remedies that *they* are not part of the problem for consumers. One example of such a proposal is the "pretrial screening board" of physicians in each state. This board could act as a pretrial consultant to patients and their lawyers. If the board figured the patient had a good chance of winning—that good medical grounds existed for a law suit—they would go ahead and the risk of cost to both patient and his lawyer would be lessened. On the other hand, this solution assumes that the board (composed of physicians, after all) is neutral on the subject of medical malpractice accusations. Second, the proposed solution doesn't deal with the bad medical practice aspect. *This* is also being considered by the medical profession, but look at their solution. They are recommending giving greater disciplinary power to state medical licensing boards or to state medical societies to stop local physicians from making mistakes.[32] But these organizations have a miserable track record for self-policing, an issue we will consider in detail in the final section of the book.

Another proposed method of handling the situation is through a "binding arbitration" process, where a third party gets the patient and the provider together and they agree to abide by the decision of the arbitrator as to who should get what, if anything. This solution is not popular with the trial lawyers, and thus has political opposition, and in addition everything depends on the particular arbitrator—a risky process, in the view of most patients and physicians.

The most important method proposed yet, in terms of the power groups supporting it (the AMA and the insurance industry) involves combining aspects of several of the other proposals. They recommend a "workmen's compensation" type system: call it a "medical mistakes compensation system" in order to get the basic idea. The *patients*—all patients—and the providers would pay into a fund to repay patients for "medical accidents". A panel of experts would decide if they are actually entitled to compensation. The aim is to remove lawyers and huge cost awards from the picture. Regardless whether you could get rid of lawyers this way (they represent clients in the Workmen's Compensation board hearings), there are other issues. The history of the *model* here—Workmen's Compensation—is not very impressive, if patient rights are of importance. That is, the Workmen's Compensation system has been drastically underpaying and underawarding workers for years for industrial injuries, according to the findings of the National Commission on Workmen's Compensation Laws.[33] It forces workers to pay for their own lawyers before the board, it underpays them if they win, and in many states is a machinery used by corporations to protect themselves from real responsibility for paying the costs of improving industrial safety and working conditions. Administered through the states (as this medical accident compensation system is proposed to be), it is easily subject to pressure by industry. What is to prevent a "medical accident compensation" board from becoming co-opted by the medical profession and denying most of the claims made before it by consumers? And who will pay the lawyer's fee for the consumer, who surely won't be able to argue his own case before the board of experts. Finally, why should patients pay for insurance against physicians' mistakes?

One final way of handling the problem—asking the government (HEW) to insure all physicians—is not really a possibility so far as the medical profession is concerned. For they are busy fighting attempts by HEW to increase regulation of their activities in general, and cannot turn to the very organizations they demand independence from for a solution in this particular area.

To sum up, each of the interest groups to date feels that they are suffering from the malpractice situation, with the possible exception of lawyers. But each of the solutions proposed is little more than self-serving to the groups proposing it. None of the solutions make the assumption that the skill level of physicians and the basic patterns of service need changing. Mistakes, after all, are made more frequently by poorly-trained people and by those who are in a hurry. In the case of private, fee-for-service medicine, speed in running patients through the office means money, as it does in the hospital, in terms of costs saved. Here most basically the industrial model influences the way health service is delivered. The increase in mistakes in turn leads to suits, and anger which makes the consumer bitter both about the mistake and the rush.

THE HEALTH MAINTENANCE ORGANIZATION: BREAKTHROUGH OR BAD DREAM?

Paying for the misfortunes that come upon us has always been a worry. Out of this concern grows the idea of social insurance; that is, placing money in a pot ahead of time to draw on in time of need. In any given plan, after a few years, the chances are worked out which forecast approximately how much money will be needed by how many. If it is a lot, more money may have to go into the pot. But the mechanics of these arrangements should not distract us from asking a key question: *who owns the pot*? A cooperative insurance arrangement is one where the people who contribute own their own pot and pay a little to a potkeeper, whom they hire on salary. A profit-making insurance system, or a nonconsumer–owned one that is "nonprofit" in nature, operates differently. Here the pot is owned by the potkeeper and each person who wants to use the pot must pay an extra fee to the potkeeper as well as their overall contribution for insurance purposes. This basic issue of insurance—who owns the pot—is critically important in understanding the debate over a particular form of insurance arrangement, namely the Health Maintenance Organization (HMO). It has been pushed by some and condemned by others, as a solution to our health-care problems.

205

The HMO Idea: Origins and Ideals

Health services have almost always been delivered with some type of fee-for-service arrangement. In the time of ancient Greece the Hippocratic physician was usually paid in produce or some other material way as often as he was paid in cash. But it was still a payment made at the time the services were delivered. In the Middle Ages the Church may have served everyone in its hospitals, but "contributions" were expected in proportion to the income of the patient. In more modern times, different forms of insurance grew up. For America, when the West was opened up in the 1800s, the mining and lumber camps began to sign contracts with individual physicians to come up once a week, to check out all the men and to see to emergencies. The idea of *group* practice by contract, with some way of paying ahead for the service, began to grow with the Depression; at this time, any way of saving money in a critical human need area began to look more attractive to many people.

It was 1929, the year of the stock market crash, when Dr. Michael Shadid set up one of the first regular, community-based group practice arrangements in Elk City, Oklahoma. This was a consumer-owned, cooperative plan in which Dr. Shadid was *hired* by the community, who legally owned and controlled the plan. As the years went by other interest groups developed prepaid insurance, but these were not usually cooperative plans.[34] For example, Blue Cross was started for and by hospitals to guarantee that more money would be available to them from hospital patients, and Blue Shield was begun by physicians who wanted more security over bill paying by their patients. But these were not *contracts* between a given provider and the patients. For example, Blue Cross, as hospital insurance potkeeper, does not provide services, it pays the hospitals for them, as they give them to the people who pay Blue Cross: *If the potkeeper is also the service provider, and if the contract*

206

is between a specific potkeeper service-provider group practicing as a group of health-care specialists and a specific set of consumers who are going to use these services almost exclusively, then we have an HMO. This long and somewhat technical description is necessary because many of the struggles over money and power in the health field are over the "fine print" of money-flow in health insurance, such as the difference between *this* type of arrangement and others. In the sixties and early seventies, the HMO idea had been pushed hard by health-care economists in the academic medical elite by some of the HEW planning bureaucracies, and by several national administrations. Cost saving and efficiency are supposed to be some of the advantages, one main reason for the increasing interest of some in the most recent historical period.

The theory of why an HMO is supposed to be a superior way of arranging money and services is fairly simple. In fee-for-service practice, the physician gets money to the precise extent that he can get sick people in the door, or can *treat* people as sick even when they are not. Since the income depends on the number of patients treated, there is a built-in bias to overtreat, to take out the tonsils and the appendix even if it may not be necessary. By contrast, in ancient China, there was an arrangement that could in some ways be considered the earliest ancestor of the HMO, but it had more consumer power than the present arrangement. In the ancient Chinese version, people paid the physician to keep them well, and the physician had to pay the people if they got sick. In modern days, people pay a sum of money as individuals or families to an HMO, which must then take care of them for all, or nearly all, of the illnesses they have. Here, the theory goes, the HMO has a built-in economic bias to keep people well. This is considered to be the case because the more frequently people belonging to the HMO get sick, the more money and staff time and drugs will be needed to get them well again. An HMO, therefore, has an advantage if it can keep people well; if money is left over at the end of the year it can be used to purchase new equipment, raise salaries, or be turned back to the members as lower payments for next year. This is the *theory*, and the assumption of how the money is to be saved; that is, by increasing the health level of HMO members.

The Reality—Cost-Cutting through Refusal of Service

The reality is something else. Notice first that the stress is on cost saving. Then we must ask: aren't there other ways an HMO can avoid paying back out the money it has already collected from the members, besides by keeping them well? The answer, observed by most close students of HMOs in recent years, is that many pathologies of the fee-for-service system are simply turned around completely, but they remain pathologies. For example, in the old fee-for-service systems, patients might be operated on for diseases they *didn't* have. In an HMO, one can simply make it more difficult for the consumer member to get in the door of the HMO clinic and get help for the diseases and problems that they *do* have. If the patient is not allowed in the door, or is discouraged from coming, then no HMO staff time and money is spent on them, and the money pot is kept from diminishing. "Utilization", or use of a health-care setting by consumers, can be kept down in an HMO through a variety of strategies. Mechanic lists some of them:

> There are many mechanisms through which a clinic may regulate utilization by increasing the difficulty and inconvenience required to obtain treatment. Busy medical practices, such as HIP and Kaiser, regulate utilization by making it difficult to schedule an appointment by requiring patients to wait, and the like. Demand tends to adjust itself to the manpower available as a consultation becomes more inconvenient for the patient.[35]

Notice that the costs to the HMO are kept down by inconveniencing the ones who paid the money into the pot in the first place. Some consumers, in such plans as Kaiser and the Harvard Community

xperiments in the
e as a respectable
a staff member of
sic "demonstration
veness of care are

physicians and have
HMO's service. Note
pocket, but not the

epaid group practice
nce Program. It em-
ling preventive care,
for individuals and for
facility . . . (and the)
it is needed—in the
e facility. Services are
37

zations) may operate
service is the profit
part because the
and make its own
money as well as
f care. Geist calls
for it represents
insurance com-

observations on cost-
e (long waits while in
f patients) which have
be found in this plan,
ccording to individuals
s of this plan. Welfare
experiment, and they
trol of or input into the
es immediately availa-
h the services available
in HMO building more
t downtown district next
the academic medical
interest in the HMO. The
a stream of articles and
and administrators of the
e government, something
the HMO as a pattern for

onventional actu-
ies have availa-
and physicians
s available (in-
entive bonus to
attempting to
ability if he or

t. Who is for
in govern-
ossibilities
are costs.
s such as
grew and
of "suc-
ed from
Harvard
ants from
Commu-
licy of the

medical school had been changed to include e[...]
financing and delivery of community medical ca[...]
area for "medical" research. Note the wording b[...]
the Plan, and note the extent to which the clas[...]
project" claims of perfection and comprehensi[...]
made:

> The Harvard Community Health Plan is a pr[...]
> meeting the guidelines for a Health Maintena[...]
> phasizes a comprehensive health plan, inclu[...]
> provides complete personal health care services[...]
> families. These services are provided at the mai[...]
> neighborhood health center, and wherever els[...]
> home, in the hospital and/or in an extended ca[...]
> available 24 hours a day, seven days a week.[...]

Sounds good, doesn't it? Yet the precise [...]
saving techniques and the patients' experien[...]
the care setting, deliberate discouragement o[...]
been found to exist in Kaiser and HIP can [...]
according to the community literature, and a[...]
interviewed by the author, who are member[...]
patients were put into the plan as part of a[...]
began to organize politically for greater co[...]
decisions being made concerning the servi[...]
ble to them, when these were contrasted wi[...]
for middle-class people who used the ma[...]
frequently, since they lived in the high-re[...]
door.[38] The medical school, like many i[...]
elite, had and has still primarily a *research* [...]
new program has meant the possibility o[...]
books on the subject for the researchers [...]
program. Thus for the university, as for th[...]
could be gained by the establishment of [...]
serving the community.

Organized medicine fought against prepaid group practice from the start. They ostracized Dr. Shadid in Oklahoma, and they refused local hospital privileges to members of new groups across the country, such as the doctors in the Russelton plan in Pennsylvania, who had to sue all the way to the Supreme Court to win their privileges.[39] Pressure against HMO physicians exists even today, for any HMO in a community is a source of organized economic competition for the community physicians.

In recent years the government itself has decided, in the absence of much clear evidence, to codify the rules for the ways HMOs must be set up, if they are to receive government money for payments. In a strategy concerning money which is perhaps a new height in sophisticated cynical manipulation, the AMA "helped" the government set such impossibly high service standards for HMOs that it is very difficult for new ones to get off the ground economically. High start-up costs are required until enough people sign up (for the health team must be paid at the start), but the new law (The HMO Act of 1973) makes it rather unlikely that many new ones will be started. Furthermore, as overall health-care costs rise, the premiums in HMOs must rise along with them, making the plans less able to compete than before with other insurance systems. Or, and this is the equally undesirable alternative, benefits must be cut back along the lines we have indicated, and possibly staff in HMO-related hospitals cut back as well. As of 1975, only four percent of the population had joined HMOs, and a significant proportion of these individuals were members of the original groups: the Kaiser, HIP, and Washington, D.C. area plans.[40] The experiment has not caught on for many reasons. Primarily, we expect the main ones to be: the money motivation of the HMO operators; the distrust of new patterns of service; the bad track record of some of the new HMOs; and the lowering of standards in some of the old stand-by groups, such as Kaiser.

To sum up, the HMO situation at present illustrates almost every strategy we have described. There was certainly carrot-and-stick behavior by government in the early million-dollar demonstration phase in the mid-sixties. Profit-making organizations were welcome as carrot-eaters and HMO operators. Some have talked about a future use of a stick by government—shaping up the existing HMOs—but few in the early period of action in this direction guessed how slowly the idea would catch on, or why. Monopoly games can be played by the HMO once it has the consumer's money for the year, since the HMO is in control of all services for which payment is already in hand. Consumers who are not members of consumer-controlled, cooperative HMOs constantly confront this problem. Budgetary politics are played by internal HEW bureaucrats and external large HMO organizations, toward getting larger appropriations for the idea, or getting new laws passed which would allow HMOs to be nourished in the future on unregulated government money. But of all the strategies involved, *cost shifting* seems to be the basic one. Costs in terms of inconvenience, or even lack of treatment, are avoided by the HMO and passed on to the consumer, after his money is in hand. Finally, technocratic politics have characterized the development of the HMO program. The abstract idea and the few case examples were pushed by a combination of academic medical elite planners and government bureau planners long before much evidence was in.

Reviews of the HMO program and idea indicate that it provides care that is technically at about the same level as fee-for-service medicine or slightly superior (*when it can be obtained*), is cheaper per patient only in the most successful and largest plans and only there by cutting corners, and is by and large unpopular with consumers, for reasons we have documented above.[41] But struggles over money, power, and service patterns are not basically decided on facts, or on careful testing to see whether "ideas" really mean what they say. As Mechanic observed, "It is, perhaps, the character of medical care politics that encouraged proponents of HMOs to advocate this form of practice as a national goal with so few qualifications and so little good data".[42]

THE MEDICAL-INDUSTRIAL COMPLEX

"Technology", as such, does not exist: it is an abstract concept. What do exist are drugs, machines, techniques, processes, the people and corporations that sell them at a profit, and those who use them with both advantages and costs to themselves. In order to understand the political consequences of the use of technology in health, it is necessary to stay at the concrete level of real groups acting in their own interest. These groups, whose mutually dependent relationships form what can be called "the medical-industrial complex" include primarily the following: corporations in the health business, medical research physicians, university-medical school teaching hospitals, rank-and-file hospitals and physicians, and the federal government.[43]

The Elements of the Complex

Myers reviewed the role of American corporations in the health business as follows:

> The market economy is very much present and at work in what is coming to be known as the "medical-industrial complex", the business of manufacturing and selling the various equipment, from bandages to two-million-volt cobalt machines, that doctors and hospitals use. The demand for such products is so strong that many new companies, some of them giants in other fields, have joined the old-line manufacturers in a bid for new profits.[44]

The word *profit* is critical here. It must be kept in mind that a great deal of money can be made in the health field—at the 4.5-billion-dollar level, per year, in drug sales, for example. But the nature of the medical-industrial complex is in the *relationships* between the private profit-making corporations and the other elements: those to

213

whom the materials and technology are sold, what their role is in the system, and the role of the federal government as a "marriage broker". In effect, what we need to inspect is the parallel between the military-industrial complex and the medical-industrial complex. There are important differences in detail between the two subsystems, but in both cases we can consider the process as an end-run, where the citizen's money is spent in a "strategic" area (defense, health) by relationships between government funders and private contractors, under little economic control, with the government under the outside pressure of the interest group to keep the surveillance light and the arrangements favorable. The expertise of the sector's spokesmen (military strategists, university and government technological planners) is used to perpetuate the relationship, as citizen criticism of its cost or imperviousness to their influence is met with accusations of, "You couldn't possibly understand the real needs of the society in this area". The ultimate end is profit making by the private corporations in defense or health, unchecked in any realistic way by the taxpayer. How, then, do the corporations in the medical-industrial complex relate to (a) the medical research physicians; (b) the hospitals and medical schools; and (c) the federal government? What are the patterns of relationship between them? What are the consequences for the cost of medical care and the perpetuation of a two-class system?

The first group which is an interested party as a buyer of technology is the research physician group in medical-school teaching hospitals. Since for them career advancement (as a medical professor) comes with research findings, their own natural bias is toward maximum adoption of technology. Many also have a personal interest in developing refinements in the machinery, and may work as consultants to private firms outside who actually make the equipment. Second, competition among medical centers is at least in part a competition in terms of who has more of the equipment, a competition in the area of "technological prestige". For example, in the recent past, several teaching hospitals in the Boston area each wanted to purchase multi-million-dollar radiotherapy units, and could not be persuaded to share the existing ones or cooperate in buying just *one* more. The *cost* of such technology, whether purchased by a research physician or by the medical center itself, can be passed on to the consumer. Recent attempts to control costs by regulation can be nullified in the technology area as they can in the personnel field—a topic to which we will return.

In private offices, general hospitals, and in the less-sophisticated smaller hospitals, the desire to compete is as evident as it is in the university teaching hospitals, but the capacity to *evaluate* the technology is not as extensive. For example, private practitioners and smaller hospitals are often targets of "technological oversell". A businessman who himself sells health technology comments on this:

> I believe there is a violent upswing of unethical practice . . . from two sources—one from large companies trying to overwhelm and dominate the field by splashy advertising and a complete disregard for qualified specifications. Many of their salesman have no qualms about selling equipment regardless of the application or the need.[45]

It is also often the case that the community physician in private practice and in the smaller hospitals does not have the technical staff or the resources to keep the technology in good working order. For example, a firm of radiologists may keep careful watch over their office x-ray equipment and have a maintenance contract, while a rural general practitioner may routinely use an old, outdated, and dangerously malfunctioning machine for x-raying broken arms, which in turn is replaced by a newer, much higher-powered unit which can do even more damage if misused. The Nader study on the subject noted such equipment sometimes falls into the hands of shoe stores, which have dangerously overexposed children's feet to radiation.[46] In another area, the physician does not always pay the necessary attention to the fine print on the side effects of prescribed drugs, a main area of importance in much postgraduate continuing education for community physicians.

Acting as a "marriage broker" in the complex is the federal government, which in health has as important a role as it does in defense. For example, new laws, or appropriations under older ones, can earmark money for technological development in medicine. Both the private corporations and the academic researchers will push for this. Each outside interest group will work with its internal counterpart interest group within HEW to develop the new law and push for the appropriation of funds. An example of this is the pressure to increase the delivery of services, which has led to a deflection of some of the "technology" money toward financing of new experiments in patterns of care, such as the HMO. Here one outside interest group—physician groups or university planners— pushes to swell the funds available for start-up projects, working with those inside HEW interested in the same thing, while the "machine buyers" and *their* inside partners vie for control over the development and spending policies over the next few years. Notice that this may change the particular *set* of actors within and outside the government, but not the nature of the symbiotic relationship in general. If the dollars are spent in a given year for computers and television remote units, as part of an experiment in health-care delivery, instead of on new heart-lung machines, one corporation's position may rise and another's fall, but the interrelations are still there. The overall cost of such technology, if adopted systemwide instead of in million-dollar demonstration projects, is seldom considered as a reality factor.

The University as Corporate Research Laboratory

Finally, there is a new development in the interrelationship between business, the university, and the government. While in past years university or medical-school professors might work on a technological prototype under a development grant from government, and then work the idea out to the point where outside profit-oriented corporations might pick it up, a newer and more direct relationship is developing between medical schools and corporations. In the old pattern, the government covered the start-up costs. In the new pattern, these are picked up by the corporation, which works out a direct contract with the university to turn the medical school into an arm of the research lab of the corporation, in the direct and literal meaning of the term. In part this is a consequence of the shift noted above, when "technology" money stopped growing from government sources, while universities remained hungry for it. This new institutional relationship is symbolized by a grant in 1975 to Harvard of twenty-three million dollars, from the Monsanto Chemical company, for twelve years of research toward a cure for cancer. Beneath Harvard's official glowing accounts of the new relationship, in their house organ, *The Harvard Gazette*, which stated that this would be "a new and effective relationship between an industrial organization and an academic institution", lies the economic base. [47] Previous to the grant, Harvard's policy was that all proceeds from patents arising from research had to be given to charity by the Harvard researcher who obtained them. The Harvard Corporation then voted to change the patent rules. Now, according to the student newspaper, which obtained the details of the contractual arrangement (which was checked out by the author):

> Under Monsanto's agreement with the university, however, the company retains all patent and commercial development rights to the products of work done under its grant. [48]

In other words, Harvard will develop a cancer cure for Monsanto to patent and sell at a profit. In effect, this enlists the medical-scientific elite *directly*, without the need for a broker, in profit-motivated activity with respect to consumers having cancer.

In summary, the funding patterns of the medical-industrial complex perpetuate its present structure, as a part of the overall society where corporations wield much political power. As is classically the case in capitalist society, in times when businesses are in economic difficulty, the larger corporations, having accumulated capital, are in a position to move in and buy up not only smaller business competition but, it would seem, the university medical research elite itself. Government cutback of research and development funding (at least in part at corporate suggestion) pushed the scientist and medical researcher directly into the arms of the corporate capitalist class. In this way, the corporate sector of the medical-industrial complex simply is behaving the way corporations have classically behaved in any field. Their attempt to corner the market, drive out small competition, and arrive at mutual protection pacts between the giants that are left, while co-opting any critical voices, is standard operating procedure. The consequences for the people are not different here than in energy or automobiles: excess cost and increased risk, to increase the profit margins of those in control of the system.

PROFIT, POWER, AND STRATEGIES:
A REINTERPRETATION

Thus far we have presented the obvious or manifest struggle between the parties involved, in a series of topic areas. At this point it may be helpful to step back and make a more general theoretical analysis of the underlying dynamics. A Marxian theoretical framework points toward the broader context within which these struggles are taking place: advanced capitalism, with the specific American condition of a far more decentralized government apparatus in human services than has been the case in Europe. The *constraints* within which all these struggles are taking place are ultimately set by the needs and requirements of an advanced capitalist economy, especially if this economy is under stress from outside. The limits are twofold in nature. Services must be developed in such a way that corporations can be "dealt in"—and a profit made off them. Second, overall costs of the public sector of health service, whatever its size, may not be paid for in the long run at the expense of corporate profits. Third, both the legitimacy of the capitalist role in health and the limits on the support of public programs by the capitalist class must be interpreted to the bourgeois occupational groups (such as physicians), to the employee class, and to the poor in such a way that *they* consider both the profit making and the limits on support legitimate and normal from their point of view.

Each of the strategies we have seen in action ultimately amounts to a defense of the existing system of power, one in which the capitalist corporations and the bourgeois professional groups cooperate with respect to the employee class and the poor, with the result that there is one overall system of care for those needed by the capitalist class, another offered to those not needed by this class. In the future, some of these strategies can be turned by the capitalist sector against the health occupational groups who presently have been cooperating with them, if the present partnership no longer serves their interests.

Examples of each strategy can be reinterpreted within this broader framework. The *carrot-and-stick* technique is primarily workable only by those with the most carrots (e.g., the capitalist class), in such areas as drug regulation and research funds for universities, or by the state operating on behalf of the capitalist class, advocating its reasoning and strategies. Cost cutting of service through the use of HMOs is advocated by government when told by business to do so (not that planners haven't also recommended it). Profit making in blood goes on at incredible cost to the population. The examples are many, but the corporate sector has not only the funds to stall the functioning of proconsumer government regulation—to throw legal sand in the wheels—but to co-opt the direction of future planning as well.

Other strategies have to be looked at from this perspective. Monopoly strategies have been in use by professions for a long time, and in the goods and services in health the drug and medical supply giants have almost complete control. But there may come a time when the capitalist class may wish to monopolize the delivery of service, and the employment of the health occupations themselves. If so, this de facto division in monopoly power may disappear far more quickly than many health occupations think.

Budgetary infighting operates within the constraints set by the capitalist class: the size of the pie left for human health services after the more "basic" needs of corporate economic health are taken care of. As Miliband notes, so long as it is primarily a *corporate* economy, then maintenance of that economy can be used as a rationale for cutbacks in services to both the employee class and the poor. Cost shifting is also inherent in the system. The share paid by the corporate sector, as against the share paid by the employees, may trend slowly toward the employee paying more and the corporation less, with the government being the agent for legitimating the shift. In addition, the poor are not paid for when they are not needed by the corporation; we, the taxpayers, pay the costs of welfare and food stamps for those who are not needed by the capitalist class, as well as the disability costs of those who are injured in the factories, through disability assistance at the federal level. It is not that corporations do not presently pay taxes—they do—but not in proportion to the costs they create for the whole society. Yet the limit is reached when they say they are being "hurt" by tax policies to support human services.

In general, then, it is important to remember the owner of the baseball park within which the various games are being played. Challenging the overall legitimacy of the power of the capitalist class—their right to set the outer limits of human service support—can thus be seen as a necessity if any major change in the picture is to come about. Otherwise, in almost a Buddhist sense, we are doomed to the eternal wheel of reinventing useless strategies.

PART THREE

Power: The Politics of Health

7

Power, Participation
and Planning

America was founded as the consequence of a revolution, one in which a major issue was lack of participation by the governed in the decisions which directly affected their lives. No such revolution is apparent yet in the health-care field of the present day. But a few warning signs are appearing. Present-day rulers, in their turn, are meeting the trouble with King George III's tactics: ridicule, stalling, minor reforms which refuse to recognize the basic issues. Yet the medical profession, and the corporate power elite, may succeed where George III failed. The situation will change, or will not, depending primarily on the balance of power existing between the groups concerned.

This basic thing called power has been discussed only at second hand thus far: as something we have observed in terms of its consequences; as the results of struggles already concluded or presently in process. We will need to consider it now as a basic fact of life, and relate it to other terms describing the arrangement, control, and legitimacy of the use of force in our society and others. Power and *influence* are related but are not the same. We must return to the concept of ideology to discuss how the two are related, and what the consequences are for health care. Next, citizen or consumer participation as a general issue has to be briefly reviewed. Will the citizens make their own revolution? If they don't, will the one made for them in their name be the one they really want? Finally, it is important for us to carefully review the major national health care *planning* programs of the last two decades, for they are going to become a part of the new expanded federal government role in health. We need to look at the impact of interest groups in the planning process in great detail, and program by program, in order to understand the sophisticated use of these programs by the groups in control as a way of disguising protection of the status quo with the clothes of "planning for change".

THE NATURE OF POWER

In a famous movie on the theme of the Russian revolution, *The Battleship Potemkin*, by Sergei Eisenstein, the climax finds the great battleship with its giant guns lowered for firing, steaming straight toward a small destroyer which is now in the hands of a mutinous revolutionary crew. At the last minute, just before the destroyer is seemingly to be blasted out of the water, the Potemkin's guns are raised again. We now see that the sailors on the battleship have turned on their own officers and rounded them up. Sailors on the two ships cross over to each others' decks, and embrace. This is the first, and the last, lesson about force. As long as it is ever in the hands of people who can think, and change their mind, no ruling class is ever safe, nor can any social order be preserved forever through the use of force.

Power is the ability of one individual or group to compel another individual or group to do something which the compeller wants done, whether the compelled wants to or not. Force alone can achieve this in the short run, but legitimacy and ownership of resources are critically important additional factors if we are to understand the difference between a transitory ruler on the social scene and a strong established power structure. We can begin with the nature of legitimacy and ownership, and their implications for power. Then the key issue of government power, and its limitations, can be considered. Strategies for action, viewed as attempts to gain power for desired ends, will conclude this discussion.

Force, Legitimacy, and Ownership

For most of the world's history, force in the form of armed might has been the primary factor in determining the status of nations with respect to one another. Within nations, those with the arms kept them from the masses. Yet no nation is held together by force alone, not even an unjust and unequal one. Max Weber found that three ways of legitimating the power situation were what he called *traditional*, *charismatic*, and *rational-legal*.[1] Tradition was the main explanation given to, and believed by, most of the world's people in answer to their questions about why the so-and-so family were always kings and landowners. Power and control had always belonged to them. Since traditional ways rule all in a traditional society, there was no other way for those on the bottom to question this aspect of life without questioning all of them. Charismatic authority—the hold of a Luther, a Hitler, a Ghandi, a Castro over followers—is a second source of legitimacy. Here, power and force may well be exerted apart from tradition or law in an existing regime, because the *leader* wants it to be, and the people who follow him have the guns. Certainly the process works elsewhere besides in armed revolutions, and is always an important factor in getting people to really do what they have already promised to do all along. Finally, and theoretically the most important method for us today, legitimacy comes from law, law made by government, a government which is democratically elected by the people. Laws function as *laws* and not as customs when they are backed up by the police power of the state. But again, in a democracy the limits on the use of this power are also defined in law, and those who misuse the power of the state, even presidents, are subject to dismissal, again through legally spelled-out processes. The "rational-legal" method, Weber stated, was the only sensible one for modern states interested in exerting power fairly, for laws were subject to the people's will and could be repealed or changed if they so desired.[2] Tradition and charisma were less manageable, less predictable, and both quite *irrational* as methods for controlling power in society, Weber, being a realist, viewed the rational-legal use of force as an ideal, just as the others were ideals in their pure state.[3] People don't always obey the law and the power of the state is often misused, when the government doesn't follow its own rules.

The medical profession has a special place in the power structure of medical care. It is no longer alone, as we saw when we considered all the other interest groups involved. But its special position can at least in part be understood by Weber's categories. The profession has traditional authority, by virtue of its long history in human service. It has some charisma as well, in the interpersonal situation when many patients find themselves following the words and advice of a physician as if he were more important, more valuable, and more of a leader than they. And the profession has rational-legal authority, by virtue of all the laws it has gotten passed in legislatures, especially at the state level, laws which give it and it alone the legal control over health work and the health care decision-making process. Notice that the profession had these things even before specific actions to gain more power. We may be coming into a period of change, however, as the traditions of all professions become irrelevant to conditions and no longer hold people, when the people sue their doctors instead of looking up to them, and when other interest groups lobby for laws limiting the power of physicians.

Marx observed that the nature of the lawmaking process was related to the patterns of ownership and wealth in a society. The ones who owned the main wealth-producing processes were often the rulemakers, the rule interpreters, and the ones in control of the power of the state. They did, and do, use their wealth and position to influence law making, law interpretation, and the use of force to protect their own power position. In effect, Marx said, each age has primary *owners:* landed barons in feudal times; merchants in the age of exploration; capitalist industrialists at the time of the Industrial Revolution and afterwards. In each period, they will so influence the way rules are made and the way they are enforced (or not enforced) that they make the power of the state a kind of private possession, an auxiliary army. [4] In a mixed or welfare state, where private ownership is concentrated in a few corporations, and the government is centralized, this very centralization makes the job of controlling the government easier. In Europe and America, for instance, another kind of ownership is occurring: international corporations so strong that they frustrate not only the aims of individual nations, but even the goals of the European Economic Community. [5]

This general issue—the size and shape of corporate and other interest group power as it relates to government power—will concern us next. But one final issue is basic to rounding out the introduction: the relation between power and morality. Millions have died in religious wars in which each side believed that they were morally right, that God was on *their* side. Perhaps a kind of universal humanistic set of values some day may guide all use of power by all; but for the present, it is always necessary to be concerned that the use of power by anyone, including one's own group, does not invalidate in moral terms the goal achieved. What *price* will the revolution demand? Do the ends justify the means? Think of the battle report from the front lines in Vietnam, when the

United States Army explained to the American and Vietnamese people that "it was necessary to destroy the village in order to save it."

In general, therefore, power is qualified and legitimated by a series of factors: tradition, charisma, law, and ownership of resources. How this power is *used* is critically important. One place to begin is with the state itself, in terms of the way governments actually operate, in contrast to what people expect of them.

Government Power: Who's in Charge?

No government known ever really has a complete answer to that question. On the other hand, at least the broad outlines of an answer appear when we compare capitalist nations of the American type, Western European parliamentary welfare states, and socialist states. In each, the architecture of power, inside of and outside of the formal organization chart, gives us some idea of the situation and some concept of its implications for the organization and delivery of health care.

In the American system, the theoretical system of checks and balances has been torn apart and then put back together to be played as a broken piano by outside interest groups. The push by interest groups is threefold, directed at each of the three parts of our system. Congress is a target for new laws favoring the existing power groups, while HEW, in all its little bureaus and fiefdoms, becomes a target for the same set of interest groups. Here they are trying to get the day-to-day administration of some particular program altered to suit their particular needs. Interplays can get very complex, as pressure can also be exerted directly on the President, who is (in theory at least) the boss of the health bureaucracies such as HEW. The courts are used to challenge existing laws and programs, a legal harassment game more easily played by wealthy and powerful groups with the money to pay skilled lawyers than is usually in the hands of some group that might be benefitting from the new law.[6]

In spite of the continuing chaotic interplay, a general trend can be seen for the federal government to become increasingly involved in quality and cost control, because it is paying an increasing share of the money for care. The training of the health professions, the funding of research, and possibly soon, the insurance for health care, are becoming primarily governmental functions. But because the federal government's power and influence has grown, this does not mean that it has grown systematically and with the consumer's needs in mind. It has, in fact, been pulled from one side to the other from outside, while at the same time indulging in every form of petty bureaucratic wrangling. The consequences for the shape of the eventual organization are the same as for a tree that has had to grow in an exposed area with strong winds constantly blowing. The result is knarled and twisted, hardly recognizable as a tree, with each crooked branch a monument to a lost struggle with an outside force. Charles Edwards, a weary veteran of five years at the top of HEW in the early seventies (he left for a senior vice-presidency in a firm within the medical-industrial complex), described his attempt this way:

> We were, in my judgement, challenged to bring stability and a sense of direction to a federal health enterprise that has grown and expanded over the years with almost no planning, no competent guidance, and no rational assessment of its impact either on the health of the American people or on the capability of the health-care system to meet its diverse obligations to society.[7]

Our own brief investigations of many of the programs tried by HEW, and the further explorations of planning and regulation in this chapter and the next, indicate the reasons why there has been "none" of this and "almost none" of that. Interest group intervention, at least in this latest expansion phase, has been primarily defensive in nature, and aimed quite successfully at stalling, paralyzing, and diverting various federal attempts from getting "implemented" once they have been voted into law.

England and the Scandinavian welfare-state systems share as many differences as similarities. But one historical tradition and one political tradition interact to create a more integrated governmental function. The historical tradition is the professionalized civil service within an insulated orbit, and the political tradition is the far greater latitude handed to government bureaus to "do their thing" once the program has been enacted. Certainly the English and the Scandinavian situation are full of cases where the medical profession tries to influence the welfare-state bureaucracies, but unlike the situation in the United States, it is not possible to play the executive (President and HEW) off against the Congress, for the executive and legislative are together, with the ruling party in Parliament directly running the administration of government. Thus a whole range of pressure-group games is eliminated.[8] Further, there are other traditions in Europe, especially in the health and other human service fields. Consultation is carried out informally by the party in power with the interest group before the new plan is written, but then it can be, and is, pushed through with far greater force and efficiency within the system. For one thing, "states" in the American sense do not play the role they do in our complex, three-layer system. More governmental efficiency is possible because of this centralization of power, at least relative to the American situation. But note one very important possibility: if one can co-opt and control a *strong* central government as the capitalist corporations have done in Europe, this efficiency may be directed at other ends than those of health care. In 1974, for example, England spent more on drugs for patients of general practitioners than it did on other salaries.[9] The drug firms are large, powerful corporations, in England as in the United States.

Finally, the specific structure of *socialist* governments makes the political party bureaucrats an interested pressure group operating at every level of decision making. Ironically, it is just this power that may give them the ability to ignore citizen desires for change in a particular pattern of health services, and they may have the ability to brand professionals or consumers as "counterrevolutionaries," or as "an enemy of the state" for objecting to orders to change a system. Labor unions in the Soviet Union do have some protective functions for Soviet workers, and are the main watchdogs for occupational health and safety. But they were rather silent on the subject when Stalin was in control of the Communist Party.[10] Other socialist states, of course, are more serious about citizen participation in planning; Yugoslavia is a good example.

The state, in other words, can become the strongest pressure group of all. And it is this possibility which indicates the need for some guarantee of citizen leverage and control, whatever the system. Consumers have always had difficulty impressing their desires or needs on the health-care system. Their role, actual and potential, is our next topic.

THE ACTIVISTS: PROFESSIONAL
AND CONSUMER

Activists come in all shades of opinion, and with differing degrees of acceptance of the existing status quo. Consumers represent primarily a group that Marx would have called "a class in themselves": a collection of people who can be *labelled* as a group, but do not primarily represent a group *acting for themselves, in an organized fashion*. This goes for the many important life issues which affect consumers. Ultimately, they have two alternatives. The first is to work for basic political-economic structural reform. The other is to organize issue by issue and try to fight against an overall economic power structure which works on many fronts: oil, automobiles, food, health care. It is quite difficult to win on any particular issue if the aim is structural reform on the single issue alone, for corporations stick together, as do parts of an occupational group, if they are under pressure. Giving up the idea of structural reform, the consumer can work alone, with a group of fellow consumers, or with a professional

231

reformer group and attempt to better a bad situation without getting at the basic cause of the problem. We would like to discuss the role of the consumer, first as an agent of basic social and economic change, second as an ally of health-care activists and citizen-oriented professional groups, and finally as a participant in the planning and administration or review of health-care programs. We may then get an idea of the several kinds of limits on what consumers can accomplish if they do not aim at basic structural reform.

To begin with, what is the aim of the change? Many have observed that the overall lack of organization of consumers prevents their taking a clear stance as a group toward a particular issue. Folk boycotts, such as the meat boycott of 1974, do arise, but their effect is short lived. In general, the consumers' most effective strategy to date has been money support to "professional consumer groups" such as the Nader organizations and Common Cause. Here full-time legal, economic, political, and sociological expertise, as well as technical consultants, can be put to work on one or two "hot issues." In general, though, these organizations do *not* get at the issue of the profit motive itself as a structural cause of problems, as a motivation for disregarding the consumer interest. Nadel, in a study of "consumers in the policy process", summarized his findings on presidential consumer panels, governmental regulatory agencies, and the Nader organizations, and found that Nader's group is more effective than others primarily because of their skill in the use of the media. But these media will not provide a platform for more radical critiques of the system that affects consumers, since they themselves (*NBC, CBS, The New York Times*) are profit-making corporations. "Realism", as the Nader organizations would say, thus dictates a strategy of minor reformism rather than structural change. These results then become inevitable:

While the activists have been successful, . . . this success is within a narrow range of issues. There has been a clear trend in consumer legislation in which proposals which would confer economic benefits to the poor have consistently failed. The activists have been successful, with one possible exception, only in enacting legislation of collective benefits to all citizens—primarily health and safety legislation—the costs of which are readily passed on to consumers. While consumer protection has become an issue which has led to legislation and administrative changes, none of the new policy significantly disturbs existing power relationships between major producers and retail consumers.[11]

This is a clear verdict of failure, not one of even short-term success. If consumers pay for the costs of their own reforms, who benefits?

The basic issue on consumer influence over the health-care field is almost symbolized by this field report from an OEO-funded Neighborhood Health Center, on the role of the Consumer Advisory Council:

> When the crisis developed at the health center, one of the major problems centered around the representation of members of the current health advisory council. However, there was the related issue: did the Council have advisory or policy-making powers? . . . The first project director [used] the guidelines of the local poverty agency, which stipulated that a policy board should be formed. At our first interview with the Chairman of the advisory council, he admitted that the council thought they had more power than they actually did.[12]

This situation is related to the "physician domination" issue, or the politics of medical expertise. Physicians tend to extend their rightful area of expertise far outside the direct delivery of service to an individual. They can argue, sometimes with good reason, that what might appear to be a strictly political or economic issue to a citizen board might also have direct implications for the quality of care delivered. However, the existing power situation and the legal framework do not usually make this a clear case, since laws on who may operate health centers, or plan for new programs, often specify physician control or physician dominance. In our consideration of health planning programs, we will see that physicians are certainly *not* the only interest group at work in citizen-interest programs. But their expertise is the ultimate ideological weapon, still very powerful among many citizens: the weapon of legitimacy.

Activist Organizations in Health

Professional activists who are proconsumer in nature appear in at least two major varieties: health-care activists who are themselves trained in health-care work; and sympathetic experts with training in areas critical for structural change of the system, such as radical economists, sociologists, and political scientists. Among the health professionals, the oldest continuously functioning organization that has consistently taken a committed position for basic structural reform is the Medical Committee for Human Rights (MCHR), which began as an organization of health-care students and professionals who wished to accompany the civil rights activists in the American South, during the great era of voting reform, when beating and injuries were a routine problem. Primarily a northern organization, they ultimately returned home and began a national series of chapters that would work more broadly in health care reform, by carrying out active research and enlisting new students, or at least providing all of them with some idea of the conservative political biases of their professional institutions and of the health-care system itself. The Medical Committee for Human Rights has remained primarily a health student organization, although they have a small full-time staff, and they may have peaked in membership in the late sixties. But they continue to operate as an important organization in major cities, working with professional groups, unions, and consumer groups, attempting to provide another, more critical interpretation of the propaganda statements on "the health-care system of the future" which emerge from the offices of the academic medical elite, the AMA, or the corporations. Criticisms, in the recent past, of their being elitist, ivy league, sexist, and physician dominated, had some validity. But they have reorganized and made a real attempt to

234

involve other health-worker groups. For this group, as for others, the past is not the only thing to look at. With every rise in the cost of living, the radical interpretation of events and recommendations for the future which they and other groups propose, sound less like phantasy and more like common sense.

Organizations whose membership tends to be far more interdisciplinary, though primarily still professional, are the primarily research-oriented groups, such as Health Policy Advisory Center, Science for the People, and the Union of Radical Political Economists, and those political movements which involve health care as one plank, such as the Women's Health Movement.

Health Policy Advisory Center (Health PAC) was born out of the anger and frustration of young researchers and health workers at what they saw happening in the health politics of New York City. Setting up an action research center and publishing a bulletin and a book (*The American Health Empire*), they made the "mistake" of telling the truth in angry tones, without footnotes. They have constantly been under attack by the academic medical elite, whom they did the first real job of studying from the political angle. It is true that the research is sometimes uneven in quality, as well as primarily being focused on New York City. But issue after issue which they raised in the late sixties and early seventies ultimately results in a study by an "authority" which seldom credits their group for first ringing the alarm bell, or for making the first correct analysis. A second group of this type is *Science for the People*, a small but important group whose aim is to take science and social science out of the mystery category, where they are used by existing elites to "snow" the consumer into believing that whatever is being proposed is "scientifically necessary." Science for the People basically aims at consumer education and the political involvement of the scientists themselves in proconsumer work: in lecturing, in providing technical advice to activists working on a problem, as they have in the fight for occupational health and safety standards reform. Another such group is the *Union of Radical Political Economists*.

Their aim is to provide comprehensive and understandable alternate explanations of the nation's present political and economic problems. Health care is one of their main interests, and they are willing to speak to all and sundry, including, whenever possible, middle-class groups such as Rotary, American Legion, and other such service clubs. They report that demands for their services as speakers to such organizations are on the upswing.

Women have organized in many areas and the women's liberation movement is one of the politically most significant movements of the decade if not the century, in terms of implications for structural reform. Within health care women have been treated badly in ways documented earlier. Each area of mistreatment—the doctor-patient relationship; the side effects of female contraceptive drugs; the nature of the abortion laws—has been the basis for women's political action at the community and state level, as well as nationally. Each consumer issue and each pathology of the health system is becoming a focus for political organization, or for the creation of self-help groups and special health-care settings. Women are the major consumers of health care, and as such are becoming an important force.

But all consumer action and professional action takes place within our existing framework of institutions. These institutions are capable of using consumer participation, and even the planning of new services, as a way of protecting their existing interests. Since planning is always a political activity, ideology plays a major role in it. We will need, therefore, to make an extensive case study of the health service planning process, at the national, state, and local level, to see the ways in which power is exerted skillfully, to prevent significant change in the present situation.

THE POLITICS OF HEALTH PLANNING

A number of years ago W. I. Thomas observed that a social fact which is perceived as real is real in its consequences.[13] The purpose of our analysis is to show that health planning, in any reasonable sense of the term, is a process that simply does not exist in a majority of cases. The fact that the general public believes that it does has major consequences for groups entrusted with such planning, major consequences for the preservation of the status quo in the health field, and thus major consequences for the public itself.

Technocrats and Planners:
The Politics of Occupations

The functional power of expertise lies in the fact that it is a necessity in our complex world. Meynaud observes that technocratic power (the power of organized technical experts in public and private bureaucracies to influence public opinion and to gain ends they may have chosen) may work for the technocrats themselves, or that these individuals may serve only as spokesmen for other interest groups.[14] "There is a risk that technocratic powers, acquired by dispossession of the politician and working apart from any opposition, may be used to benefit one portion of society, or be confiscated by it.[15] The potential co-optation of technocratic skill and influence is made possible by two factors: a common social background and education of those within the cental service bureaucracies and those in control of outside interest groups, and the circulation of people from inside government to outside groups and vice versa.

Mills noted this phenomenon in discussing the "power elite", with special reference to the military-industrial complex, and it applies as well to what we could call the "medical school-teaching hospital complex".[16] This is a technocracy. No one who has beheld the physical presence of the block-long, multiple-wing, seventeen-story Parklawn building of HEW in Rockville, Maryland can deny it.

An analysis of technocracy must identify who the actors are "inside", who pushes them inside, what interest groups they collaborate with outside, and the role, if any, of the general public. Inside professional reformers working in the health bureaucracies are often the first ones to propose ideas such as "the community mental health center", "regional medical programs", or "comprehensive health planning".

Planners constitute a group of individuals only now on the verge of creating themselves as a clearly delineated occupational group. The essential problem is twofold. First, as Carr-Saunders and Wilson were the first to point out, most professions possess a central theoretical body of ideas which undergirds their specific skills.[18] But planners do not even agree among themselves as to what their skill is. Second, as Freidson spells out in detail, a strong profession has control over its work.[19] Planners lack autonomy as an occupational group. In most cases they are hired processors of data to reach goals set by the interest groups—governmental or other groups which employ them. Altshuler, a well-known professor of planning, suggests that "the decisive question is not whether planners have or want power, but whether they are well-equipped to advise those who have it."[20]

Planning has no developed theory but usually consists of the ad hoc application of various skills and technologies to a goal defined by others. Even these amorphous skills appear to be absent in the health-planning area where those "doing the planning" are primarily from the fields of medicine and public health, or with some kind of engineering or systems analysis background, without the training in geography and transportation planning common to city planners.[21] However, to state that planning—of cities or health systems —has no central theory is to miss politically the most important fact about it. It requires the ability to handle complex abstractions and types of jargon, and complicated interorganizational, interbureaucratic relations, and grantsmanship skills as well. A college-educated individual with graduate training in medicine, law, business, economics, sociology, political science, or city planning can learn the specific skills in the health area in a year or two, for the field is essentially undeveloped and undifferentiated, and the process is very much an ad hoc activity in spite of graduate programs in "health planning".

The Politics of the Planning Process

Even if there were a truly effective, rational health planning process, it would have to take place within the existing reality of American metropolitan, regional, and state power structures. Such authors as Wood and Almendinger in *1400 Governments*, on the overlapping jurisdictions for human service activities in New York City, spell out clearly that existing political power centers effectively control the way in which any new planning activity is introduced and applied.[22] Alford notes that groups with a heavy interest in rationalizing services, especially public health officials, medical schools, and hospital power groups, want to do so at least in part to advance their own economic and power-related ends.[23] The private profit-making wings of the power elite in health, especially the organized medical profession, the health technology corporations (drugs, electronics, hospital supply) and the private health insurance corporations, also have a stake in stopping any neutral planning process which affects them unfavorably.[24] This is often accomplished effectively by the altering of legislation for new programs to ensure a strong voice, and possibly even delegated authority, for their groups in the administration of the new planning effort.

The process of planning is inevitably and basically a type of power politics involving either the preservation of the status quo or changes in it. To the degree that powerful interest groups exist in fields such as health before the introduction of any new attempt at planning, they can be expected to frustrate or twist, or co-opt, the planning process away from its original intent.

Perhaps the clearest way to illustrate what the health planning process is, is to see what it is *not* in most cases, through the results of Frieden and Peters' national study of thirty-three completed health plans.[25] First, "Typically, the reports do not include a description of the health service framework desired at the end of the planning period". Second, "the health plans in our survey devote scant attention to formulation and selection of alternative long-range goals and short-range objectives". Third, "Most plans in the survey contain no statement of goals whatsoever. When goals are stated, they are seldom specific. . .". Fourth, regarding analyses of accessibility, travel time to treatment, and waiting time: "health planning agencies have seldom adopted specific policies in regard to these issues". Fifth, only one out of thirty-three plans used comparative data on prevalence of illness rates in different parts of the area, *or any data at all to justify their stated priorities:* "These choices are usually based on more informal—and often inscrutable—grounds". Sixth, "from the city planner's point of view, health planners seem relatively unconcerned with the exact location of resources; areawide plans are somewhat map-shy". Seventh, although various types of data on population, housing, and the economy of an area are appended to the plans, "very often this information is reported without analysis, since areawide health studies rarely develop detailed system proposals requiring integration and interpretation of such data". Finally, "only a few of the plans emphasize long-range improvements or specify a target date for the implementation of recommendations".[26]

The reader might well ask, is this planning? Verbal statements made about health services systems that describe no specific ends, no alternatives, with only vague goals, with little consideration of physical or ecological variables, and almost no relevant data analysis, and no target date for implementation, may more realistically be called *ideological* statements. The sponsors of such plans may be seen as their proponents, and planning may be viewed as a simple political activity in the direct sense of the term.

FIVE NATIONAL PLANNING PROGRAMS: AN IDEOLOGY IN USE

Generally, main themes of the health-planning ideology stress such usually undefined virtues as "comprehensiveness", "democratic decision making", "consumer participation", "economy", and "improvement in overall health service".

Increasing complexity in the relationships between outside interest groups and governmental programs, combined with the growth of an essentially technocratic politics in health, characterize the progression from the Truman era to the present. This growing relationship between the "outside" and the "inside" is reflected in the growth and function of health planning as a managerial ideology.

Five major national health-planning programs will be analyzed below. The discussion of each plan will include: its legislative and political history; a description of what the plan entails; the ideology in use; the proponent-client situation; and the consequences of accepting the proposed ideology for all of the parties. The analysis will suggest some historical trends in the use of health planning as an ideology.

Hill-Burton Program

Immediately after the Second World War, political pressure began to be applied by organized hospital interests for government subsidy for hospital construction, with opposition by organized medicine. The Hospital Survey and Construction Act of 1946 (Public Law 79–725) provided significant support for hospital construction in rural areas, as the formula for state support favored such areas.[27] Citizen participation in planning, in the sense that we now think of it, was not required. A single state agency, usually the Department of Public Health, was designated as the overall administrator of the program for each state. Provision was made for the creation of an advisory council

> representative of government and non-governmental organizations and groups, including persons familiar with the facility needs of both urban and rural areas. The council as such is not vested with any administrative authority, but serves the state agency only in an advisory capacity representing the various interests and geographic areas affected by hospital planning.[28]

The program was popular from the beginning, except with civil rights activists who objected to the separate-but-equal clause which allowed government funding of Southern rural segregated hospitals, a fight which the activists won in 1963.[29] Present-day activists are fighting to have recent amendments enforced and effective guidelines written to guarantee Hill-Burton service to the poor.[30] But the fighters are outsiders due to the structure of the program. Hospital boards and hospital-planning councils are primarily composed of the business and professional elite of a community, and continue to resist democratization or interference with decision making by citizen groups with respect to Hill-Burton funds or in other ways. Transferral of planning functions in 1966 to another government program (which will be considered below as Comprehensive Health Planning) changed the venue but not the results.[31]

Hill-Burton, initiated as a program in a time of shortages of hospitals and funds for them, continued and was refunded over the presidential veto in 1970, a time when excess hospital construction was becoming a problem and a source of extra cost to the consumer.[32] The increasing ability of hospitals, in a Blue Cross/Medicare era, to borrow money from banks for new building against a guaranteed input of hospital fees means that Hill-Burton money is no longer a major factor in hospital construction. The program's own reports indicate a trend toward renovation instead of construction, and toward more use of funds (by congressional amendment) for community clinics.[33]

The Hill-Burton program essentially had no significant ideology. It was what it claimed to be, a program of funds to support the building of hospitals. It provided a baseline against which to judge the increasing use of ideologies. Perhaps the ideal of "hospital planning" was a type of low-level ideology, but it was not broadcast far and wide as a political solution. In this case there were proponents including hospitals, HEW technocrats, and legislators such as Mr. Hill and Mr. Burton, the public as a target, and client groups. The medical profession eventually benefitted from the use of the new funds by having more work settings to operate from, and organized hospital interests helped establish a "no-strings" support policy. There was no significant planning or claims of planning, and no ideology.

Comprehensive Mental Health Planning

Crusading for improved conditions for the treatment of the mentally ill can be traced back at least to Pinel in France and Dorothea Dix in this country.[34] Yet in the early sixties—the Kennedy era— came the fruition of a long-term drive by the mental health lobby. During the late fifties this was made up of the American Psychiatric Association and other mental health professional organizations, academic psychiatry, the voluntary associations in mental health and retardation, and eventually, the office of the President himself. The Joint Commission on Mental Illness and Health reported in

1960 that mental hospitals should be phased out and replaced with community clinics and a new "community psychiatry" movement.[35] The Commission operated as part of the academic psychiatric establishment elite and proposed a major role for their inside compatriots at the National Institute of Mental Health (NIMH), an increase in funds for mental health programs, the development of a new professional orientation toward the community by mental health workers, and thus, a role for the writers of the report themselves.

In 1963 two events, orchestrated as part of a plan, occurred: planning money was allocated to each state in a state agency which was in most cases the Department of Mental Health, to develop a statewide comprehensive plan for mental health services, and the Community Mental Health Centers Act of 1963 was enacted.[36] The money for state planning was handed directly from NIMH to the states, and they were required "to include details on how information would be secured, and the methods to be used to insure active and continuing participation by all relevant state and community groups". Citizen advisory groups primarily consisted of the organized middle-class voluntary associations, i.e. state "Associations for Mental Health" and "Associations for Retarded Children". The Centers Act of 1963 providing construction funding for community mental health centers, also required "representatives of consumers of the services provided by such centers and facilities who are familiar with the need for such services"; all groups were "to consult with the state agency in carrying out such a plan".[37]

The ideology in use was both general and specific. In general, the rhetoric of a political movement—a "new wave"—was used to promote the idea of mental hospital reform and community treatment to a recalcitrant and suspicious public. Specifically, the ideology did make claims about the community role of the mental health professional and the mental health center, but not about the community role of mental health planning for such professionals or centers.

The ideology was used primarily by mental health professionals, especially in NIMH, the state Departments of Mental Health, and medical school departments of psychiatry, and was directed both at client groups such as the voluntary associations, and the general public. For example, the skills of the mental health professional included "his vision of what the institution's potentialities are for the job of helping individuals achieve more effective skills of living".[38] The role of the community mental health center was also specified.

> Ultimately, the overall goal of a community-oriented mental health center becomes that of community improvement. The major efforts and energies of the mental health team then become devoted to gaining a better understanding of basic community processes and to developing the means for making them more conducive to the emotional well-being of individuals.[39]

As Meynaud notes, this is a classic characteristic of a technocratic ideology—to suggest that a community's well-being is basically worked out not in direct politics but rather with the help of the technical expert, in this case the community psychiatrist.[40]

The ideology was accepted by the client groups in general, believed in strongly by the proponents, given lukewarm acceptance or ignored by the citizenry, and perceived as the direct threat it in fact was by other interest groups at work to develop a community constituency. But the ideology did not make excessive claims in the *planning* area. Thus Halpert in NIMH's own evaluation of Comprehensive Mental Health Planning in 1967, studied six representative states.[41] The findings led him to conclude that "The planning effort was, to a considerable extent, a public relations operation". In critically important detail, the study found the following:

> (Georgia) Many agencies and organizations were involved through the state and regional meetings. The purpose of this involvement was to prepare for implementation of the plan, rather than to assist in writing the plan.

(Maryland) Planning staff adopted the approach of working around vested interests, both at the state and local level (particularly in Baltimore City and in the metropolitan counties surrounding Washington, D.C.

(Illinois) The Commissioner of the Department of Mental Health did not believe in "total involvement" of others during the planning process. In advance of planning, he determined to use a small, "power-structure" professional group to make decisions, and a series of broader groups to modify, approve, and disseminate the decisions.

(Minnesota) There was minimum emphasis on communicating to the general public aboiut the need for such services. . . . The Minnesota proposal was prepared by the planning director. [42]

To summarize, the ideology of community mental health services planning, and a closely connected technocratic-professional elite relationship and lobbying system, created an action program with a consciously formulated political message. Participation was not stressed, since the need for it was not felt at the time the programs were started. The strong demand for citizen participation and the creation of an ideology to deal with this demand, was the consequence of the program described below.

OEO Neighborhood Health Centers

The history of the foundation of the Office of Economic Opportunity (OEO) in 1964, and the creation of the now famous "maximum feasible participation" clause, has been written in detail and evaluated in a series of studies. [43,44] In general the "professional reformers" within OEO headquarters and in the field used the clause and the guidelines of the program as an ideology to incite the poor, especially in black areas of major cities, to organize for militant protest action against the (often racist) city halls of their metropolises. Belief in the overall ideology led to action by poor citizens (conducted by professional community organizers), then to reaction in the form of funding cutbacks for the Community Action Program

(CAP) and an amendment which placed the OEO/CAP program under the control or approval of the local mayor. In the health area, the original provisions for health services were the basis for a series of pilot projects establishing neighborhood health centers.

The ideology of the OEO/CAP program and the now engaged activist sentiment of the local community shifted over to the health arena, where a new structure—far more sophisticated and prepared for OEO-style conflict than was that of the mayor's office—stood waiting. The ideology of planning in this program focused on participation. In OEO's words, "high quality comprehensive health care services are to be readily available to the poor in a manner most responsive to their needs and with their participation".[45] But the medical elite administration of the programs was already an established fact. As OEO noted in 1971, medical schools administered more than half of the programs, and most of the rest were given to public health departments, group practices, and other physician-operated organizations. As the Health Policy Advisory Center observed,

> Community representatives were supposed to be able to participate in a common venture with the men who ran the local medical center, with its hated wards and clinics. Somehow, the medical center representatives were supposed to suddenly show respect for the judgment of the people they had formerly seen only as teaching material.[46]

Several reasons can be found to explain why the escalation in ideology from Hill-Burton and Community Mental Health Centers to OEO Neighborhood Health Centers was not accompanied by any significant increase either in citizen participation or in rational planning. First, professionalism itself is an ideology protecting the autonomy of the physician, and was extended to the day-to-day administration of the center itself on *all* matters, even when evidence showed that citizens were not interested in interfering with strictly medical matters. Second, as in all participatory schemes, the "community" is a fiction. In the OEO program, two main groups expressed interest in the program: "professional citizens" seeking status, and job-seekers interested in the range of paraprofessional occupations offered by some of the centers. Third, *deference* to the physician exists in the lower class as elsewhere, and fourth, *dependence* on health settings is major, since the poor cannot afford the services of private practitioners.[47] Finally, grantsmanship skills were required of Neighborhood Health Center administrators at the community level. Time shortage and complex program renewal applications often meant that even the best-willed administrators (and these were rare) had to exclude the citizen from planning and to use them as a rubber stamp board one day before submitting next year's application to OEO. Thus participation was ineffective or irrelevant to the structure of the program as it had been set up. It is doubtful whether the new idea of community corporations in neighborhoods will change this because the same actors are still involved. A means test requirement added to the procedure for qualifying as a patient in these centers in 1967 will hardly serve to provide services "in a manner most responsive to their needs.[48]

Only in retrospect did the final irony of the Neighborhood Health Center program become evident. Local clinics for the poor have been present in urban settings since the turn of the century. Only the participation in administration would have been new, but this was as ideological in fact as it was in the previous two programs. But the expectation of citizen participation in planning remained as a legacy of the OEO program, and later in the sixties, Ralph Nader and consumer activism escalated this pressure.

Regional Medical Program

The Regional Medical Program (RMP), the Heart Disease, Cancer, and Stroke Amendments of 1965 (Public Law 89–239) is an excellent example of a program that was turned into an ideology in the process of pending legislation. The academic medical elite had been writing for years about the importance of the university teaching hospital as the center of a new complex of health services. But when legislation to create such a teaching-hospital-centered, service-providing complex was suggested by the DeBakey commission, the AMA rose in protest. Health-PAC speaks of a bargain between President Johnson and the AMA, i.e. the AMA would not obstruct the new Medicare program if President Johnson would guarantee that the Regional Medical Program provided no services, but became simply another grant mechanism for innovative education or research projects following the model of the familiar Public Health Service-National Institutes of Health model, with grants, review commiittes, advisory councils, and all the usual trappings familiar to the academic.[49] The focus of the program was to be categorical, centered on cancer, heart disease, and stroke, the cause of seventy percent of mortality in America. Support from the voluntary agencies interested in these diocuses was important, as was support from the medical schools who would be the primary recipients of the grants. But there was no real support from other interest groups. In a commissioned study of the Regional Medical Program, Arthur D. Little, Inc., asks:

Who would support it in the long run? To whom would it really belong? Not, presumably, to the Public Health Service. . . . Apparently not to organized medicine; the AMA never endorsed it in the course of its passage. Not the President's Commission; this law was not what they asked for. Possibly the medical schools, although not quite all asked to join. Certainly not the hospital associations.[50]

The Regional Medical Program is best described by what the legislation said it could *not* do while "regionalizing" and "improving services". Its purpose was "to improve the health manpower and facilities available to the nation and

to accomplish these ends without interfering with the patterns or the methods of financing, of patient care or professional practice, or with the administration of hospitals.[51]

This clause, which could be called the "American Medical Association" amendment, would also be inserted into the Comprehensive Health Planning legislation to vitiate it, as it did the RMP, as a vehicle for change of the health-services system. *The advisory group for each RMP* (there were fifty-five by 1971) *was to be chosen by the applicant* and would include:

> practicing physicians, medical center officials, hospital administrators, representatives from appropriate medical societies, voluntary health agencies, and representatives of other organizations, institutions, and agencies concerned with activities of the kind to be carried out under the program and members of the public familiar with the need for the services provided under the program.[52]

The ideological message contained the assumption that enlightenment traveled in one direction only, from the university medical center to the community doctor and hospital. The Regional Medical Program would "afford to the medical profession and the medical institutions of the nation . . . the opportunity of making available to their patients the latest advances in the diagnosis and treatment of these diseases".[53] The headquarters of RMP in HEW expressed the following about its future grantees:

> Because we have invested heavily as a nation in strengthening medical center capability, we have available a magnificent resource which should be used more effectively for strengthening health care at the community level.[54]

The medical school and teaching hospitals were to be asked through RMP "to strengthen and improve the personal health care system in order that the quality of care received by individuals may constantly be improved and the capacity of that system be enhanced".[55]

The proponents were twofold: university medical academics, especially professors of public health, and the inside technocrats at

HEW, with whom they sometimes exchanged places. The main client group, besides the proponents, was the special-interest disease-related organizations. The headquarters of RMP in 1969 hesitated about attempting to widen their mandate to include all diseases. They questioned

> whether the support and participation of powerful voluntary health agencies such as the American Heart Association and the American Cancer Society would be lost through decategorization, and whether Regional Medical Programs could afford this now.[56]

The targets of the ideology were the community practitioner and community hospital, who were supposed to play the role of unenlightened peasant, and the general public, who in paying the bill were to be convinced that "regionalization" (a) was happening, and (b) had consequences for health care. Neither appeared to be the case as of 1970. In a nationwide study of the RMP done under contract to its federal headquarters, Arthur D. Little, Inc. studied eighteen RMPs in depth, and concluded (a) there was no focus to RMP; it was simply a funding category for demonstration project grants; (b) its impact was not measurable; and (c) it was not effecting any significant regionalizing.[57] These conclusions are not surprising since, by statute, RMP was not allowed to change any patterns of service. The study allowed that a few minor special continuing education programs for physicians and nurses and some special surgery were being funded by RMP (the money for these could come from other programs), however,

> in our field work, we saw no fully developed center-periphery example developed as a result of RMP. In fact, it is difficult to see how center-periphery regionalization can ever be achieved if it entails any significant redistribution of power in a region where there is even moderate opposition to it. . . . One of the reasons for this, we believe, is that the center-periphery regionalization by definition fails to recognize the centrality of the practicing physician.[58]

In summary, the process by which the Regional Medical Program was created, which changed it from an alternate plan for health services to a trivial demonstration program, was not an accident. In a power struggle between the academic medical elite and the practitioner-AMA elite, the practitioner group and their interests won, reducing the program to an ideology from the start.

Comprehensive Health Planning

The Partnership for Health Act of 1966 (Public Law 89–749) can be likened to a group of people closely gathered around a table, holding their breath and watching one of their number delicately building a castle out of playing cards. Suddenly someone sneezes, and the house of cards collapses. The act was conceived by professional reformers as a means to tie together into one cooperative whole the federal government, the state government, the voluntary hospital, and especially health and welfare councils. The intent was to involve all of the forces—including consumers—in the health-planning process. But Congress, in noting that it had "given" both OEO Neighborhood Health Centers and RMP to the medical school, deemphasized the role that these agencies would play in the original legislation. Since the AMA had compromised with Johnson on Medicare, there was a self-destruct clause here, as there was in RMP. As the legislation reads, the aim of the Comprehensive Health Planning (CHP) program was

> to support the marshalling of all health resources—national, state, and local—to assure comprehensive health services of high quality for every person, *but without interference with existing patterns of private professional practice of medicine, dentistry, and related healing arts.*[59] [Italics mine.]

Once again, the program was created as an absurdity. Obviously, nothing real can be accomplished if the program is not allowed to correct inadequacies in the present pattern of services. But once again, this has been the central argument of the analysis. Planning in CHP became a rhetoric, an ideological cover for the strengthening of existing interests, a process aided by the very real money that came to the designated planning organizations.[60]

Consumer participation was to be a major goal of this act, at least on paper. Referring to the advisory councils to the state planning agency (A agency), and to the planning agency at the local, areawide level (B agency), the act provided that "a majority of the membership of such council shall consist of representatives of consumers of health services".[61] In general, there would be a federal headquarters, the Comprehensive Health Planning Service in HSMHA (an HEW agency), one designated state comprehensive planning agency in each state (A agency), and a set of regional planning agencies within each state (B agencies). The A agencies, and often their advisory boards, were chosen by the governors, with bank presidents and political supporters along with government officials as prominent "consumers". Anderson and Anderson note that the A agencies obtain the majority of their data from health professionals and existing information, but only thirteen percent of the agencies believe that the consumer should be the main source of ideas and goals for the program.[62] According to the national evaluation of the CHP program in 1971 by the Organization for Social and Technical Innovation, Inc., (OSTI) under contract to CHP federal headquarters, the A agencies are primarily either in departments of public health or in governor's offices, but whatever their location, their function is unclear both in the original legislation and in practice. They are often ignored by B agencies, who work directly with the federal program headquarters.[63]

The B agencies—the official, local, areawide health planning organizations—were designated by a procedure that varied from state to state, but Ardell observed that the approved agencies were, in most cases, recently augmented and reformed versions of existing agencies in the voluntary health planning power structure. The majority were either former hospital planning councils or former health and welfare councils.

> Basically, both hospital and health and welfare planning councils are restricted purpose agencies without public mandate. Both are somewhat elitist in structure, lack procedures for due process and effective implementation of proposals, suffer from insecure funding bases, are dominated by special interests, and offer unexceptional track records of achievement.[64]

The Organization for Social and Technical Innovation notes that the single-function B agency tends to predominate in urban areas, and that they seem to operate primarily as "review-and-comment" agencies, evaluating the planning proposals of other groups.[65] Boston's experience was typical, and agrees with OSTI's overall national data. The Boston B agency "has given up the pretense that it was engaged in any areawide comprehensive health planning. Instead, its staff considers that its major responsibility is limited to comment and review on the projects and proposals initiated by other organizations".[66]

The primary role of urban B agencies—reviewing others' proposals—entrusts to them a kind of protoregulatory responsibility, since other divisions within HEW and other legislation are beginning to require approval of the B agencies before action can be taken in several areas. In some states such as California, the B agency is given actual regulatory authority. Hollister and Shapiro doubt that these agencies will make a *real* contribution here, however, as a symbolic (ideological) response is enough to satisfy the public—in the short run—that "something is being done".[67] But even here the issue of who they are—primarily representatives of private agencies and professional groups—and what they do—approve or disapprove their own plans—leads Curran to wonder whether a "legal crisis" is developing.[68] While the Federal Aviation Administration, the Securities and Exchange Commission, the Food and Drug Administration, and other federal regulatory agencies

254

make some pretense of neutrality, they *are* public agencies; the CHP legislation, and especially some slated for the near future, deliberately invests power of this kind in the private voluntary hospital elite in the community.

The CHP program had the most diffuse ideology of the five national health planning programs inspected, with the most grandiose claims and the greatest number of proponents (everyone *did* get into the act) while showing the least amount of discernable concrete activity. The CHP federal headquarters, the state A agency, and the state B agencies, once established, began to advertise that they were doing comprehensive work (seldom defined in any precise way), and that they were concerned with health (but not in any specified way). Clearly, they were not planning, The review of thirty-three health plans by Frieden and Peters described earlier was primarily an inspection of the paper products of CHP B agencies. The Expectations Project (planning staff and consultants at one of these agencies, with support from headquarters) summarizes the ideology by stating that CHP is expected to be characterized by "comprehensiveness", "democratic process", "consumer participation", and "public accountability". These messages have to be evaluated against the reality of the program. The ideology stated:

> Comprehensive health planning exists to use all means to meet the total health needs of all of the population by resolution of problems and as an advocate in the public interest in all circumstances and actions that can affect health.[69]

The fifty-one percent consumer participation rule in the legislation and the federal guidelines was interpreted with absolute cynicism. OSTI's national evaluation concluded:

> There is much less difference between B agency usage of the term "consumers" and "providers" than is frequently assumed . . . "consumer" lists often include professionals such as retired physicians, administrators of homes for the aged, and directors of social service

departments. . . . Our interviews frequently yielded statements to the effect that "there is no difference between consumers and providers" . . .

Minority consumers, ten percent of all "consumers" in our sample, tend generally to be professionals, such as a black professor of community psychiatry. In a sample of 57 B agency "consumers" we found only two "consumers" who were both poor and black or brown.[70]

Any pretense of objectivity in the functioning of these B agencies was belied by the way they were funded. They had to obtain almost half of their operating funds from the groups for whom they were supposed to plan, evaluate, and regulate. As Linton, Mields, and Coston, Inc. point out in their national (contracted) evaluation of the CHP program, in larger urban centers, the program was a battleground between interests which would usually withdraw their support if they couldn't control operations. For example, "Cleveland was able to replace a declining local government contribution by sizeable funds from Blue Cross and . . . it must remain sensitive to the issues of concern to this supporter".[71] The New York Expectations Project observed in 1972:

Because of the need to "panhandle" for its basic support, an agency frequently can be placed in an awkward position when making decisions affecting the operations of its contributors. In order to survive, an agency may see as its constituency its financial supporters rather than the community.[72]

In conclusion, the CHP program, as evaluated by the governments' own contracted evaluators and by the reports of its own participants, was a thinly disguised rationalization for the funding of the existing power structure in health services, combined with a cynically-used ideology directed at the general public. The people were led to believe that some kind of public-interest-regarding "comprehensive health planning" was occurring. This nonexistent process was paid for by them both directly in terms of government funding, and indirectly in terms of the continual escalation in health-care costs.

This analysis has indicated that "health planning" in its most important national examples, is primarily an ideology. It is a managerial ideology, used by combinations of federal human services technocrats and outside interest groups in health, especially either the academic medical elite or the practitioner-community hospital elite. From 1946 to the present, the use of ideology escalated on several dimensions. In focus, it widened from a concern with special areas—building hospitals, clinics for the poor, specific—to cover the planning of everything. The claims for the process increased markedly relative to the actual accomplishments. The number of proponents and client groups increased, with the steady presence of the inside technocratic professional reformers being joined first by simple outside interest blocs, and then by complexes of groups.

Although the earlier targets of the ideology were in part specific subgroups in the population, the general public has always been the main target. The theme of citizen participation in planning grew with each program, while its actual absence remained constant. In short, the increasing demands for public accountability, participation, and control of health-services planning is being met with the increasing use of ideology as a symbolic, not real, response to the demands. This process is the inevitable consequence of technocratic rationalization within a system where the inside technocrats work in mutual cooperation with, or as agents for, outside interest groups primarily concerned with the perpetuation of profits and the maintenance of their existing power and control over the system.

No major changes in health services can be expected through a *planning* process while the existing political economy remains in control of the legislative process. A change toward a more nationalized or socialized economy will not remove the problem of controlling technocratic power in the interests of the people, but it might make possible a legislative and planning process that would neither create programs as absurdities nor lead to their systematic destruction after enactment.

POWER, PLANNING, AND
CULTURAL HEGEMONY

Antonio Gramsci coined the concept of "cultural hegemony", within a Marxian theoretical framework, to get at a phenomenon similar to that which others, such as Weber, have called "legitimacy". But the idea of hegemony is even broader in scope. Cultural hegemony is the concept which refers to the precise ideas which are used, at a particular time and place, by the ruling economic class, to win the hearts and minds of the people over to an acceptance of the existing status quo. When a particular ideology is truly in a position of hegemony, then "one concept of reality is diffused throughout society in all its institutional and private manifestations, informing with its spirit all taste, morality, customs, religions, and political principles, and all social relations, particularly in their intellectual and moral connotations".[73] Citizen or consumer participation in the planning and delivery of health services is a challenge to this concept of reality only if it is carried out in conditions where citizens have real power.

The *appearance* of participation, powerless limited participation, or the short-run victories of the consumer activists such as Nader or the various health-activist groups, have quite the opposite effect. They tend to legitimate the status quo precisely because, to the majority of citizens, "something is being done" while the overall economic structure and the patterns of basic ownership and control (inside and outside health concerns) remains unchanged. Viewed in this way, power groups in our modern era often *want* a limited form of powerless citizen participation in the planning process. The five planning programs reviewed here, or the new Health Planning and Resources Development Act of 1974, which is built on three of

the programs reviewed here, rearrange slightly the existing processes but do not essentially change the functional role of the planning
process in health.[74] The activity is itself ideological, for people
think inevitably that if they talk and plan they are having some real
effect on the real decisions that have, in most instances, already
been made behind closed doors. Viewed in this way, a boycott of
co-opted participatory planning schemes, by those affected, may in
reality be a truer form of participation than playing the game by rules
designed to favor the house at every opportunity.

Genovese, following Gramsci, summarizes the problem:

> It follows that hegemony depends on much more than consciousness
> of economic interests on the part of the ruling class and unconscious-
> ness of such interests on the part of the submerged classes. The
> success of a ruling class in establishing its hegemony depends entirely
> on its ability to convince the lower classes that its interests are those of
> society at large—that it defends the common sensibility and stands for
> a natural and proper social order.

At present, the "common sensibility" accepts the token participation of powerless or carefully chosen consumers, plus an occasional gadfly consumer group, within an advanced capitalist
economy that uses the state and the legal system to protect the
existing interests. Rejecting all of this at once—totally—is a hard
task for anyone. One place, however, where many start is the legal
system. "At least let's change the law", the consumer group says.
The limits of this strategy are our next topic.

8

Action through Law

Generally accepted customs have always functioned in human societies as rules of conduct. Law in the modern sense of the term slowly evolved out of custom, but now constitutes something qualitatively quite different. For in our present-day world, customs and values may go one way, the formal letter of the law another. Our need for courts, judges, lawyers, and policemen testifies to the disagreements over what is acceptable behavior. Durkheim called this condition anomie: a lack of shared agreements about socially valuable and desirable behavior. Attempts to patch over basic disagreements with *laws* could lead to situations where a slight majority passes a new law through a legislature, and the other half of the society then ignores the law, rejects its enforcers, and defies them to do anything about it.

An example of the ways the political system intersects with the legal system is provided by the things which happen when an interest group is barely successful in getting a new law passed.

When such a law is used as strategy for change, the government, if it is not in sympathy, may attempt to get the administration of the law "handed off" to groups or individuals that were not in favor of it in the first place. This creates a "toothless law" situation, such as when a president unsympathetic to school busing announces such, in his position as president of the nation and supposedly as moral leader. In general, laws, lawmaking, and law enforcement occur within a social and political context. Only when the context is understood can we see the limits and possibilities of action through law.

Health care is increasingly becoming a legal battleground. It is first an arena for struggle in the law-making process—a struggle by different groups attempting to place their stamp on the future pattern of services. We can begin with a brief inspection of the complexities of this law-making process. Two cases can be observed which illustrate some points in the process: abortion law reform and cancer research programs. Then we turn to the law enforcement, or regulation, process. We will be concerned with those agencies whose job it is to enforce the rules relating to health care which have been passed into law. How regulatory agencies operate in general can be considered first, and then how regulatory programs work, or don't work, in the health field. Here we will briefly consider the regulation of people, places, medical supplies, and costs. We will conclude with an assessment of the strategy of law-making and regulation as an effective tool for change, within the framework of an advanced capitalist society.

THE LAW-MAKING PROCESS:
POLITICIANS, EXPERTS, AND INTERESTS

Legislation—the law-making process as well as the resulting law—has long been a subject for study. The ideal view of this process portrays law making as a kind of arbitration process, in which the different affected interests have a chance to put their opinions and inputs on record. The lawmaker then calculates the compromises needed to get the law passed against the goal that was the reason for going ahead and making a new law in the first place. If the opposition is too strong, the attempt is given up early. If broad support exists, the inputs will help "refine" the law, making it more "realistic" and making its chances of being effective after passage that much greater. Thus maximum communication between lawmakers and those potentially to be affected is considered desirable, even necessary, to the making and passing of a valuable, effective law. The interested parties are assumed to be of somewhat equal weight in their influence on the bill. The support of the society is reflected, according to the ideal, by the votes of the elected representatives. Support is necessary for laws before and after passage is considered. It should be noted that socialist states have laws, and they too have problems in enforcing some of them if the people are unwilling. The Soviet Union, for example, has trouble in enforcing its law requiring new medical graduates to spend their first two years in the rural areas, because of the systematic sabotage of the rule by those in the medical profession who have close ties to the party elite.

Theory or ideals and practice are different, of course, and the function of studies of the law-making process is to expose the difference. For example, two decades of research by political scientists on the tyrannical committees of Congress and their authoritarian chairmen, who held up many possible reforms and new laws because they did not meet with the approval of interest groups friendly to the chairmen, may have had an effect. Regardless of the degree of ultimate success, the congressional committee "revolution" of 1974 was caused in part by young congressmen who had first heard of this system through critical studies by academics and reporters.

The specific structure of the law-making process is a key problem, especially as it compares to the simple or diagrammatic view found in the textbooks. In the federal system, a law is made by a complex maze of committees, panels, amendments, and parliamentary procedures, different for the House and Senate. Different details exist for each state. Mastery of the details of this process— the way the committees *really* operate at any level in the political system—necessary for all and is usually achieved first by the pressure groups, the interests who lobby "on the Hill" on a daily basis. Such familiarity with details is central for an interest group, including consumers, who wish to influence the passage of new legislation. Yet, as we will see below, that is just the first stage in the process, even if it is successful.

Input into the Law-Making Process: Groups and Strategies

Politicians, experts, profit-making corporations, and consumers are four main groups that often attempt to use the law-making process for their own ends as well as for the creation of the law itself. For example, a particular politician may become an informal expert over the years in the health field, by virtue of committee assignments, personal interest, and a series of popular public stands on health issues. Once a politician has developed a "legislative image", other interest groups with similar approaches and values may turn to him for support, and he to them. In turn, the creation of new laws bearing the politician's name can do much to create a niche in history and a feather in the cap of the politician, at reelection time. Senator Fulbright, for example, probably got much mileage and prestige out of the student aid program for foreign visits being called the "Fulbright" program. In addition, a health-care image is usually a good one for any politician, second perhaps only to support of motherhood (and with the rise of female liberation, perhaps in a class by itself!).

But the complexities of the field, which have been hinted at in this book, demand so much time, even for those senators and representatives who have large staffs, that dependence upon outside experts for advice, and for bill writing, becomes a necessity. *Which* experts the politician depends on will have critical implications for the shape of the bill, and the possible future it may have along the way toward the final decision. Thus one of the most important choices a politician makes when he get into the health policy area, is which experts to choose, and how much to depend on them. Several types of experts have begun to play an important role in nearly all the legislation in process in Washington. These are professors in the academic medical elite who specialize in "systems design" and health-care economics; planners and strategists working out of the AMA headquarters; insurance experts in both the private companies and Blue Cross, who have built up experience in administration of health insurance; proconsumer groups such as the Health Research Group of the Nader organization; and radical activist study centers, such as the Institute for Policy Studies.

Experts cannot usually be *bought*, if by buying we mean bribing them to say what you want said. But basic values and attitudes toward the usual issues of concern in health legislation—that is, who should have power and control in a new project, where the money will go, who will benefit, and the role of different interest groups—these priorities and choices are worked out early. Thus the AMA works with *its* economists, usually conservative and free-enterprise oriented; the planning and manpower economists work within the academic medical elite; and radical economists do critiques from outside, or at places such as the Institute for Policy Studies, and try to help consumer groups who are pushing legislation. The point here is that experts seldom influence the law-making process directly (although this has happened more than once when a professor is hired to completely draft a bill), but rather usually through sponsors who already have taken a basic position on a new law. On the other hand, some experts, such as the Nader group, find that their expertise is listened to only when they have first created a stir in the media, and in a sense they have to force their expertise on people who don't want to listen to it.[1] One final note is in order on "experts". The leadoff witness in congressional hearings on a new law—the official expert—is often only the formal spokesman for a team of graduate students in health-care research or a group of senior law students working for a law professor specializing in health care. Their round-the-clock work, sometimes on short notice and lasting for weeks, may well lie behind the polished presentation by the "name" witness. In turn, if "their" bill succeeds, their own career as an expert in later years will in part be based on their role in the new law they helped to make. The ferocity and intensity of work by the dedicated and anonymous assistants to experts needs mention here, for it is usually their effort that makes or breaks a new innovation in health care through law.

Profit-making corporations, especially the great insurance combines, swing weight in health legislation for three reasons. The first is their key role in the corporate capitalist class. Many other corporations have stock owned by the great insurance combines. They may call on *all* these corporations to help them if it looks like a major insurance interest is being threatened. For example, any national health insurance bill which writes profit-making insurance companies out of the picture can be vetoed not just by *their* strength in Congress, but by their ability to call on the services of the lobbyists of most of the 400 largest corporations, if it looks like their interests are in great danger. Second, the profit-making firms have stables of experts on their own payroll, and are willing to lend them free of charge to a sympathetic but understaffed congressman. Any politician's image is improved in the view his home constituency simply by virtue of introducing bills in Congress (even if this eventually loses him the respect of his colleagues—unless they are really well worked out). Again, the corporations—as well as the other interest groups named—will be glad to write the entire bill if asked. Nonprofit corporations, especially Blue Cross in the health-care field, act as interest groups who can claim on some issues both expertise and a heavy role in administering the existing system. Their trump card, as they see it, is that they have the experience, and should thus be given the right to design and run a new national insurance system. Those opposed to their using this claim point out the inequities in the present system (including some within their own organization) and say, "Yet *look* at that system!" This, unfortunately or not, is another aspect of the expert consultant game: the challenging of the legitimacy of the opposition experts and their objectivity. When experts disagree, as they do in each of the cases we will consider, their expertise is neutralized and the issue pushed back almost completely into power politics.

Finally, there is no one strategy which works in all cases. Each bill, each committee, each month of each year presents specific problems. It may be a good year for a new law, or a bad one. (For laws which endanger corporate interests, it is *always* a bad year.) A sympathetic chairman may be ill, a war may be going on between two congressional committees, a particular politician may decide to run for reelection or for president on the health-care ticket. Strategies are therefore very much an up-to-the-minute thing, and power in Washington is a fast-moving thing as well. Roller-coaster ups and downs have affected the fate of every new bill, whether it goes through or dies in committee. Thus it may be helpful to look at some of the factors affecting such laws by considering two areas: abortion law reform and the creation of a new cancer research agency.

TWO CASES: ABORTION AND CANCER RESEARCH

The history of a law consists of two closely related parts: the history of the way it is made and the history of what happens to it after it becomes official. Groups that have been active in opposing or supporting a law before passage do not usually change their minds afterward. The opposers before passage shift to a series of new strategies that aim at opposing the immediate consequences after passage, while the supporters aim at insuring that the changes actually do take place. One exception can occur with some frequency, if the opposition group is offered a piece of the action after passage, or some compromise is made with the original aims. Both of the two cases we have are compromises. The first is the issue of what happens to a law after passage, in the courts; the second, what happens to an agency which is created by a compromise.

Abortion: Who Owns a Woman's Body?

Abortion had been illegal for many years—though in fact widely practiced in settings both medical and kitchen—when the proabortion interest groups decided to organize and fight the idea of antiabortion laws themselves. A broad coalition developed in the fifties and sixties and began to work systematically to influence public opinion by challenging the legitimacy of the laws themselves.[2] But until the rise of the women's movement, no real mass support existed. Seizing on a central issue—that a woman's body belongs to her alone, and that laws against abortion interfere with her basic rights as an individual—efforts were made in several states to bring the challenge to the courts and up to the Supreme Court if possible.[3] In addition to organizers from the women's movement, other proabortion groups were important. First, obstetricians and gynecologists could testify in court, and did, to the maiming and permanent injury done to women by incompetent and untrained abortionists, damage they had to repair if they could in the emergency rooms of city hospitals. Civil liberties groups believed that the antiabortion laws were an attempt to legislate morality, and as such were not fair. Some lawyers, active in general civil liberties work, lent their services to the legal fights against specific state laws. Population control people were involved, for abortion is certainly a clearcut form of birth control—although they, as well as

267

most proabortion people, would prefer contraception techniques for this purpose. Also, the poor and organizations working for the poor were in favor of it, for it could lower the overall costs of welfare and also lower the pressure on a given welfare family which already had children and could barely survive as they were.

Those ranged against the proposal were against it for a number of reasons. The Catholic Church viewed the abortion law reform campaign as a direct attack on their theology and a threat to their centuries-long prohibition on abortion as well as birth controls, when carried out by technological means. As Pope Paul said, "Everyone has a right to sit down at the banquet of life".[4] Who would put the food on the table was not an issue the Church explored in detail. The antiabortion campaign was strongest in Catholic areas, but it was also effective in areas where a fundamentalist, strict meaning of "morality" excluded abortions; and it was more effective on the east and west coasts than in the heartland of the country. Of course, illegal abortionists stood to lose business as a consequence of the legalization of the process, but few were in a position to openly campaign for its continuing illegality.

Finally, New York State passed a reformed abortion law, and in another case, the legal activists took the case up to the Supreme Court, in 1973. But the Court did not agree that a woman owned her body under all circumstances. She had the right to terminate her pregnancy freely and legally under any condition only in the first three months. After that, in the next three months medical approval was needed, and in the last three months only when the mother's health was in danger was termination allowable. It was *qualified* victory for the proabortion forces. In the words of the Court,

> A woman's right to terminate her pregnancy is not absolute, and may to some extent be limited by the state's legitimate interests in safeguarding the woman's health, in maintaining proper medical standards, and in protecting potential human life.

Just as with the Brown vs. Board of Education decision by the

Court in 1954, which made segregation illegal, a change in the law does not necessarily mean a change in society. In fact, just a brief time after the Supreme Court ruling, a Boston physician who performed a midtrimester (from the fourth to the sixth month) abortion found himself in criminal court on a manslaughter charge. In heavily Catholic Boston, the Right-to-Life organization had been campaigning for a repeal of the state's new abortion law. The judge told the jury that Dr. Edelin—a black physician who was at the time a chief resident in obstetrics at Boston City Hospital—was performing an operation on a legal nonperson (the fetus) and that manslaughter conviction required a *person* to die. The prosecution held up pictures of the fetus and told the jury to disregard the testimony of most of the nation's leading experts on prenatal medicine, all of whom had testified that the fetus was too young to live outside the mother's womb. In addition, the judge told the jury that abortion was *legal* by the Supreme Court's own rule.[6] In spite of all of this, Dr. Edelin was convicted of manslaughter. The shock wave hit every operating room in the nation. Eventually the Supreme Court will probably get this case as well; but in the meantime, a finding on the record throws into question the legality of every abortion after three months, except for health reasons. Since many poor people cannot get the money together for such operations quickly, and they tend to be less sophisticated sometimes on pregnancy in general, more of them are likely to go over the time line. City hospitals, not known for risking their necks on behalf of the poor, are now under even more pressure to wait. Thus regardless of the long-term implications, there will be many unwanted babies born before the case is finally resolved.

One considered verdict on the importance of this trial was given by Ingelfinger:

The Edelin case is a fiasco. As Dr. Kenneth Ryan has said, "This court trial on abortion has not established what an abortion is and certainly has not defined the moral issue any more than the Scopes Trial was the last word on evolution." In addition, the trial has hardened the positions, inflamed the rhetoric, and disrupted rational exchange between the pro-abortionists and antiabortionists.[7]

This statement, correct as far as it goes, misses the basic point of the trial in the first place: that it was a political trial staged by the antiabortion forces to do just what it did, namely harass the legal abortion process and the physicians carrying it out. The jury simply cooperated, on the basis of values they shared with the opponents of reform.

To sum up, the strategy for stopping a new law can include obtaining judicial interpretations of the new reform which limit its effectiveness as a vehicle for change, as well as simultaneous attempts to build a movement to repeal the law entirely. For if extensive support does not exist among the people in a democracy, the life and usefulness of a law is limited indeed. Unless it is a law which directly threatens the interests of corporate capitalism, the people usually have some influence on whether the judges and the law enforcement procedures are brought to bear or not. For example, the Prohibition era in America occurred *after* the passage of the law, yet the law had become disregarded and a force protecting crime created long before the repeal. This is the ultimate irony; to pass a law without much support may create a backlash of great proportions. On the other hand—and it is a point that many believe outweighs the risk—to have the new law on the books may be far better than not to have it, as a tool for change if not to produce the change itself.

Cancer Research: Science Politics and the Research Establishment

In politics, almost anything can happen in the way of temporary alliances, and in addition last year's friend may even be this year's enemy *because* he was last year's friend. The politics of cancer research give us an example of the way that interest groups build up a stake in a system. Also, especially in the case of the drug corporations, successful passage of a new law may create a new interest group that may oppose others in future attempts to create yet another new law or program which affects the new creation. Medical research was a small item in the federal budget until the Eisenhower era. Then a combination of academic medical elite professor-researchers and private lobbyists went to work on Congress. Prominent in this group was Mary Lasker, an independently wealthy woman active in civic affairs and health care. She used not only her own skills in political infighting but also the aid of experts within and outside her family in the area of public relations work. Strickland sums up the skills needed for this kind of work as threefold in nature: "the ability to translate ideas, whether clearly good or of questionable merit, into popular causes; the sense to document . . . cases so as to make them persuasive to policymakers on a cerebral as well as an emotional level; and total dedication and relentless pursuit of desired goals".[8]

An example of the way Lasker operated, using support from the specific disease agencies (National Heart Association, National Foundation for Infantile Paralysis, etc.) and the researchers, was the way she approached the Republican chairman of the Senate Appropriations Committee, Senator Styles Bridges of New Hampshire in 1947:

> She made her case in two brief parts. Knowing that he had been bothered by heart trouble, she pointed out that no funds had ever been earmarked for research into heart disease and circulatory ailments by the National Institutes of Health. She also knew that Bridges was already concerned that President Truman was going to try to label the 80th Congress as a do-nothing Republican failure, so she suggested that Bridges take the lead in doing something that would be important and popular. Her idea was to have Congress direct NIH to step up its investigations into heart disease and provide more money for the effort.[9]

Bit by bit, the giant campus of the National Institutes of Health was built in Maryland, with its complexes of in-house research and outside academic research advisory boards. By the time of the early seventies this had become its own interest group, tying government based researchers in with academic ones. And by this time, both Ted Kennedy and Richard Nixon had come upon cancer research as an issue, and were anxious to have a new agency set up to specialize in it. The argument, in preparing a new law, came down to one of expanding the small existing National Cancer Institute in NIH (Kennedy's view) or the Nixon view, of a War on Cancer to match John Kennedy's race to the moon or Johnson's War on Poverty—hopefully with the success of the first and not the second effort. A War on Cancer struck the Nixon White House as good public relations, and the Lasker/private-agency forces were interested. But ironically, the scientists affiliated with NIH—which the Lasker group had originally put in business—now felt that this was a bad idea, that science had grown up and was now too respectable for the old ways of getting things done, a la Lasker and Nixon. The issue, always a fateful one in the politics of law making, was the bureaucratic location of the new agency: inside NIH, or directly under the President, as the space program had been? If we remember the issue with the Medicaid program, the location of a new program has great consequences for its future. The academic medical elite was insistent on this point. One of its leaders said in 1971: "To proceed with the establishment of a cancer program separate from and independent of the essential process of scientific decision making represented by the National Institutes of Health would, we believe, gravely impair the objectives of a national attack upon cancer".[10]

The battle eventually came down to one between the versions of the bill in two congressional committees: one in the Senate which would set up an independent agency under the President; versus one in the House of Representatives, which didn't want it this way, figuring that it could become a "political football research agency" that would be ineffective in doing cancer research. The House delayed and worked carefully in preparing its version. Mary Lasker, thinking that their stalling was directed at her, declared war on the House:

> At the suggestion of the honorary chairman of the American Cancer Society, Mary Lasker, the Society raised funds for full-page ads in major newspapers across the country and in some less-than-major newspapers located in the Congressional districts of the Rogers sub-committee members. The Message addressed to the people implied that a small handful of willful men in the House were hamstringing the effort, staunchly supported by the President and the Senate, to conquer cancer.[11]

The House was furious at this tactic. Eventually each side, and the President, took three or four positions for or against a structure or a fund-granting proposal review process for the new agency. Finally a compromise was reached which put the agency on the margins of the NIH and in close contact with the President. In turn, Lasker chose the highly political "old line" first director of the new agency.[12]

Three years later, the agency remains semipolitical in nature, giving a large portion of its funds out to large profit-making corporations which charge high overheads, and whose proposals to do research are not under the usual careful scientific review of the regular NIH scientists or outside researchers. Greenberg, in a study of their information policy, finds that the agency does not, in the classic NIH mold, produce accurate data on disease, but rather politically censors its disease statistics to make the executive branch and the President look good. He compared many sets of data produced by the agency on the cure rates against a more complete set of data and interpretations from outside experts. He found the agency implying that progress made decades ago was being made now, as a consequence of their new organization's efforts. His well-documented opinion, widely respected in the research world, was:

The vast and ill-conceived undertaking that was created by the National Cancer Act of 1971 has inevitably spawned a monolithic bureaucracy with a heavily supported public-relations apparatus that is simply misleading the American public on a dreadfully serious subject. That the intentions are sound and humane is no excuse for the snow job that is being performed by these tax-subsidized institutions. [13]

What this case suggests is that interest-group activity in the law-making process can create ill-conceived agencies dealing with the most critical of problems. Furthermore, though the academic research elite has definitely moved in many areas beyond what many would call basic medical research, within this specific area they do have competence to judge worthwhile research proposals. It was precisely here that they were steamrollered by the lobbyists from the special disease agencies outside, and by the drug lobby. The need for a law and a program to work toward a cure for a dread disease became yet another victory for the politicians and the corporations for whom they were earmarking many of the new research funds.

To conclude, both of these cases indicate that the specific language of a law is fateful to the future of the program and its success. Courts can interpret the law and modify it, or the process of law making itself can alter the program, even before it is fully conceived, so that it cannot fulfill its original function. But another kind of law is possible, as well as those which prohibit or allow processes, or which create and fund new programs. These are the laws which create permanent "watchdog" agencies to look after health-care activities. These laws, and the rule-making, regulatory agencies they create, are our next topic.

THE NATURE OF REGULATION:
IDEALS VERSUS INTERESTS

Reglation is a process attempting, in theory, to protect the public in vulnerable areas. The passage of legislation enacts rules relevant to the area to be regulated, or creates an administrative (regulatory) agency to deal with the relevant problems on a day-to-day basis. If the regulators are the guardians of the public interest we must still ask the question, *who guards the guardians*? To what degree are attempts at regulating any area critical to the public (mass communications, power, air transportation, or health) frustrated by interest groups whose own agenda in these areas conflicts with those of the public? The consumer movement, especially the series of studies by the Nader group and other investigators, has singled out regulatory agencies and regulatory processes for special attention, because the risk of co-optation of the regulators by the regulated is always high, and evidence exists that many agencies have had a long history of working in tandem with their target groups and against the overall interests of the public.

But by no means is this the entire story, nor are "co-optation", "special interest", and "public interest" always easy to define. There is also the important dilemma of the growing social role of technical expertise. If a process is highly technical, and yet of basic importance to a society, then experts must be enlisted to supervise and guard the process in the interests of the public. But they must guard their fellow experts (perhaps personally known to them) and often these are members of exactly the same profession. The public does not have the option of ignoring its need for expert consultation, nor can it ignore the possibility that experts in the regulatory role might work in the interests of the regulated rather than in the general interest. In perhaps no other area are these two issues—of co-optation of the regulatory process and dependence on expertise—raised more strongly than in the health field. The present crisis in health care, especially problems of health manpower availability, health-service system quality, and health-service cost, have never been so severe as they are at present. These problems are promoting a reinspection of our existing mechanisms for regulating health service in the public interest. The basic question is: *can regulation work, in the present political and economic context*? In each of the subareas of regulation, does it protect the public interest and lead over time to an improvement in the quality, availability, efficiency, and cost of health services? If so, how? And if not, why not?

We can begin with a review of the problems that regulation has *elsewhere*, outside of health, as a method for protecting the interests of consumers. Then we may look at two main political dimensions in health-service regulation: intergovernmental bureaucratic politics and topic-oriented interest group action by those concerned with specific areas of reglation. Then we will briefly consider the political action of these interests as it affects the regulation of *people* (credentialling), *places* (certificate of need, etc.), *things* (food and drugs, blood, etc.), and *costs* (rate-setting). The possible (and unlikely) role of consumers will be considered.

The Functioning of Regulation: General Issues

Proposals to reform the regulatory process in federal regulatory agencies (SEC, FPC, ICC, AEC, FAA, etc.) have centered around three basic issues: *administrative procedures, the scope of regulation*, and *the effectiveness of regulation*.[14] In the first, or procedures area, well-known texts in administrative law consider all the complex possibilities and technical details.[15] Legally the delegation of power from the legislature to the regulatory agency has several dimensions, and raises several functional questions. Has the legislature given an agency too much leeway, so that they may make up the regulatory process as they go along? Or have they not given it room to act, to truly cope with the variety of problems it confronts? Has it been constructed to be responsive to changed environments, and new problems in the area it is regulating?

Most important, the judicial and rule-making (legislative) powers handed over to agencies have many legal implications. The regulatory agency can decide cases before it on whether the public interest is being served and it may write and distribute rules and regulations which have the force of law. Immediately we can see that the health

276

field at present is composed of many different protoregulatory agencies in this sense, each of which has a "piece of the action": e.g., licensing boards judge fitness to practice; hospital accreditation and licensing agencies approve health settings; and state insurance commissions, rate-setting commissions, or the federal government approve insurance rates for third-party payers, and the ceilings on more than half of any state's health care charges. Note, however, that though there is one field (health care) there are many regulatory agencies, usually not working together, and sometimes even working at cross purposes. Each has been given some regulatory functions, but they are not closely related to one another. For example, a decision in licensing manpower can affect the functioning of settings or health-care costs. The issues of fairness and efficiency in procedures for health regulation are only in the early stages of inspection, in spite of the fact that they are, if anything, more vital to the public interest than in such areas as power, mass transportation, communications, and air safety.

A second area, the scope of regulation, is clearly also a critical issue in health. In general terms, *total* regulation of a field of activity may not serve its original purpose, for the regulated may fight to stay totally under regulation *once they have co-opted the apparatus to work in their favor*. In general, how much of a field should be regulated and how much left alone? And in the regulated process, what specifically should be regulated: details of day-to-day operation, all results, or only those results which are considered to have direct impact on the consumer? The naive idea that a strong regulatory agency in total control of the entire range of consumer-relevant issues in an area (as the best of all possible worlds) must be compared against the possibility of what could happen if the agency remains strong but becomes co-opted in its aims by the regulated group.

Third, the *effectiveness* issue has been the focus both of general studies of the regulatory process by such authorities as Friendly[16] and of specific consumer-oriented probes by the Nader groups. Such studies as *The Interstate Commerce Omission*, *The Closed Enterprise System*, and *The Monopoly Makers* all concern themselves with the effectiveness of the regulatory agency in terms of its working in the interests of consumers.[17]

Four related sociopolitical processes seem to aid in the breakdown of regulatory effectiveness. First, the regulated group is almost always politically organized and is in day-to-day business contact with the regulators; for the politically unorganized consumers the area of regulation is important but is more remote from daily life and not the top priority item it is to the regulated industry. Second, the relative amount of expertise available to the regulators and the regulated industry usually involves the frustration of the agency's aims, as a wealthy, powerful, and well-staffed industry battles an underfunded, understaffed and harassed regulatory agency. Wall Street lawyers and the "Washington lawyer" are examples of the technical experts on regulation usually marshalled by corporations to frustrate the aims of regulation and regulatory agencies.[18] Third, there is actual co-optation: appointment of agency heads who come from the field to be regulated, and career opportunism by members of regulatory agencies, who are overly solicitous to regulated firms in hopes of a later job in such firms. Finally, bureaucratization in the sociological sense is a problem; the overly complex rules and slow movement of the regulatory process frustrate the consumer's ability to know what is happening and delays decision-making that might be in his interest until the action is effectively "too late". In general, the regulatory process is conceded by most students of it to be a flawed one. Yet it is considered by these same specialists to be preferable to the alternatives of total state ownership or total deregulation. Our review will conclude by returning to this question.

Political Dimensions of Health Service Regulation

There exists to date no extensive body of literature that is clearly concerned with the politics of regulation in health. On the other hand, a broad body of literature is concerned with two problems: those of intergovernmental relations and the nature of interest-group intervention. In each of these areas a few studies are now available concerning: the human services in general and in health in particular.

Studies and surveys of the literature in health service have highlighted the political action of at least the following interest groups: the practitioner wing of the medical profession (AMA); the academic professorial elite (major medical school and teaching hospital directors); national voluntary accrediting agencies (such as the Joint Commission on the Accreditation of Hospitals); and the federal health bureaucracies; state government executive agencies; state legislatures; corporations in the health field; consumer groups; and the legal profession. Evidence already exists which indicates that each of these major groups acts politically with respect to regulation.

Representing the interests of *the private practitioner*, the AMA has attempted "professional dominance" over the political field of forces relevant to regulation. As Friedson points out, the skill and expertise of the physician relevant to the field being regulated is used as a primary political bargaining tool for physician control of the regulatory process, e.g., "only doctors can regulate doctors".[19] The AMA, through its representation on the Joint Commission, directly makes policy on the voluntary accreditation of hospitals, while through its action groups and lobbying efforts it affects legislation relevant to the regulation of office practice and the quality-cost relationship.[20]

In the vanguard of groups advocating systematic regulation of personnel, health-service settings, and financial schemes are members of the *academic medical elite*, who are in some cases the major students of the regulatory scene, and the authors of bills on state and federal regulation. They and their close allies, the nonmedical economists and planners, advocate what Alford has called the "rationalization" of health service.[21]

Organized hospital interests, especially the American Hospital Association, are affected in many ways by changes in the regulatory picture. As a consequence, in their journals, such as *Hospitals*, editorials and articles regularly appear on issues of regulation and the position of hospitals toward its use, or changes in its nature.

National private hospital-accrediting associations have a major interest in regulation. In his brief history of the formation, present nature, and potential future activities of the Joint Commission on the Accreditation of Hospitals (JCAH), Schlicke stresses that the original vanguard position of the JCAH as an "uplift" organization for the elite in hospital services has given way to a functional role as the de facto quasi-public national organization for hospital regulation.[22] But recent legislation is changing this rapidly. A JCAH administrator points out a future of increasing pressures by federal government and consumer groups to (1) open the regulatory process to greater public responsiveness; and (2) increase the degree of inspection of process within the hospital.[23] New direct federal roles, to be discussed below, can be perceived as interested action by government taking back what they had informally given. But governmental staff shortages and association pressures will probably preserve a role for these groups in the future.

The federal government (especially HEW) has been given an increasing role in regulation of health service, with each step toward greater public participation seeming to grow from each new law. The present regulatory role of the federal government is not extensive, but with the new legislation on comprehensive health planning (as of

December 1974) and the PSRO legislation (discussed later in this chapter), the potential exists for a far stronger role. The research wings of the federal establishment, and the evaluation divisions of each operating program, check their own activity to increase its effectiveness. On the other hand, the federal health bureaucracies exist in a highly political context, with administrations and executives potentially changing every four years. Successive administrations may take different positions on the degree of federal involvement in actual regulation, and on the degree of evaluation of existing programs needed before pushing to expand existing ones or proposing new ones. Nevertheless, the escalating manpower/cost crisis in health care exists for all national administrations, and increased consumer pressure on congress usually results in an ever-increasing involvement by HEW in regulatory activity. They may perceive themselves as neutral, but the regulated groups may not.

State-level executive agencies, especially in the office of the Governor and the Departments of Health, Public Health, or Human Services are among the primary agencies carrying the burden of regulation of manpower, settings, and costs. To act by carrying out their mandate is to directly affect, for better or worse, the interests of the regulated groups. Thus it should not be surprising that major political pressure by the practitioner interest groups is brought to bear on these agencies. The process of their co-optation—and their strategies for resisting it—are critically important political activities. In addition, if as in some states a number of the regulatory agencies are staffed with young, activist proconsumer administrators, the "action" of these state regulatory agencies is real and important.[24]

State legislatures can play an important role in regulatory politics. Interest groups can affect the regulatory process at the state level in two major ways: lobbying for the passage or defeat of regulatory legislation affecting their interests; or influencing the distribution of funds to existing agencies, as a way of hindering their effectiveness.

Thus a thorough understanding of the political context must include the activities of the state legislators, and the interest groups lobbying before them.

Profit-making corporations in the health field have an interest in selling their products to the maximum extent (be this product heart-lung machines, drugs, disposable syringes, or health insurance) while minimizing the costs involved. Until quite recently the cost could be passed on to the consumer indirectly through Blue Cross/Blue Shield or welfare. Attempts to control costs, or to monitor the expenditure of funds for such technology, have been and will be resisted politically by firms whose profit motive conflicts with the aims of regulatory agencies in controlling costs.[25]

The consumer movement antedates Nader and will continue after he is gone, but it was given major impetus by his organizations and others of similar type; at present the most active concerning regulation is the Health Research Group. At the state level, some statewide newspapers have concerned themselves with cost problems for consumers, and the need to control them. But consumer protest, or consumer participation, is difficult to organize around cost-control issues in health, for the technical economic details are seldom simplified by the other political actors to the point where the consumers can make realistic choices among alternatives. The Nader organizations, by being elitist in the sense of using full-time technical experts in proconsumer work, are effective at times precisely because they share knowledge on the level of the interest groups, rather than only knowledge on the level of the average consumer.

Regulations, rules, and their interpretation, through the judicial process, are the special province of *the legal profession*. Although to date lawyers have been primarily involved in important but essentially peripheral areas, such as financial advice and malpractice cases, they now are bringing their technical or "legal process" view of the law and of regulation into the health field, causing some culture shock and puzzlement to those more traditional occupations in health care that are not familiar with the viewpoint of the lawyer. The interest groups have a major stake in finding skilled administrative lawyers, but the socially conscious consumer-oriented legal activist also has a possible role to play. Whichever side the bulk of the expertise is on in a given regulatory program, the recent explosion of regulatory activity in health unquestionably demonstrates the legal expertise commands great leverage in building a regulatory process in health, and also that others are beginning to feel that the lawyers are running away with *their* field.[26]

To sum up, interest-group activity in regulatory processes plays such an extensive role in the health area that here, as elsewhere, regulation becomes a form of interest-group arbitration, but with the proviso that usually the regulatory body arbitrates between strong and well-organized health provider groups on the one hand, and weak, disorganized consumers on the other. This is typical for regulation in general. But what singles out regulatory politics in health as an extreme example of the process is the head start which health providers have over consumers at the initiation of the regulatory activity. There are three overall reasons for this: the real need for their expertise and participation in the regulatory activity; their prior degree of political organization; and the degree of status, prestige, respect, and even deference which lawmakers continue to show the health field's organized interests, in terms of the way regulatory legislation is framed and enacted into law.

AREAS OF REGULATION: PEOPLE, PLACES, THINGS, AND COSTS

In health care, four areas of action can show what happens to the ideals of "regulation" in the health-care field: the regulation of *people*, of *places*, of *things*, and of *costs*. We can only deal with the broad outlines of the process, but a pattern is apparent.

Regulating People: The Credentialling Process

Three major studies of regulation of manpower have found a pattern concerning the credentialling of health occupations in America.[27,28,29] The medical profession, through its practitioner wing and especially within the education committees of the AMA, continues to control not only the accreditation of its own training programs, but also those of most auxiliary programs. Since such accreditation is usually necessary for the kind of federal money needed to keep schools going, the profession has the power of life and death over innovative training programs which might threaten its interests. Licensure, through state licensing boards, remains routinely in the hands of local physicians with no particular distinction as practitioners or scholars in their profession. The main pathway to board membership is through medical societies, which "all too frequently . . . ignore professional and educational attributes, endorsing some faithful political stalwart who has worked his way up in the councils of the medical society".[30] Other private roles of the usually politically conservative state medical societies involve fighting bills in state legislatures which would threaten their existing prerogatives, or attempts to force the board into more disciplinary activity.[31] In fact, the most striking finding of all studies is the near total avoidance of any policing of peers by the licensing board members even in cases of extreme malfeasance. Cohen and Miike suggest several reasons:

(a) There is a natural reluctance on the part of board members to invoke disciplinary action against their fellow practitioners; (b) disciplinary actions often result in lawsuits against the boards thereby causing boards to drop certain actions if an adverse ruling by the courts is anticipated; (c) board members function both as the rule makers and rule adjudicators in deciding disciplinary matters, thereby causing confusion and overlap of roles; and (c) statutory provisions delineating the grounds for board sanction generally are ambiguous, leading to judicial reluctance to enforce them.[32]

A revealing exercise is to compare the recommendations of the major studies, concerning changes in the above situation, with the action taken. An example is the set of recommendations made by the HEW study in 1971, as against their degree of implementation reported by Cohen and Miike in 1974. The general recommendation, to increase board staff and step up the surveillance of the profession, simply has not occurred in the vast majority of states. The recommendation to use national licensing exams, while heeded in many states, has not been heeded in the sense of using one standard score as passing and failing across all states. In fact, in Arizona, those who fail but near the state's passing line are allowed to practice provisionally in that state's rural area![33] Relicensure and reexamination or a course of instruction as requirements were recommended by all major studies: as of 1974, two states have such a requirement for physicians, and two more have it on the books but "have no present plans to implement their laws".[34] Consumer representation is enacted as classic tokenism in state after state, with one consumer on a board of five to fifteen members. Ideas concerning institutional licensure, and plans to combine licensing boards, routinely meet defeat at the hands of the local practitioner/ state medical society/state legislator combination. Reformist ideas by HEW planners, medical professors, consumer groups, and activist state executives, have met overwhelming political defeat.

Regulating Places—Conflict over Settings and Programs

Private and public programs for the regulation of the settings relevant to people's health share certain features, though the essentially internal federal bureaucratic political dynamics are missing from the private model. Still, the private model came first, in the form of the Joint Commission on the Accreditation of Hospitals, and thus it is appropriate to consider it briefly before considering three public (or quasi-public) activities: occupational health and safety enforcement, comprehensive health planning, and certificate of need. In each case, we cannot even begin to go into the details of these complex programs, which are constantly under review and recombination through new legislation. But we can highlight certain similarities they share in the form of strong interest-group action successfully directed at nullifying the effectiveness of regulation.

The Joint Commission's early role as a leader in hospital self-regulation, and its "thereness" as an existing organization in the early days of Medicare and Medicaid, gave it the opportunity to perform a quasi-public regulatory role, whereby its accreditation was necessary for government reimbursement for an institution. Over the past several years, as the government's direct role has increased, the JCAH has increasingly devoted itself to the development of quality measurement, in what amounts to a division of labor with the government, with its interest in cost.[35] The JCAH could in a sense be seen as doing pilot work of the sort that might be needed under the PSRO legislation, to which we will devote some attention later. It is devoting more attention to nonhospital, community settings as well. Its politics are simpler than those of the government's regulatory programs. As an organization of constituent members dependent on fees for staff support, it was for many years rather lax concerning enforcement of standards. Though government pressure in recent years has been exerted on JCAH to get tougher, and to some extent it has rejected a larger number of applicants for accreditation and reaccreditation, it has a basic social-structural problem limiting the effectiveness of its sanctions. A nonaccredited or a refused hospital is often still in demand as a facility by those who have no other alternative, especially in urban and rural poverty areas. The consumers have actually exerted political pressure to keep the public, state license of a recently disaccredited hospital active, for fear of having the doors shut of the only place that serves them. Even the federal government is not immune to pressures to discard its own qualifications on reimbursing nonaccredited hospitals, for Senator Ted Kennedy once intervened to keep the federal funds coming to Boston City Hospital, during one of its worst periods concerning services and accreditation status. In sum, because of dependence on the regulated hospitals for support funds, functional delivery problems which are created by disaccrediting a hospital, and an essentially conservative operating philosophy, the JCAH uses primarily an educational rather than a regulatory-policing strategy. While this may be realistic under the short-term circumstances, its limitations on improving the quality of service are obvious.

When we take three public regulatory or semiregulatory programs—all the result of federal legislation—we may see certain similarities in interest-group activity in a series of phases. First, in the law-writing phase, direct political intervention by the affected interest groups usually results in a weakened bill and a role for the target group in their own regulation. Second, in the administration of the law, in three main areas—federal headquarters, state level, and in the local setting—interest groups act to nullify or divert the intent of the law. Finally, interest group activity is constantly directed at decreasing the effectiveness of the regulatory agency itself, through lessened funding and amendments to the initial legislation which restrict the scope of the regulatory activity.

Our first example is the field of occupational health and safety. Page and O'Brien document the extreme health hazards in American industry and the long fight by industry against the passage of the Occupational Health and Safety Act of 1970.[36] In the most significant section of their book, the study of the first postenactment years, they document a deliberate cutback in enforcement staff by the Nixon administration. There is also evidence from the Watergate investigation that some corporations were promised immunity from federal investigation in this area, as a quid pro quo for large campaign contributions. In addition, the state governments, who were handed the main operational responsibility, performed as the interest groups hoped they would: business as usual, in the state context where corporations have even more power than they do over the federal government. The law has become a shell, a tool for legal activists, but not the basis for regulation of the work-place in the health interests of workers. In 1974, two new exposés, by Brodeur[37] and Scott[38] appeared, almost as if the Act had not been passed, and the Nader study not done.

Comprehensive health planning (CHP) has been discussed, along with four other health planning programs, primarily through the use of the government's own contracted evaluations of these programs.[39] The interest groups early paralyzed the effectiveness of CHP activity in several ways, primarily through its successful push for a provision to require at least fifty percent funding of the program locally by the groups to be planned for. When the Certificate of Need legislation of individual states was built into federal law a possibility existed for illegal conflict of interest. The agency was to "review and comment", for example, on proposals to expand hospitals—but the hospitals paid for part of the upkeep of these agencies; and the new "Need" agencies were involved in this situation as well.[40] Early in the establishing of some state processes for hospital expansion control, Curran commented that the legal requirements were being set up in a strange way indeed if cost control and antiexpansion were the issue. For there was plenty of provision for a hospital to appeal a negative decision against their expanding, with very little formal avenue for *consumers* to appeal the bulk of the other, positive decisions. This created a bias which favors expansion on the hospital's terms.[41] Finally, all the above programs have been put together in a new bundle, the National Health Planning and Resources Development Act of 1974, an act which hands even more power to the regulated, under the guise of the reverse, for "consumers" can now include, on planning boards, both elected and appointed public officials, and boards do not have to have public elections. Federal review processes are supposed to take care of any local biases, but the federal agencies themselves are under tremendous pressure from outside lobbying groups in health.[42]

Regulating Things:
Food, Drugs, Machines, Blood

The materials which prolong life and cure illness include food (in nontoxic form), drugs, technological equipment for diagnosis and treatment, and blood, along with other biological products. In each case, the American situation is one of strong interest-group action toward co-optation of the regulatory process. Turner's extensive study of the role of corporate pressure in limiting the effectiveness of food regulation,[43] and Silverman and Lee's analysis of drug regulation,[44] both deal with branches of the Food and Drug Administration, a classic federal regulatory agency whose political history antedates many of the later regulatory efforts which we have considered thus far. Reform efforts in the last few years have led to some revival of regulatory effectiveness in the activity of the FDA. But structurally there still is circulation of leaders between the outside industry and the inside jobs in regulation. Political compromises, especially in the food area, continue to be made for "levels of allowable filth". The classic capitalist argument against strong regulation continues to hold water with the administration and the agency. "Too much regulation and our profits suffer, and you will hurt us. Don't do it, especially in a time of economic hard times for the nation".

Blood provides us with another example. Titmuss's study comparing the nonprofit English blood distribution system with the American profit-making system, which is totally unregulated, suggests that the absence of regulation is not necessarily an improvement over its existence.[45] Surgenor's analysis of the open warfare between segments of the blood collecting system (referred to earlier) illustrates that in the *absence* of any state intervention and administration, *ownership* of the system is the key issue. As long as it remains in private hands "regulation becomes a cover or a legitimizing tool for profit-motivated activity".[46]

To sum up, in food and drugs, by limiting the effectiveness of regulation through the use of skilled legal expertise to fight cases through the courts—for a decade if need be—and by direct political intervention at the top of the executive branch, regulation of things seems to remain at a cosmetic level. Occasional high-visibility court suits are mounted to show the agency is alive; however, they are followed by long, unreported court battles in which the corporation either wins or succeeds in stalling a negative verdict for an interim period, resulting in continuing profits for the corporation. In other critical "thing" areas, including blood and much of technology, the absence of controls creates great danger for the consumer.

Regulating Costs: Government Control as a Wet Noodle

The traditional issue in regulatory politics has been that of rate setting: the role of the regulatory agency in deciding what a "just" and "necessary" profit level is for an industry, after which decision and the industry's profit seeking has the governmental stamp of approval. Here above all the technological expertise of the economist and regulatory lawyers combine on the side of the regulated interests to fight a war justifying the regulatory agency's raising the allowable costs: a war fought with charts, establishment of "trends", and the use of legal and economic jargon that pits the skilled staff of the interest group against the usually understaffed regulatory agency and the technically naive consumer. In health care we have had several types of cost-control efforts to date. In addition to the Certificate of Need attempt, already discussed above, we have had (a) federal requirements on review of Medicare and Medicaid spending; (b) federal freezes on costs through the Cost of Living Council; (c) state rate-setting commissions (usually in departments of insurance); and (d) the new Professional Standards Review Organization (PSRO) program, aimed in the introductory language of the bill at "quality" control by peers—physicians reviewing physicians' decisions—but clearly also aimed at cost control of medical care for the poor and elderly.

In the early years of Medicare and Medicaid, mild cost-control activity did not work by the government's own admissions and its own data. The first time prospective charge ranges were set, the medical profession and the health-care settings immediately charged top rate for everything listed. The Cost of Living Council, which froze all prices and wages during a brief period and continued the controls in health until the expiration of the program, did not have control over some of the input costs to the health-care settings during the time controls went off the "thing making" corporations and the unions. Thus immediately after the expiration of controls, during the first six months, costs rose at a rate which, if it had been continued annually at that speed, would have reached thirty-nine percent, per annum.[47] Finally, state insurance rate-setting commissions perform with the typical handicaps of federal regulatory agencies, but with the difference that the political power of insurance companies is often national in scope and is exerted within each state against a governmental organ that is far weaker on its own.

Finally, there is the Professional Standards Review Organization (PSRO) program. Enacted in 1972, it did not by law even intend to designate its administrative regions until January 1974.[48] The basic review of care for the publicly-supported patient is to be done by local physicians, usually through slightly reconstituted regional and statewide medical society groups, with an occasional nonsociety member involved to satisfy technical aspects of the law. Cohen observes that several federal checks and balances are possible to total physician self-regulation here, such as the development of "regional norms" under HEW consultation, and HEW's power to disenfranchise a "bad actor" PSRO. But Cohen is suspicious of the idea, based on the long history of performance by physicians on licensing boards.[49]

As of February 1975, according to HEW's Office of Professional Standards Review (the governmental group administering the program), they have ninety-one planning contracts out to physician groups, twelve or thirteen conditionally approved PSRO units, and *none* officially and totally approved.[50] While there will no doubt be slow progress here on a month-by-month basis, the slow pace is not an accident. HEW staffers admit that political pressure by organized medicine has been a factor in slowing the speed of implementation.[51] Physician groups wish to stop it or administer it directly from their state headquarters, or failing that, to hassle it, stall it, increase its controversiality, and use resulting problems as reasons to press Congress to repeal the program before it goes further.[52] In addition, the overall cutback in funds for human services programs definitely will include, if the conservatives have their way, a cutback in the funds available for implementing this program, with its costs for staff time, data-gathering, state-level panels, and federal staff as well. Organized medicine can get contracts from HEW to develop "standards" for this program with their right hand—while their left hand is urging a congressman to vote against appropriating money to operationalize the program, to starve it in infancy.

The history of the Bennett amendment, which is the PSRO program legislation, shows that organized medicine had the inside track from the start.[53] Early study-committee versions of the bill hand regulation to the physicians, as if the long history of physician-run licensing boards did not exist. Other systematic aspects of the program include the philosophy behind it, which is ageist, racist, and antipoor in intent, forcing physicians and hospitals to justify treatment for the poor that they do not have to justify for the middle class and wealthy, since *they* are not regulated by the PSRO program. Caper notes that quality of care is talked about in the legislation, but the government wants hard data primarily only in the area of costs. Thus even a conscientious physician who *wants* the PSRO program to work as a quality improver may be driven to save money in the care of the poor by pushing them out of the hospital a little sooner than the middle class.[54] Others observe that the cost of administration of the program may well exceed the amounts of money saved by the review process. On the other hand, various types of planning strategists, especially those in government and in the academic medical elite, have grander plans for this apparatus and don't consider its present use—or its present costs—as the most important thing about it. To sum up, cost regulation in its different forms has not worked. A new program which effectively is not really in operation yet shows signs of costing more than it will save, at no increase in control except the control of the regulated over their own regulation.

IN SUMMARY: ACTION THROUGH LAW

The making of laws and their fate after passage constitute a continuous process, with the interest groups working actively for or against the change at every step of the way. It is necessary for those who wish to use legal strategies to consider carefully the field of forces as well as the wording of the laws. We began with a consideration of the legislative process, and noted the increasingly important role of technical consultants in writing the legislation. We then took two cases—abortion law reform and the National Cancer Institute—to see the ways laws can be remade after passage in the court system, or remade in bureaucratic politics similar to those which resulted in the form of the agency in the first place. Then the critically important area of regulation and regulatory agencies in health care was developed. We found that credentialling processes are being used at present at least as much to protect the interests of the occupational group as to protect the interests of the public; that programs to control the growth and efficiency of health-care settings have been

293

given to the hospital interests; that regulation of food, drugs, technology, and supplies, where it exists at all, is very carefully limited by corporate interests in their influence on the executive branch; and that every indirect attempt to regulate costs has failed, because the politics of the formation of the law gives a place for the spenders in the regulation of their spending.

From a Marxian theoretical perspective, one is led to ask whether one could expect anything else but the above. Specifically, within the context of advanced capitalism, what are the basic functions of "law making", the judicial system, and the regulatory apparatus? A law-making process which can always be nullified by the corporate capitalist class when its interests are significantly threatened can still function ideologically to get people to believe that they are taking a hand in creating the rules by which they suffer.

The cases of abortion and cancer politics, while complex, can be viewed from this perspective. In the abortion case, the tendency to work against change has been pushed primarily by organized conservative religion, which through the centuries has, as Marx presented it, worked against the development of class consciousness by the oppressed. The cancer agency is one of a large number of examples by which capitalist corporations—in this case drug corporations—willingly pervert the function of a new government agency *before* its birth, to guarantee it will not function as an economic threat. Then the cancer agency funds anticancer *drug* development (with its attendant profit) to fight existing cancer, rather than supporting basic research to find its cause, research which might not bring profit to corporations and which might *prevent* the development of cancer in the first place—totally eliminating it as a source of profit.

Regulation is the clearest case in which a more general interpretation is needed in addition to the interest-group approach. In general terms, the state uses its relative autonomy from the employee class to act in ways which appear legitimate; the state licenses, it "regulates" hospital growth, it "controls" costs. Yet

294

these processes often are simply a cover for anticonsumer activity. Regulation, just as planning, is badly in need of some demystifying activity. Even to begin here is to find oneself challenged not only by the direct economic interests, but also by the new class of regulatory experts which have come to have a stake in the new status quo. It can be a lonely occupation—for a writer or an activist group—to take on *both* wings of the medical profession as well as the organized hospitals and corporations. Yet some consumer groups are coming to the realization that they must speak out because no one else will, for they are among the few that have both the technical knowledge of the process and the value position that favors consumers at the expense, if need be, of providers and the capitalist class itself.

9

The Sickening Environment

At present, for far too many people, home is a place that makes you ill, work is a place that maims your body and spirit, and the environment is a place that functions to finish the job started by home and work. The politics of health has, as its most important issue, the politics of the causes of disease. All our previous investigation of the relationships between server and served, of the manifest and latent functions of the service system, and the role of the state in the politics of planning and regulation, are but concerns with the consequences of attempting to cure illness within an advanced capitalist society. What we must now consider is the distinct possibility that this form of political-economic arrangement may guarantee the perpetuation of *causes* of disease, disease which is only partly handled by the service system. As modern scientific advances have increasingly dealt with the problems of contagious disease, to the point where the death rate has been brought down in these areas, it is important to note that the problems of poverty, psychological stress, and physical assaults to bodily integrity related to work and nonwork environments, have risen in importance.

The role of the state here is even more strictly limited than in the area of planning and regulation, by the nature of state functioning in an advanced capitalist society. Profit—the aim of capitalism—includes profit in the areas of urban slum housing, the manufacturing plant, and the wider environment. Actions by the state against these sources of illness would constitute, in many cases, action against given sectors of capital. How does this work out in practice? The topics necessary to answer this general question are, at a minimum, the role of the state in alleviating poverty and promoting health, in dealing with disease-producing environments at home, with conditions in industry, and with disease-relevant processes in the wider environment. All these areas can in turn be related to the broad political-economic issue of the fiscal crisis of the advanced capitalist state.

POVERTY AND HEALTH:
THE ROLE OF THE STATE

Poverty and illness form an interlocking and interdependent relationship. From poverty comes illness, from illness, the inability to escape poverty. The cycle is perpetuated generation after generation, and the available evidence indicates that *the official organs of government intervene only when it is in the interest of those groups in control of government policy*. But poverty is only partially alleviated, it is never eliminated, for it is a condition that the powerful can use, to force people to work under conditions that they would otherwise reject. Piven and Cloward have reviewed the relationship between the capitalist class, government, and the administration of welfare. They show both the historical and the modern American evidence for the political and economic gains to be made in using the welfare system for the oppression of the poor. Since the Renaissance,

> Historical evidence suggests that relief arrangements are initiated or expanded during the occasional outbreaks of civil disorder produced by mass unemployment, and are then abolished or contracted when political stability is restored. . . . Expansive relief policies are designed to mute civil disorder, and restrictive ones to reinforce work norms. In other words, relief policies are cyclical—liberal or restrictive depending on the problems of regulation in the larger society with which the government must contend.[1]

Their careful review of several periods in American history relates the official employment data to government action and power group intervention in policy making. It shows that the response of the Roosevelt administration, in the earliest years of the Great Depression, was a massive expansion of relief to mute the turmoil and radicalism that was building. This aid was drastically cut back even though the Depression was still on, after 1936, because the immediate danger of revolt had passed.[2]

With the onset of the seventies, the dying down of protest and the rise of the politics of racial backlash have led to another wave of cutbacks in welfare. It is this refusal of basic, minimal support which perpetuates the extreme poverty that produces the illness we will now consider. In each case, and in each period, the absence of protest and strong organization by the poor leads to cost cutting by terminating people on welfare, refusing support for new applicants, discouraging people from applying, and shaving or cutting back on existing support to those already on the rolls. In addition, the fiscal crisis of the state itself may be forcing the support levels down, where they stay because of this absence of political organization and mass action.

Thus it should be no surprise that definitive surveys of rates of physical illness among the poor—as measured by infant mortality rates, mortality among adults, and illness rates as well as rates of disability—find the rates for those in poverty areas exceeding those for other people, urban or rural, by rates varying between 1.5 and 2 times as high, depending on the study.[3] Political opposition in Congress has prevented, year after year, the routine gathering of statistics by income level, and administrations for two decades have not pressed HEW to do so. As a consequence, the picture for physical illness levels must be pieced together. The picture for mental illness is clear, with a mountain of evidence collected by studies over the last two decades. According to Fried, the evidence here

> is unambiguous and powerful that the lowest social classes have the highest rates of severe psychiatric disorder in our society. Regardless of the measures employed for estimating severe psychiatric disorder and social class, regardless of the region or the date of study, the great majority of results all point clearly and strongly to the fact that the lowest social class has by far the greatest incidence of psychoses.[4]

But studies, and summaries of studies, which simply indicate that the poor are sicker than the middle class, take us only part of the distance we need to travel. What needs to be looked at are a series of lacks in the home environment of the poor. For each area of existence, we must ask: what is the evidence that the problem is serious, what perpetuates the condition, and *who benefits* by the continuation of the condition? We can do this for areas that affect both children and adults, but especially children, and which scar these children for a lifetime.

THE POLITICAL ORIGINS OF MALNUTRITION

Severe malnutrition is endemic in American society, among that sizeable segment of the poor on welfare or working at subminimum wage who must skimp on their food, or do without it, in order to pay the rent and take care of the other necessities of life. This affects especially the unborn and recently born children of the poor, for the brain must grow rapidly in the first year and a half after birth, and *must* be well nourished in order to avoid retardation. Shenour, in *The Malnourished Mind,* sums up the growing literature in this area, as of the mid-seventies:

> The evidence indicates the negative effect of prenatal malnutrition on brain development and on cognitive faculties. It suggests that part of the damage induced by this nutritional deficiency is long lasting and may even be permanent. But whether or not it is permanent is not as important as the fact that it persists at least long enough to interfere with learning during the critical early years and thus interferes with the adaptation of the child to society.[5]

In the words of a former assistant director for health at OEO,

> Five percent of the children in the United States are born mentally retarded, yet by the time that age group reaches 12 years of age, 11 percent are retarded, which indicates that we *produce* almost as much mental retardation as is born.[6]

In the city, interns and residents at any city hospital will testify that major cause of infant deaths is pneumonia, which no longer kills anyone except those who are weakened by poor food and chronic illness.

The Politics of Food Distribution

But what about the programs of food for the poor? If such conditions exist, hasn't the government used the commodities (surplus food) program, the food stamp program, and the school lunch program to prevent malnutrition? Briefly, the answer is no. Commodities are distributed by the Department of Agriculture to aid the farm economy, and are often incomplete for a normal diet. Food stamps cost too much for the truly poor to purchase, and the school lunch program works best in the suburbs, not in the poverty areas, for the state must put up more money than the federal government for the program. States cut the budget first in the areas where the poor are affected. The dynamics of food deprivation, or the perversion of the food support programs in what Kotz calls "the politics of hunger", works in several ways. These are, briefly: the action of powerful farmers in state and national areas, to protect their use of indentured labor; the antiwelfare stance of the U.S. Department of Agriculture; the priorities of national presidential administrations; and the use of food aid as a weapon to supress dissent against the present system.[7]

First, there are the class-based economics of hunger. Much agricultural work in the South, Southwest, and West is carried out by individuals—children as well as adults—who are paid far below the minimum wage. During the off season, local welfare departments, working closely with growers, provide minimal food in commodity form. Then when planting time begins, *they cut off the food,* acting for the planters and forcing the people to work, in the seventies for about three dollars per day. The Poverty Subcommittee and the Citizen's Board of Inquiry (on hunger) found that:

Food aid programs in agricultural regions throughout the nation were turned on or off to suit the convenience and labor needs of the growers and planters. Coal companies in Appalachia, cotton planters in the Deep South, and vegetable-fruit growers in the Southwest all tried to keep their cheap labor, in virtual bonded indebtedness by advancing them survival funds which they could never repay.[8]

Second, the U.S. Department of Agriculture, not HEW or OEO, is the bureaucracy in Washington which is in control of both the commodity distribution program and the food stamp program. They have a decades-long history of fighting against use of commodities which will be of disadvantage to the large farmers that are their primary political constituency.[8] "Their" congressmen, those who head the agriculture committees in Congress and vote on their yearly appropriations—decide how they will be able to spend their money from year to year. These chairmen in the past have invariably been racist, politically conservative Southerners who have fought against expanding the amount of food distributed to the poor and against lowering the cost of food stamps. In the midst of the War on Poverty, with far more pressure on local bureaucracies, as well as on the Department of Agriculture, than exists at present, this was the result:

> Representing the black poor of Mississippi, Mrs. Myrtle Brown explained how a woman with $68 monthly income could afford to pay neither the $28 monthly to participate in the food stamp program nor the 25 cents apiece daily for each of her five children to participate in the school lunch program. At noontime the five children walk a mile to and from school in hopes of lunch. "Some days they come and find me with food," she said. "Some days they come and don't find me with anything."[9]

A third reason for the continuing illness and death of children and adults, directly attributable to malnutrition, has been the low priority which three succeeding presidents and their administrations have placed on relieving it. Under Kennedy there was rhetoric but no action; under Johnson, much in the way of early promises but cutbacks because of spending in Vietnam. Under Nixon/Ford, there was talk of welfare reform in the early period, but this did not materialize even though *it* was the excuse for waiting on food support reform. Then Watergate intervened and distracted attention away from all domestic issues. Under Ford, the policy against inflation seems to be more cutbacks in domestic spending. This means, as usual, a policy of "let them eat promises".

Finally, the threat of starvation has been used consistently by those in control of the food supply as a selective tool for repression of dissent. The poor are often afraid to testify by name before congressional committees, for the food of others has been cut off after such appearances. Those who testified before the groups that wrote the *Hunger USA* study were investigated by the FBI as well as being harassed or cut off the rolls by their local welfare departments.[10] In addition, overall government policy changes, such as cutting back on commodities and increasing the importance of the food stamp program without cutting the cost to the poor, has lead to mass emigration from the South by the blacks. This changeover to food stamps was pushed by southern politicians as a way of diminishing the power of blacks by diminishing their numbers, as a strategy to counteract some of the power they might gain from their new ability to vote. But they landed in the North to face the restrictive policies of the seventies, and the inflation which now threatens not simply malnutrition, but clinical starvation, in both North and South. When the poor scream, "stop killing our children", this is part of what they mean.

HEALTH AT HOME

Poor people do not own their own housing. The people who *do* own it view it primarily as an avenue for profit making, and the profit is available only if the expenses of operating and maintaining the rental property are less than the money taken in. In considering health at home, such facts as these are critically important in understanding why we cannot assume, as we might for the middle class, that the home is a place to recuperate from illness instead of a place that causes it. Two kinds of stresses produce the illness: physical stresses and sociopsychological ones.

In large cities, some of the major contributors to mayoral campaigns, or campaigns of city offices of other types, are the owners of large numbers of slum properties. They are rewarded by lax enforcement of building codes, in such areas as building sanitation, fire safety, and room temperature in wintertime. Consequently, the physical environment of children in poverty is characterized by extreme stress and stress-producing conditions. If we enumerate a series of such stresses, we must ask in each case what would be required to alleviate it and who would resist.

Sanitation. In migrant camps, enforcement has been traditionally lax, and in urban slums, almost nonexistent. New plumbing is expensive and plumber's fees steep. Most slumlords and employers of migrant labor are successful in resisting the attempts of reformers on grounds of "inability to pay". In rural areas, ourdoor facilities are still the most common in poverty areas. Thus in both the city and the country-side, the poor facilities lead to infectious diseases such as dysentery. As a consequence of such disease, severe diarrhea lead to dehydration and death, in the case of small children especially. Other diseases directly related to sanitation are also common.

Heat. The recent energy crisis gave slum landlords a patriotic excuse to do what they have done for decades: cut heat in apartments to save expensive fuel, down to levels of heat which can maintain life but not prevent the chronic colds which weaken resistance to flu and pneumonia, and which ultimately take their toll. Combining this type of temperature stress with malnutrition leads to markedly higher illness rates in the North. In the South it also gets quite cold, and in poverty areas the shacks and shanties often have no fireplaces, and certainly no modern heating equipment. "Energy conservation" has effectively been used in cities as a countervailing force to prevent the administration of penalties even in clear-cut cases of violation. In addition in many cases advance warning of building inspection is given by the city inspectors, so that for the brief period of the inspection the heat is at normal levels. *Public* housing has been almost as bad as private in this respect, with many cities conserving funds by cutting off all heat in sections of the city in the evenings except for the height of midwinter, especially in public housing projects.

Building safety. Both in structural safety (such things as fire hazards and rotten stairwells) and in biochemical safety (especially the presence of lead-based paint which chips off and which children eat because of its sweet taste), the dwellings of the poor are a primary cause of disease and death. Some activists have set up lead-poisoning screening programs in cooperation with some local hospitals in ghetto areas. But the number reached by such programs is only a fraction of those reached by the poisoned paint.[11] Slum landlords argue that they cannot afford to repaint all of their buildings and the cities almost invariably refuse to force them to do so. The consequence is children with retardation as a consequence of early childhood lead poisoning.

In sum, the physical environment of poverty remains so because it is in the economic interest of those who own such environments *not* to improve them. To pay for sanitation, heat, and safety improvements would diminish their profits far more than the relatively cheap bribes and campaign contributions that are necessary from time to time to protect their investments.

In addition to the physical causes of disease in the environments of poverty, there are social and psychological consequences for a child, or any human being, if they are never sure of their physical survival. We have presented the statistical evidence earlier, in terms of the rates of psychosis in the lowest social class group. The clinical evidence is equally striking. Robert Coles has spent much time with children undergoing the stresses of food and shelter deprivation described above. Here he speaks about ghetto black children who migrated north from the Mississippi delta, but he could be speaking of poor whites in Appalachia, or chicano migrant children:

> They become tired, petulant, suspicious, and finally apathetic. . . . They ask themselves and others what they have done to be kept from the food they want, or what they have done to deserve the pain they seem to feel. . . . The aches and sores of the body become for the child of four or five . . . a reflection of his own worth, and a judgement upon him and his family by the outside world, which he not only feels but judges himself.[12]

In adulthood, the years of stress result in either one of two consequences: a majority of poor people who have been tempered and toughened far beyond the limits usually demanded of the middle class, and a tragically large minority that have been broken or badly scarred by the experience. Brenner's study on the relationship between rates of mental hospitalization and economic cycles adds statistical verification of a dynamic sort to the years of studies relating social class position to frequency of psychosis. As economic conditions worsen, the rates of hospitalization go up.[13] Given that the poor have always had a high rate, the conclusion leads us toward an observation of the fate of working-class and upper-middle-class people when they too are brought under the stresses of poverty.

In all of our focus on nutrition, physical environment, and psychosocial stress, we have primarily been concerned with the poor. This is a matter of analytical as well as social priority, for the greatest pathology exists here, and the relative power of profit-oriented groups with respect to citizens is most unbalanced in the case of the poor. Yet nutrition is a problem for the middle class, especially in the area of food adulteration and food value. Housing is often overcrowded for many blue-collar workers in deteriorating neighborhoods, and the stress of work and aging hit those at all socioeconomic levels.

But perspective is needed here, especially if we are dealing with health over the entire life span from childhood to old age, and if we are dealing with a reporting system for illness that picks up most of the problems of the middle and working class while it ignores the illness of many poor people, or does not record them because they are not at the place (usually work) where the "absence rates due to illness" are tabulated. For example, sets of data are often used to "refute" the idea that the poor are sicker, in terms of overall illness rates for chronic conditions and short-term illness rates. Both are higher in the older age bracket, but these age brackets are reached far less frequently for the poor, who die before they can become a chronic illness statistic. Second, acute or short-term illness rates are found to be as high, if not higher, among the middle class, as recorded by the absence rates from work or school. Records are kept only on those working and those at school, two groups in which many poor adults and children simply do not hold membership. The absence of major national surveys keyed to income level, relating these levels directly to health care and illness levels, simply has the effect of deflecting our attention away from the facts.[14] Certainly executives do die of heart attacks. But look at the way they have lived for their fifty-five years and look at their children, and compare both them and their children with a black sharecropper of fifty-five and *his* children, who have never had a good meal or a healthy week since the day they were born.

Occupational Injury, Disease, and Death

As with the home, the place of work can either be a place for achievement, pride, and health, or it can be a place where illness is created and life shortened and cheapened. Most of blue-collar America works in factories, or in craft work with major hazards of one sort or another. We can begin with a report from the front lines, from a man who worked in several locations in a large automobile plant. He speaks now about the area near the welding department, and the consequences for him of doing welding for several years:

> Was there noise? Oh yes. We had some big presses in there, twelve, fourteen, sixteen feet long. And when you cut that steel the sound was like thunder. I know quite a few people that have taken sick. If it wasn't the eyes, it was the mouth, their teeth rotted out. And there is quite a few heart conditions.
> Ever since I started working there I had trouble with my eyes. Well, not right away, but in two, three years. My eyes began to run water and they kept getting worse and worse, you know. Then when I left there it was the same thing. I didn't have no dreams of compensation when I left.[15]

Doctors examining this man for the Nader investigating team that interviewed him concluded that his eventual problem—almost total blindness—was a consequence of beryllium poisoning in the poorly ventilated plant. The chemical had been vaporized by his welding arc, and he had not been protected from the fumes. Nor have workers in most American industries *ever* been protected. A congressional committee interviewed a man working in a plant with mercury and chlorine in the air in dangerous doses. This was his perspective on his situation:

> And, well, my father worked in a chemical plant right next door to the one I work for: about twenty years. He's dead now. I had an uncle; he also worked in a chemical plant, the same plant right next door to me. He died of cancer, this cancer in the throat. He had a tube in his throat, and it was a result of working in this chemical plant; he didn't have it before he went there. But a certain chemical that he inhaled got in his throat, and his throat was a mess and he died. . . . We're a small bunch but we've got a problem. These chemicals are going to kill us all.[16]

National evidence is developing which indicates that the industrial work-place is a primary generator of illness and death. Certain direct causes will be considered, for both physical illness and mental illness. We will then briefly review the strategies successfully used by many corporations to deny, end-run, or subvert laws on occupational health and safety in the work-place. For example, in 1968, the U.S. Public Health Service, estimating from a study of California, calculated a national rate of 336,000 cases of job-caused illness per year—a figure which didn't include in the estimate diseases not found in California, such as coal miner's black lung or pneumoconiosis.[17] More recently, the National Institute for Occupational Health and Safety estimated in 1972 that *about 100,000 Americans die each year as a consequence of working in American industry, of industrially caused diseases, and another 390,000 become ill each year as a result of working in industry*.[18] This is a death rate that exceeds that of our servicemen in Vietnam at the height of fighting in that war, and it continues year after year. It is almost surely an underestimate as well, for the bulk of the data used by the National Institute on Occupational Safety and Health comes from corporation and factory physicians, working for management and prone to diagnose anything as extraneous to work that they possibly can. The rates are far higher among those who are poor; agricultural workers have the highest rates of all. Rates are higher by far for blacks than for whites; and least for those in white-collar and executive jobs. Such extremely high rates are clearly caused by the environment of the work-place to a far greater extent than they are due to worker carelessness. This is easier to see if a series of the main industrial diseases are briefly considered: black lung or pneumoconiosis, asbestosis, metal and solvent poisoning, and pesticide poisoning. (This is not a complete list, by far.)

Black lung, a form of pneumoconiosis, is perhaps the best known of the occupational diseases. There has been a long fight in Great Britain and the United States to get it recognized as a *disease,* instead of an unavoidable consequence of work in the mines, which mine owners claimed was the case. The possibility of inhaling coal dust as a consequence of working underground has been escalated by the modern technology of mining, for the new automatic coal diggers shatter and powder coal much faster than the old hand methods. Thirty years after Britain legally allowed payment to miners for the disease, and within the past ten years, the United States coal industry was still refusing to admit the disease existed and refusing to pay any medical expenses for miners suffering from the respiratory damage and lung cancer that were its regular consequences.[19] The environmental aspect of this disease is shown by the problems of miners who wear protective equipment, yet work in poorly ventilated mines, and who still routinely come down with the disease. *Asbestosis* is the related lung disease which is found among workers in the cement, roofing, insulation, and housing industries. The critical danger is of lung cancer, and another rare cancer that affects the tissues that encase the lungs. *Industrially-caused cancers*

309

are common from other sources. In Dickens's England, the chimney sweeps, while still children, got cancer of the scrotum from the coal tar in chimneys. Today:

> Cancer of the skin, particularly of the face, neck, limbs, groin, and navel, affects those who work with coal products such as tar, pitch, anthracene (used in the manufacture of synthetic dyes and in wood preservation) and creosote (used in wood preservation.)[20]

Metal poisoning and solvent poisoning are two other major areas where the industrial environment causes disease and death. Mercury, used in the manufacture of chlorine and other industrial acids and gases, causes mercurial tremor as an early symptom. It can be absorbed into the lungs as vapor, dust, or mist, and then paralyzes the action of essential enzymes needed for the functioning of the kidneys, liver, and brain. Lead poisoning, already mentioned for ghetto children, is an insidious and slowly-building disease in factories which manufacture paints, batteries, pipes, bullets, chemicals for cars, auto radiators, and other related products. The consequences for one worker were: "My joints hurt, I can hardly talk anymore—I shake all the time—sometimes I don't think I can get up in the morning". This particular employee had worked for the National Lead Company for fifteen years, yet they refused to admit any responsibility for his condition.[21]

Solvents, either in direct production or in use in all types of actories, usually contain ingredients which dissolve the human tissues they come in contact with when employees are assigned cleanup work. *Gases* such as sulfur dioxide, to take another example, were found in a 700-factory survey in New Jersey, Pennsylvania, and Michigan, to be in concentrations about four times that found in the London killer smog of a decade ago.[22] Finally, agricultural workers are constantly exposed to one of the greatest risks of all: the nerve gases which are marketed as *pesticides*, such as 245-T and Parathion. These can cause almost instant death to children or old people if the rules on exposure are not followed by planters—rules which they seldom consider.[23]

As we noted above, blacks tend to have higher industrial illness and death rates than whites. Primarily this is because of two kinds of factors: the willingness of blacks, for economic reasons, to take some risky jobs that whites avoid; and deliberate racism on the work setting, which assigns blacks to the more hazardous of two jobs, both carrying the same pay. Another group constantly exposed to many of the dangers above is women. Their rates of occupational disease are high in several areas dealing with assembly work, where women are preferred to men. Their rates are pushed higher by the special biological vulnerability of the female system during pregnancy. In addition, the fetus is susceptible, and in industrial work in the presence of chemicals such as lead, far higher rates of miscarriage and congenital malformation are found than average for women elsewhere.[24]

Economic pressures complicate the extra disease risk and have consequences for infant mortality:

> The policy adopted in many industries of dismissing pregnant women as soon as their condition is known causes women who wish to continue working to conceal their condition until it becomes obvious, which frequently is not until the middle of pregnancy. Since the most dangerous period, as far as spontaneous abortions are concerned, is during the early months of pregnancy, these women continue to work during this critical period with no medical supervision and no regard for the type of work.[25]

Thus with women we have a double risk, with the health of two generations being affected by the conditions at work.

Occupational disease is not just a physical thing; it has a psychological component as well. Studies of "executive stress", such as that by Levinson, and long-term studies of heart disease do definitely show that executive and upper white-collar workers have physical problems related to high pressure and anxiety on the job.[26]

But what tends to be neglected here is that the psychological stress on blue-collar workers is, if anything, higher. They may not choose psychotherapy as a way of handling the pressure on the assembly line, since they are not comfortable with "talking cures" and they may also view the psychiatrist as a manipulator paid by management. (One union has a contract which includes its own mental health staff.) But clinical psychosis, severe neurosis, and the more common headaches, weariness, and deadening to experience which are the consequence of prolonged individual stress, are a real problem for most blue-collar workers. In addition, some of the alcoholism found in industry among workers developed initially not as indulgence but rather as a form of painkiller to get them through the work day. The same motivation results in benzedrine addiction for long-distance truck drivers. Hypertension is another consequence. Eyer's exhaustive survey concludes:

> Two primary features of modern society which contribute to the elevation of blood pressure are community disruption and increased work pressure. Drug therapy and relaxation therapies for hypertension attempt to counteract the physiological effects of social stress. However, it is more appropriate to use the occurrence of hypertension as an indicator of fundamental social problems which need to be solved.[27]

Finally, there is the psychological state of alienation and numb depression, caused by year after year of meaningless work, during which time the blue-collar (or white-collar clerical) workers cannot create anything, or have anything to show for their work that they can care about, and thus have any way of fulfilling themselves at work.[28] This spot welder, interviewed by Turkel, could be speaking for thousands of secretaries or clerks as well as for factory workers when he says:

> I don't understand how come more guys don't flip. Because you're nothing more than a machine when you hit this type of thing. They give

better care to that machine than they will to you. They'll have more respect, give more attention to that machine. And you *know* this. Somehow you get the feeling that the machine is better than you are. (Laughs)[29]

The Fight against Occupational Health

When the annual toll of injured, diseased, and dead is presented, a natural question arises. What has been done about it? The answer to this question immediately brings us into a consideration of the role of the capitalist class in the politics of occupational health. We can only briefly consider positions and broad actions here, but in the final section of the book a more detailed study of the political and social strategies will be presented, as part of the overall politics of health. For our present purpose—understanding why the American work-place has remained as it has—we will need to consider three periods in the recent past: the period from the thirties to the sixties; the passage of the Occupational Health and Safety Act of 1970, and the period following the passage of the law; to the present day. The political actors to be reviewed for each of these three time periods will be the industrial corporations, the unions, the state government, the federal bureaus dealing with occupational health and safety, and the workers themselves.

Traditionally, the work-place was under the complete control of management. In the period between the thirties and the sixties a minor and ineffective system of state inspections was put into practice. Workmen's Compensation, which would pay in part for injuries incurred at work, was created as a state-by-state system.[30] On the setting itself, the owner was king, and still is. Even the nurse's and physician's work is influenced by the policies set by top management. In a textbook for industrial physicians, a former president of the American Medical Association's section on occupational health explains the real priorities:

313

> The primary purpose of industry is to produce at a profit. It is not to practice medicine. . . . An industry operating without profit, or even at a loss, cannot afford a health program or even a part-time medical director; nor can it, in fact, stay in business very long. From industry's point of view the *raison d'etre* of a medical program is, essentially, to help increase profits.[31]

Implied in the position taken here, of course, is that little voluntary effort can be expected by most industries which would increase the quality of health care on the work setting at the expense of profits.

In this first historical period—from the thirties to the sixties— unions were passive or even disinterested in the issue of occupational safety and health, in the sense that all other issues were considered to first priority in bargaining with management over the yearly contracts. The corporations responded by refusing even to consider occupational health and safety issues as part of the contract. They considered it their own prerogative to operate the plant as *they* wished. Wildcat strikes (workers walking off the job without the support of their own union) sometimes occurred in the worst health situations, such as the mines. But union bosses regularly refused to consider the realities of the situation. Very few unions even kept records on their members' injuries and illnesses. Professional organizations—such as organized medicine (the AMA), industrial engineering groups, and industry-supported safety organizations, such as the National Safety Council—refused to consider conditions as critical and refused to push for legislation which would improve the conditions.[32]

Also in the first period, from the thirties to the early sixties, state governments had almost no inspectors and refused to fine corporations when they found violations. In most cases the major corporations had much power over state government at the locales where their major plants operated. As late as 1968 the AFL/CIO found, in a twenty-five-state sample, that the states employed one and one-half times as many fish-and-game wardens as they did occupational safety inspectors.[33] The federal government was characterized by several classic pathologies of regulation: (a) fragmentation of agencies responsible for parts of the problem; (b) internal infighting within the Department of Labor (which had the largest responsibility); (c) refusal to look at occupational *diseases* but only at the far narrower area of safety from *accidents* (falls, injuries, etc.); (d) deliberate shielding of information which they did have on work injuries and bad health conditions, from unions, and from the workers themselves; (e) a refusal to push for the right to enter a factory against the wishes of the factory owner; and generally (f) a deliberate disinterest by the Department of Labor in doing anything which would significantly irritate industry. The worker, as a consequence, could not look for significant support from industry, unions, the federal government, or the states, and health-care activists had yet to appear.[34]

Lyndon Johnson, as part of his program of social legislation, attempted to pass a bill which would strengthen the bureaucracies which were responsible for occupational health and safety. But he did not push for it hard, and neither did the unions. As a consequence, business carried the day: by being the only groups showing up for the hearings, the U.S. Chamber of Commerce, the National Association of Manufacturers, the American Iron and Steel Institute, and the Manufacturing Chemists Association, led the fight against the bill. It was Nixon's attempt to convince labor to vote Republican that finally led to the passage of a new federal law, with bipartisan support in Congress. The unions, while critical of its provisions, preferred it to nothing and the bill went through as The Occupational Health and Safety Act of 1970.

The Fight after Passage

Rearranging the power relationships between the interest groups—within the existing capitalist economy—was the main aim of the new law. For example, employers were required to tell workers if they, the employer were exceeding safety standards, and had to post any violation notices received from state or federal inspections. Any union, or small group of workers, can request an inspection by the federal government if they suspect conditons are bad. This inspection must be made or a letter refusing to make it must be sent; and the letter can be grounds for suing the government. Employees now have the legal right to object and to complain if they are harassed by employers for fighting to improve safety levels. States are to make up comprehensive new plans to upgrade their own industrial and health safety inspection. Then, when the state plan is approved, the state is allowed to do the enforcement work for the federal government, but always under federal supervision. At the federal level, an old bureau for health and safety was upgraded within HEW to form the National Institute for Occupational Safety and Health (NIOSH) to conduct research on individual diseases and danger levels for given chemicals, to set safety standards for the future. In summary, the new law:

> spells out in detail how safety and health standards are to be set, inspections made, and citations for violations issued. In addition to that enforcement authority, the Department also must provide training and education programs for safety and health personnel, as well as for employees and employers, and must gather information on the extent of occupational injuries and diseases. [35]

The present period resembles, in the field of occupational health, the period in the education field just after the Supreme Court declared that segregation in public schools was illegal. The group that was the primary sponsor of the new law (the Nixon administration) immediately turned toward the destruction of the new occupational health legislation, just after its passage. But there is an additional factor now, besides the usual attempt by interest groups to sabotage any changes. There is a federal standard. When each group does not live up to it, there are legal grounds for suits by activists, worker groups, and unions, and these have already begun, because the third period looks very much like the second and the first. For example, corporations have routinely refused to make the basic changes in technology which would eliminate the causes of many work hazards. Instead, they have chosen easier and cheaper methods, such as requiring workers to wear earmuffs against sound levels that penetrate bone, or goggles which fog up against steam and chemical vapor. Then, when the pressure to produce is increased, the workers are forced to discard the pseudo-protective devices. When they fall ill, the companies continue to blame the worker for carelessness, and refuse to support compensation claims on the grounds that "the worker wasn't obeying the safety rules". True improvement of the health levels in most factories would be expensive in many settings. It is this direct economic interest which motivates factory owners against major changes.[36]

As a consequence of the passage of the new Occupational Health and Safety Law, unions have a potential tool to work for change. A few unions, such as the Oil, Chemical, and Atomic Workers' Union, have developed new model programs for worker education. The "health and safety committees" in each plant can also serve as a base for local action. States have been handed back a lot of the power they lost in theory to the federal government. Interpretations of the new law by industry-favoring national administrations have led to federal government passivity which borders on sabotage of the intent of the law. For example, the Department of Labor under Nixon and Ford has refused to reply to many worker requests for the inspection of their plant to check up on conditions which workers have evidence are dangeorus. The federal "enforcers" have refused to fine companies for not posting the violation notices which they have sent out, thus keeping conditions secret from the workers. Federal agencies have agreed with corporations that they do not have to pay workers for time they spend accompanying plant inspection teams—making workers pay for their safety out of their own paycheck. The federal government agency has continually refused to require states to actually walk around the plants they are "inspecting" for the federal government. Interviews of management are allowed to suffice as data for making a decision. ("Mr. Factory-owner, do you have a safe plant?")[37]

In general, activists and organizers now have a tool in the new law, for the above strategies to stall or frustrate the intent of the law are now illegal and can be fought. The struggle will undoubtedly be long and there are other aspects to the fight which we will take up in the final part of the book. But the issues are clear in this field; for workers they are literally life-and-death issues. The struggle is fought one step at a time. One day last year the writer was in the office of Urban Planning Aid, an activist group in Cambridge, Massachusetts. A young welder walked in. "Here", said the young man in charge of the office, "read these and then let's talk". He handed the worker a series of clearly written booklets, such as *How to Look at Your Plant, Be Your Own Inspector*, and *What You Should Know about Welding*. Each was written to combine practical and immediately useful ways to check on the dangers of particular work-places and the advice needed to organize the workers on his setting to make a formal protest and a legal battle.[38] But one year later the Ford administration refused to renew the grant which kept this information office open.

Health in the work-place, to sum up, is at least in part the result of a present outcome in an almost eternal power struggle. It is not something that happens or does not happen without cause. The history of industry has been one of great suffering to workers, and only in the immediate present has a chance even existed to mobilize the power of the workers themselves against groups which have been working to preserve illness, or governments which have deliberately stayed out of the way of those groups. But in the absence of immediate change, we ultimately must ask why workers go on working in such settings, which are so dangerous to their health. *They* answer that the alternative is welfare. Work may mean sacrificing their own health, but the alternative will sacrifice not only theirs, but that of their children as well. This lack of choice is not an accident, but rather the consequence of the structure of a capitalist

318

society which forces people into such jobs even at the cost of their health in order to preserve the profits of the employers.

ECOLOGICAL HEALTH AND ILLNESS

Ultimately there is no limit to what can be considered a health-giving or illness-producing setting. Modern industry, and the modern automobile, have turned many cities into overall sources of illness. The concentration of air pollution under weather inversion layers, or the photochemical smog from gasoline fumes which lies over most American large cities, slowly but surely destroys the health of the healthiest individuals in a manner quite beyond their control. For example, benzo-a-pyrene is a known carcinogenic chemical that is suspended in the air of major cities, for it occurs in gasoline exhaust. A recent series of definitive experiments have proven the long-term effects of auto exhaust not only on the lungs but on other body systems as well, and they are striking.[39] Esposito, in the Nader study, *The Vanishing Air,* reports that living each day in a major American city is equivalent to smoking a pack of cigarettes a day. Sulfur dioxide pollution, to take another example, has caused the rate of lung cancer on that part of Staten Island downwind of the Jersey refineries to be thirty-three percent higher than that on other parts of the island.[40]

Since the problems of ecological health form simply one segment of the vast ecology literature, there are practical limitations to the extent of our considering them here. But we can consider the political or economic dimension of the pollution. Simply put, the costs of medical care, and the overall damage to the environment, are not paid by the polluters, but by the public at large. Power in the hands of large corporations is usually able to frustrate enforcement at state and local levels through influence on the local politicians. And with the resources of money and manpower behind them, corporations can afford to wait out short-term attempts to thwart them while turning out political propaganda of their own; an example is the ecology movement:

> The backlash they face comes not from the public, but from businesses and industries that are finally taking the movement seriously and are responding forcefully—with stepped-up lobbying; sophisticated advertising campaigns proclaiming their dedication to sunshine and green grass; and employee "education" programs which, crudely summed up, sometimes amount to saying: "Which do you want, clean air or a job?" (an approach commonly called "environmental blackmail").[41]

It is often the case that the same corporations, using similar stalling techniques and the same legal staffs, as well as the same arguments about the costs of change, fight one day against the occupational health and safety laws, the next against the environmental pollution laws. On both days they are in a major struggle to preserve illness in America, through continuing to put the same chemicals into both settings. Economic motivations have a genuine place in social planning considerations in any society, but the majority of individuals in our capitalist society at present do not have the power to draw the line at direct danger to their health. Whether they do in the future is not a scientific question, but rather one involving the future political activity of the groups concerned.

HEALTH, SERVICE, AND THE
FISCAL CRISIS OF THE STATE

As American capitalism advanced from the early robber baron era to the present, it worked for a much closer involvement with the state, especially with the economic policy planning, budgeting (Office of Management and the Budget) and regulatory agencies of the federal government. Increasingly, this relationship has been motivated by *defensive* considerations since the rest of the world has begun to change around American capitalism. The era of cheap raw materials from Third World nations, of cheap labor in the passive colonies of the major capitalist powers, and of undisturbed international relations between American and European sectors of capital is now coming to an end. As Third World nations begin to put pressure on the American capitalist class, as the price of oil and energy rises, as these same nations begin to do their *own* producing (thus beginning to compete with us), and as the socialist nations develop their own trade relations, American capitalism comes under pressure. To compete in the world market, while paying comparatively higher salaries to American workers now organized enough to demand them, they must push productivity up while cutting costs, fringe benefits, and their share of the national tax burden. [42]

At the same time, the neglect of those of no use to the capitalist class (created by blocking legislation to help such people) creates further problems and great costs on its own. The poor, the ill, and the unemployed demand support. The state is thus caught in a bind. To cut back on services and costs too extensively is to enrage a growing share of the population which has grown to expect them. To *not* do so is to endanger capitalist profitability and thus ability to compete worldwide. Cutbacks in services to the dependent and poor, especially when they are passive and unorganized, is a first step, but just as Gough observed in Britain, the next target is the social supports for all working class individuals, and not just in the health area. The capitalist class urges the state to relax even their present feeble enforcement of occupational health and safety laws, as well as general environmental ones. At the same time, in the office-factories and industrial plants, the workers are pushed harder and harder for the same pay and also simultaneously, their share of the overall tax burden is increased while the capitalist sector's share is *decreased*. Gough found these patterns for all OECD nations, and has quantitative data on the change in tax proportions over a ten-year period. [43]

These stresses lead to yet another series of diseases. All of these diseases and demands confront the state. The state's role, as

Navarro notes, differs here from its role in supporting industry itself. While de facto industrial subsidies, such as railroad ownership, road-building, power-line construction, and other activities help to build the profits of the corporations, the state in the human service sector acts as a rationalizer and cost-cutter concerning services to the working people themselves. [44]

Gradually, therefore, the health service system comes under observation by joint capitalist/state technocratic planner teams. The cost-benefit analysts begin to call the shots here, against the rising protests of hospitals, the health professionals, and patients who have been judged too expensive to service in top-rank settings. It's not that the professions (especially some physicians) and the hospitals, as well as capitalist sectors such as drugs and medical technology, have not been in large part responsible for the rapid rise in costs. This isn't the point. From a more general theoretical approach, the point is that doctors and hospitals are becoming increasingly irrelevant to the more basic problem—the salvation of capitalism. It is this latter problem that begins to preoccupy the advanced capitalist state. This goal relegates health and service to a minor, low-priority support role.

The role that service systems play, as part of the state apparatus in a situation of this kind, is to save "the economy", meaning the capitalist economy. Beyond this function, the limits are iron-clad. Because of the new world political situation, and its impact on American capitalism, the greater the pressure on our capitalist class, the greater its pressure on the state, and in turn, the greater the state pressure to cut back, rationalize, save and eliminate "unnecessary" health services. Unnecessary to what, one might ask. *Unnecessary to the preservation of the present economic system.* Thus the iron constraints on the deployment of service workers, on the creation of equal systems of care, on planning and regulation that is real instead of ideological, and of surveillance programs that protect the health of the employees are all now seen as part of the structure itself. It does not really matter how "moral" or "humane" a particular corporate executive, President, or technocrat is personally. It is this political-economic structure itself, not a group of villains, compatriots or political allies, that preserves the conditions and prevents the solutions. True solutions would have to be achieved at the expense of the capitalist order. But the demands for change are rising. People are saying *no more*, and they are searching for alternatives. These alternatives are our final subject.

10

Who Will Make the Future?

To some extent, individuals and groups can make their own future. But swimming against the tide is considerably more difficult than swimming with it. Throughout this book, we have been concerned with trends, with struggles, with conflicting aims and points of view. The unfairness and inefficiency of our present health-care system has been presented in detail. The issues of the present—at least some of them—were found to be previewed quite remarkably in the issues of the past. Strategies for change have been seen as consistently coming up against organized interest groups and more generally against an overall social and political order—capitalism. They have usually been frustrated or destroyed in the process. What then of the future? Is it to be simply more of the same? This ultimately may be up to the reader, but only if the reader gets involved and acts to change the situation.

But change it toward what? This last chapter will consider some possible alternatives to the present situation. First, the main trends that we have spotted throughout can be reconsidered as to where they might go, depending on who is most active in the near future. Then two alternatives for America can be briefly considered, along with the probable reaction of the existing interests: one a plan for national health insurance; the other, an American National Health Service. We conclude with a reminder on the relationship between information, values, and action.

TRENDS AND DEVELOPMENTS:
FOR OR AGAINST THE TIDE?

King Canute, as the legend has it, once placed his throne at the beach, and commanded the waves to stand still. The critical question, which we have to ask in order to know whether Canute got away with it or not, is *which way was the tide running at the time?* At high tide, a throne one foot beyond the edge of the water is safe, but if the throne is put there at low tide, both it and the king will soon be very wet indeed. But tides are quite predictable. The politics of health care are not. Trends do exist, however, which we can respond to with our knowledge of the social and political context, and suggest the possible reactions which the existing interest groups have to these trends. These are trends involving health workers, health-care settings, the patterns of service, and the relationship between costs, profits, power, and attempts at controlling such phenomena.

Unquestionably the other health occupations are on the move. As the medical profession comes under greater surveillance by non-physician groups in government, and as other crises divert them from their traditional position of professional dominance, they are less able to deal with the nearly full-time activity of the leaders of some professional groups, especially nursing, as they gain more autonomy on the health-care setting. As the technology gets more complex, fewer and fewer physicians are able to operate the dials and levers. Those who *can,* use this skill as blackmail for partial independence and a higher salary. Furthermore, other groups, especially the hospitals, see greater advantages in dealing with each occupational group separately, thereby improving their power position with respect to each one, including the physicians. Group health insurance plans often have a parallel approach, as do the large clinics such as Mayo and Leahey, which divide up the responsibility considerably. In addition, action through law, by the other health occupational groups, is gradually weakening the legal backstop which the medical professional has had for a long time as a tool in dominating the other health occupations. An active attempt by government to take the AMA's school accreditation function away from it could be yet another way to allow greater freedom for innovation. In general, consumer acceptance of the greater independence of the other health occupations will make this a greater possibility in the near future. But the way in which they do their work—in money terms—is critically important. It would appear that most occupational groups that want "independence" want it at least as much for the chance to set up shop and make high incomes (as physicians have) as they do to increase the quality and accessibility of health care. We will discuss this problem below as two alternatives for health care are presented.

Bureaucratization and prejudice may well be reversible processes. But the energy required is tremendous, while the interests that push the processes along are still alive and well in America. As health-care services pass from their chaotic unorganized pattern toward a more organized one, the dangers of the iron cage will increase rather than decrease. Remembering that the model of bureaucracy which Max Weber used to create his "ideal" of the form was the Prussian army, we must ask whether the Prussian army, the spider-in-the-web, or any such neat, geometric, and potentially totalitarian model will provide anyone with the health care they need or want. Increased government involvement, of a sort we will suggest below, may handle some of the money issues more effectively. But structural reforms on the way government itself operates, and the checks and balances of power over the operation of the health-care setting, will be a major item for the future. As for prejudice, what can be said of it that has not already been said before by many others? The moral necessity for humane treatment between people who are different is also, in the long run, a social necessity for civilization to survive. It is also true that some political and economic systems benefit from existing prejudices; but a socialist state is not necessarily an unprejudiced one, as we know from recent history. Education and exposure are critically important in ending racism, sexism, ageism, and cultural chauvinism, as are action through law—far more action on the laws we already have. If these are not handled very soon, a new system will very likely freeze the existing patterns into permanence.

Costs are always a problem, in any system of human services in any society, and the people have to pay for the care, one way or another. But they may not pay equally, nor receive equal service even if they do. In most nations the powerful have always been in a position to control the way the costs are paid, or not paid, depending on who is in trouble. Fuchs puts the issue this way. He begins with an analogy of the "crashed private plane" and asks whether a lot of effort will be expended in finding the downed pilot. He concludes that if the pilot is rich, famous, or a politician, much more time and money will be spent on the search. He continues:

> Suppose, however, that instead of a plane crash the threat of death came from an ordinary fatal disease? Would the same answers apply? The capacity of medical science to intervene near the point of death is growing rapidly. Such interventions are often extremely costly and have a low probability of long-term success—but sometimes they work. Whose life should be saved? The wealthy man's? The senator's? Society cannot escape this problem any more than it can avoid facing the other choices we have discussed.[1]

Different answers to this particular question, and to others like it, will be suggested by professors, cost accountants, and ministers of religion. But the answer will be *written* by those with the power to write it.

There will be an increase in attempts at planning health-care services more rationally, in the near future, as a way of handling these difficult problems, and an increase in attempts at regulating health workers, health-care settings, programs for service, and the costs of the service. Yet as we have seen, the ones causing the problems are in very much of a position at present to dictate the solution. Federalizing our health-care programs—running more of them directly from Washington—has in the past and will in the future always be a two-edged sword. The increased efficiency may well be there, and an increased capacity to control waste and duplication of services. But who will guard the guardians? And who is the advisor at court? We have been living in an era that can be characterized politically by the perversion of our constitution and its system of checks and balances, toward a centralization of un-checked power in the executive branch of government. A brief series of setbacks have occurred here, from the point of view of executive dictators. Nixon is gone, and his successor complained as South Vietnam fell of his "frustrations due to the War Powers Act", which Congress had just imposed on the presidency to prevent another undeclared war or our reenlistment in an existing one, without the consent of the people. We will consider two alternatives to the present situation: a national health insurance system and a National Health Service. But we must preface them with a warning. No system can be perfect which is made of fallible humans, and we are all fallible. The framers of our Constitution two centuries ago were well aware of it. There must be a set of checks and balances to our health system of the future. Even to create it, the power to do so must be seized back by the people and soon. If it is not, in the nation as in the health-care system, some of the "reforms" which may look good today could be the building blocks of a totalitarian nation tomorrow. This may sound like an extreme statement, but it would be hard to overstate its importance. There are few things that the conservative and the radical agree on. But one of them is the need to check the arbitrary power of the institutions that govern our lives.

ALTERNATIVE ONE:
NATIONAL HEALTH INSURACE

For many Americans a serious illness means financial ruin. The house must be sold, children uprooted, and much suffering created. Private insurance plans are often filled with loopholes, and even the nonprofit Blue Cross plans leave many expenses uncovered. What results is a situation where pressure is building for a quick solution—a patching job which would be paid for by the citizens—a national health insurance plan. But the first alternative to the existing system may not be an alternative at all. That is, there are several plans to rework the ways that health services are presently paid for. In many of these plans, not only are the roles of the existing interest groups unchanged but the money-flow systems proposed, if put into practice, would strengthen the existing patterns of care, permanently freeze the two-class system, and give much leverage over the interest groups to control how and in what way we receive health care. In addition it is important to remember that *we already have an existing, two-class national system of health insurance*. Few of the existing proposals do much beyond filling in the gaps, and some do not even do that. We have a system where the middle class and wealthy are insured by a combination of profit-making corporations, "nonprofit" organizations such as Blue Cross and Blue Shield, and themselves. When the money runs out for the middle class, and for the poor and old at all times, there is the Medicaid/Medicare insurance system, working with the bottom of the two-class delivery system. We can begin with the existing insurance role of one key organization—Blue Cross—and then proceed to a brief rundown of the proposals of the major actors on the insurance scene at present.

Blue Cross—The Insurer as Middle Man

Insurance is technically a way of sharing risks, and in practice becomes a way of collecting money from consumers to pass to providers for services they have given out, after a fee has been taken off the top. For a profit-making insurance company, this fee goes for both costs of administration and for pure profit. And in addition, the profit-making firm refuses to insure people on whom they are likely to lose money, such as the poor, old, and chronically ill, and often *cancels* insurance at the first sign of serious long-term illness. Nonprofit firms don't go to this extreme, but they have some ways of lowering the costs to themselves and collecting extra money to use for purposes of more interest to them than to the consumer. One such nonprofit plan, of importance at present and of future importance as well, is the Blue Cross system of hospital insurance.

Blue Cross, in addition to having about forty percent of all private health insurance, is in addition the middle man for several large governmental programs, doing the paperwork for the government here. It is a combination of a national office and a series of local plans, each of which *must* by its own rules have seventy-five percent of the hospitals in its area as members. It is a middle man, a "fiscal intermediary" between the consumer and the hospital. But its history indicates that it was originally created by hospitals and retains a close tie to them today. For cosmetic reasons, consumers have been added to many local boards of Blue Cross, and for self-interest reasons the organizations are becoming more independent of hospitals. Law and the Health-Law Project of the University of Pennsylvania, in a recent study of the Blue Cross organization, observed that the "nonprofit" status of the agency is dubious, because of the large money reserves which they collect over the years and do not return to consumers, after all costs for the year have been paid out.[2] In addition, like the middle men in the food production sector, Blue Cross plans are beginning to become independent of the primary producers (farmers, ranchers, doctors, hospitals) and are keeping payments to *them* down while selling the service to the consumer at an even higher price, while pocketing the difference. This money, reinvested, earns interest which the Blue Cross Plan keeps.

In state after state, local regulatory agencies and the federal government have been very unwilling to force Blue Cross to come up with detailed data on the use they make of collected money, or the ways in which they figure costs, while allowing them to go on raising costs to the consumer. In addition, in 1965 Blue Cross got a nationwide contract to administer many of the U.S. Government's Medicare programs, and they are also doing some of the administration of state Medicaid programs, under subcontract from state welfare agencies.[3] All of these responsbilities give them bargaining power for a large role in a future insurance system, and in addition they have built up a series of relationships with people and bureaus within government in much the same way that the major defense contractors build up a relationship with the generals and bureaus within the Pentagon. The military-industrial complex is a good analogy here for the government/insurance industry complex. But in the absence of public data on the internal finances of these agencies, or direct data on all costs and benefits, and with existing splits between them (Blue Cross as a hospital insurance group and Blue Shield as the outpatient-visit group), it is doubtful whether simply giving them even more of a role is a good idea.[4]

More openness to outside investigators—such as was not given to the Law group—might change the picture that this organization has created. But even their own public data show that these plans operate with widely varying overhead costs. For example, Massachusetts Blue Cross takes twice as high a percent off the top for administrative costs as does Blue Cross of Northeast Ohio, yet the latter plan has more complete benefits.[5] Why? For the present, Law and her colleagues conclude:

There is no reason to believe that Blue Cross will move toward greater consumer control and accountability in the absence of hard and specific requirements to do so. Despite growing consumer discontent and criticism and a rhetorical public commitment to community service, the evidence is that Blue Cross actively seeks both a major role in national health insurance and the preservation of its present orientation and autonomy.[6]

Blue Cross is important in regard to the insurance issue, because to many people it represents something of a compromise between letting the profit-making corporations have a piece of the national health insurance pie, and cutting out all existing agencies. The key justification here is "at least they're non-profit". What the Law study has put together, and what has not been refuted by Blue Cross in their informally circulated mimeographed response to the book, is that the extra funds are neither returned to the consumer nor used in ways that lower the costs in the future.[7] As a compromise between the extremes of no insurance and cutting the corporate giants in, they are under pressure to "shape up" in order to be the chosen middle-man for a national insurance plan. According to some consumer activists who work against them on a daily basis, they seem to be more capable of modification in a positive direction than the profit-making firms are.

But the tide at present is not on the side of Blue Cross. The private profit-making insurance companies presently, as of 1976, have more than 60 percent of the policies. In addition, they are trying to drive Blue Cross out of the market through the offering of package plans (auto-home-health) advertised through the mass media. By typical oil-company tactics, they can reduce the price below that of the Blue plans, and then when the Blue plans are driven under, the private profit-making companies can raise the costs. In this respect, their ability to cancel policies is legal and unnoticed by most consumers, while the Blue policy of refusing to cancel those in serious trouble puts them at a major economic disadvantage.

Thus the role of any group, in a national insurance plan, will only in part be settled on the impartial merits of the case. In part it will be settled rather by the capital, resources, and political strength which the contenders have in the Congress, and in the wider society. We already have a good general idea what the odds are here, but they can change. The proposals presented by the contenders are thus of great importance, if an insurance scheme is to be the shape of the future. These proposals are a study in themselves.

Proposals for National Health Insurance

Why do we need a middle-man at all? The answer is often given that unless we go to a directly administered national health service (which we will discuss below) then we must have someone doing the insurance paper and money processing. Given that, it is important to remember that each of the contenders in the insurance field at present, of which Blue Cross is only one, is primarily interested in getting into the plan because of that part of the money they can take "off the top" for profit or "reserves". The plans proposed by the groups are complex; they change from month to month; and they rise and fall in importance from causes that have many origins, including the political fate of their congressional sponsors. We cannot go into the details of these proposals here, for in the time it takes to print a book each statement will be well out of date.[8] But the general outlines of the strategy of each contender can be given, along with a recommendation to check each directly for the fine print of their latest plan. Several plans have been around for a while, in different versions, and we can mention them simply as examples of *who* proposes *what*. These are the plans: the medical profession (AMA); private profit-making insurance companies; Blue Cross and the hospitals; Senator Edward Kennedy's, and that of the government itself.

The *medical profession*, through special insurance committees of the AMA, has changed its strategy and its attitude toward national health insurance, from the "good old days" of the fight against

Medicare. In the late sixties and early seventies, they presented a series of insurance plans. "Medicredit" was a nonplan that simply kept the two-class system as is, while recommending that people be able to deduct costs of health care from their income tax. In the present Congress (1975–1976) they are introducing yet another plan. Two policies remain unchanged. They propose to keep the two-class insurance system. Second, "The federal government would be prohibited from interfering with the private practice of medicine".[9]

The *private insurance companies* propose covering everyone but the poor and old, letting the public's funds pay for their usually more expensive care. They want the government to let them split the pie of the wealthy and more healthy upper and middle class, profiting both from lower illness rates per dollar collected and also a guaranteed profit rate that would go into the billions of dollars. Others will be paid for in the public system and thus paid more by employee class taxes than by the capitalist sector.

Blue Cross and the hospitals, using the argument that they have local plans in most areas of the nation, the argument that they have already extensive experience at working closely with government, and the argument that they are nonprofit, want the same role as the private insurance firms, but with "administrative costs" and "reserves" instead of profits. As noted above, they have a long history of resisting open inspection of their books, even when working with government. Other nonprofit groups, such as the large HMOs in the West, the Washington, D.C. area, and New York City, would dispute their claim to be as the "sole main insurer" as well.

Kennedy, alone or in temporary combination with different politicians, has consistently advocated the government's primary administration of the plan with subcontracting to any *nonprofit* organization (at least in a recent version). His system is the only one that seriously considers ending the two-class insurance system.

The government, under Nixon, suggested a "piece of the pie for everyone" plan, combined with keeping the two-class system, a sort of path-of-least resistance model. President Ford is delaying as this book goes to press.

Although each of the proposed plans talks about reorganizing some minor part of the health care delivery system, great faith is always placed in the existing system's ability to regulate the costs. No inflation will occur, the consumer is constantly assured, because there will be *government regulation!* The previous chapter is critically important in showing the weakness of that argument, and in showing why critics of *insurance* as a solution say that whenever there is a middle man of any kind, there will be pressure to escalate costs without increasing service or coverage.

There is a final question we must ask, yet once again, about insurance. It is primarily a mechanism for paying for health care. None of the existing plans *demand* a reorganization of our present pattern of services: its two-class system and its chaos and waste. Some say it would be *nice,* and recommend some incentives for it. But no basic reorganization is required. What happens to a corrupt and unfair health-care system when it is guaranteed a continual supply of money? Will that make it change, or make it better for the consumer? An analogy might be helpful. If the government of some corrupt foreign regime is supported by the United States, it can demand more and more of our dollars to feed its inefficiency, greed, and wastefulness, as well as its oppression of citizens. Yet increasing our supply of money to such an entity is not going to reform it; it will strengthen it and feed its pathology in the short run. In the long run, however, it will not forestall the inevitable time when the people rise and throw it out.

ALTERNATIVE TWO:
AN AMERICAN NATIONAL HEALTH SERVICE

One measure of a nation's maturity is its ability to anticipate crises and deal with them constructively ahead of time, instead of deliberately proceeding with a series of stop-gap measures that do not deal with the basic causes of the problem. It is being said by many depressed and weary activists that America will have to explore the disaster of a national health insurance system first, with the existing power groups in control. Then, when the costs have escalated out of sight and the chaos has gotten even worse, we will turn to the development of a national health service. Such pessimism may be warranted. But it is not beyond possibility that the alternative of a national health service can be considered *now*. We can do so here only in broad outline, and with the understanding that a full plan would require a book in itself. But it is necessary to widen the debate from that of "this insurance plan" versus "that one" to the more important debate of "insurance" versus "an American National Health Service".

The Elements of the System

To begin with, if we wish to create an American National Health Service we must nationalize all health care personnel on federal salary as federal employees—and all health-care settings. We must nationalize as well all major *supply* sectors: hospital supply, blood, drugs. The government will be its own middle man, instead of duplicating the process, in terms of collection and payment of funds, and will be in control of all aspects of the money-flow situation. Realistically, to attempt to do this would create the most monumental kinds of opposition from any and all of the existing interest groups. The consumer will practically have to stand alone, and many will have doubts, of course. But the American people have deposed a president and forced the end of their participation in an undeclared war. But *this* will be a more difficult fight. In addition, there is no need for the process of creation to become simply another name-calling match. The first step might be a national referendum for a year-long convocation, similar to the kind called for in our original Constitutional Convention, to set up the plan. Accompanying the convocation would be a moratorium on legislation for insurance, new delivery-system programs, and new programs for planning and regulation.

Several elements of this new American Health Service are suggested by our findings. But these are simply suggested ideas, and should be open to full debate. First, we will need far more community general practitioners in every neighborhood, urban and rural, delivering primary care, in formal though flexible arrangements with small community hospitals and major medical centers. *The primary-care practitioner should be the independently practicing nurse.* Specialists in medicine and nursing, will either be in the local offices or the larger hospitals, depending on the degree of specialization and their relation to primary care. But the general practitioner of tomorrow, within the Service, should be the specially trained nurse.

The spiderweb model is suggested by the above, but one critical difference is recommended; the removal of medical-school control of any and all major general hospitals. Instead, medical education will be relocated into the community general hospitals under the community's supervision and control. This leads us to consider several aspects of the system: the nature of training, the use of existing buildings and offices, the role of consumer and citizen control of planning, financing, cost-related decision making, and reorganization or repeal of the new system, if it does not meet with the long-term approval of the majority.

Training, Teaching, and Research

Training would have as its primary purpose the abolition of the class system of medical education. Government will pay for all education and have a strong role in the location of the graduates in the first few years after graduation, with zones of prohibited practice (enough servers present) allowed and specially supported, with a quota for each area. In the years of training, universities and not medical schools will do the first two or basic science years, training all health workers together, with a graduated number of years and tracks for those going on to the status of nurse, specialist physician, and medical worker in any of the many allied areas. One will be easily able to return to school or do part-time study to go from one status to the next. The training in clinical years will be based in the community and general hospitals, but community supervision and control will replace "medical schools". In fact, our existing medical school system would be changed beyond recognition, with pure and basic research, as well as service system research, being located at five new regional Institutes of Health—one for every major region of the nation—as well as the existing national ones in Maryland. Salaries and honors of professors will be equal to those of practitioners, and a small core of permanent teachers in each hospital will share the teaching duties with sabbatical health workers, who would become full-time clinical teachers one out of each seven years. This circulation between the ranks of teachers and practitioners will help both groups in every field.

The Political Role of the Consumer

The existing health-care settings of the nation will belong to the people. The prime directive should be the immediate abolition of two-class care, in the sense of physical plants and the relation between income areas and hospital services. In the one-year period before the enactment of the National Health Service Act the use of all existing places of brick and steel will be reconsidered. A small private mental hospital before passage of the Act might become the local first-line community health center for one part of a suburb; an old tuberculosis hospital may well be sold for scrap. The process of deciding what in the way of existing buildings will serve what future function would be a political process, as it always has been in the past. But the existing technical experts and managers will not be the voters and decisionmakers; they will be technical consultants to the local consumer panels that make the final decision, working with the federal planners who can give the sense of the overall regional context and needs for an integrated system.

This leads up to the most important change of all: the political role of the consumer in the new system. The relationship between consumers and the local system will be an elective one, with consumer-planner administrators running locally, as school committee candidates must, on their qualifications and record at administering the local health-care system. Budget items beyond a certain size would have to be submitted to a formal community vote, as would the allocation of funds by regions and allocations for research versus service. The same would go for national health care administrators, who would be chosen at election time along with the President and Vice-President.

Notice that we are not saying that the consumer must take a hand in directly running the system. What he must have is the power of approval, of budgetary control, of free access to all information on the system, including all costs and all major planning decisions. Planning agencies would be set up locally, regionally, and nationally, with a maximum of one-third provider members, and these health workers must come from *all* ranks. Full consultant panels must be set up for each consumer planner group, representing the health-care workers at each level, and they would routinely be expected to answer any of the technical questions put to them by consumers. In fact, full-time consultant advisors could be on the payroll of the consumer boards, available on circuit in less-populated areas.

Costs will be a problem in this system as in any, and decisions on funding will have to be made. But they will be publicly debated first. In addition, incentives would be given in the way of salary raises for administrators of health-care regions for "holding the line"—*but only if the consumers in the area decide this was not done at the expense of quality, and only if the professional health workers and consultants decide that corners were not cut in treatment to save money*. In general, many of the regulatory innovations that couldn't work because of outside interest group interventions could work well within the system. (Remember, we are assuming the abolition of health-related capitalist sectors.) Peer review of health workers will be routine, but not directed at cost-saving, only at the correctness of the medical decision. In fact, individual decisions on care will not, under the new system, be directly related to cost considerations. Otherwise the cook-book medicine approach and cost-oriented medical decision making which characterize the PSRO program will destroy the humanity of this one. Any administrator intervening this way (forcing a medical decision directly on cost grounds) will be recalled by consumer panels, forced to explain what was attempted, and discharged if the offense is proven.

No system has acceptance on the part of all, and one of this sort could be expected to be met initially with attempts at sabotage and evasion. Although there would be a phasing-in period when private practice would continue, the funding of the new system would eventually make private practice far less attractive to physicians than participation in the national health service. Ultimately, private practice would become illegal. This is necessary to prevent the creation of a new version of our old two-class system, such as England has, with one class for the rich and the other—the public system—for everyone else. Private use of funds for profit, and profit-making activity in the supply sectors, would be discouraged at first and then, when the system is fully in effect, be replaced by nonprofit corporations providing the supplies at cost-plus-overhead operating expenses.

Lest the reader think this scheme is somewhere in the indefinite future as a serious, detailed legislative proposal, we can present here the outlines of the fully-worked-out design of a national group of health professionals, on the details of a legislative plan for an American National Health Service.[10] As with the above proposal, with which the author was not familiar as he developed his own rather similar model quite independently, there are strong requirements for consumer control, and deliberate attempts to end the two-class system through the creation of one service system. Particularly important are their purposes in the Findings and Declaration of Purpose Section of the "Health Rights and Community Health Services Act":

> To structure the National Health Service on the basis of community health centers, conveniently located to assure ready access and freedom of choice for all individuals; these centers, the primary unit for the delivery of services to be staffed by multidisciplinary teams of health workers (serving under an incentive-based salary system) providing preventive, primary, and continuing care and linked to community hospitals, special facilities and regional medical centers for advanced care.

> To assure equitable and ready access to National Health Service services and facilities for all—without regard to age, sex, race, nationality, religion, income, place of residence, political belief, or citizenship—by implementing local, regional and national planning for the construction, equipment, supply, and personnel of needed facilities to overcome present shortages, e.g., for currently deprived rural and inner city populations, minority groups, prisoners, and occupational groups.

> To establish representative and democratic administrative systems for the National Health Service, through a linkage of community, district, regional and national health boards, with a composition representative of the population served as well as of the health providers; and

341

To finance the National Health Service from national revenues, on the basis of progressive taxation, particularly of corporate income and wealth, with no payments from lower income individuals.[11]

Alternative Two: Some Trouble Spots

Thus we have seen two closely related proposals for a national health service. The *context* of the service—the advanced capitalist political-economic world of the nation—and the problems of the malfunctioning of government itself—will be taken up below. But even on a technical level we must warn that both proposals have potential trouble spots, based on the evidence in this book, especially in the final sections on the politics of planning and regulation. First, consumers will need to be educated far beyond those at present, for either total control of boards or partial control, where they share board roles with health-care workers, who make up about a third of the decision-making group. The problem is the technical nature of many of the decisions, and the limited budget available under any system, capitalist or socialist. How will the people be trained? How can efficiency be maintained without degenerating into the kind of passionate but often irrelevant political struggles that characterize our local school board systems? And do the people of the nation *want* what amounts to an amateur administrative system? Is what they want *health care* instead? The British, the Cubans, the Chinese use various forms of participatory input, but by and large rely on professional administration from a central location for the overall shape and direction of the health service. Can we really have our cake and eat it too, administratively? Or, to put it another way, what serves the people best? We might look to having two states try this out, one with a strong consumer-controlled service, another with a centrally administered service. But where would we get the states?

This brings up the second point on planning, administration, and decision making within such a proposed service. Bureaucracy is

342

already a major problem here, and we have reason to suppose that the creation of a unified system would not decrease the red tape. It is important, however, to note that much of the present red tape is caused by the complex set of relationships between the public and the private sectors. On the other hand, the government, quite independently, can and does proliferate regulations and instruction books in health at an amazing rate, especially in the early seventies. What will the impact of all this be on the quality, efficiency, and availability of time and manpower in the new system?

Finally, there is always the danger that a National Service, community-controlled or not, could become part of the machinery of a capitalist/state combine, and once in place could be used *against* most people as a cost-cutting, service-rationing device, especially at a time of fiscal crisis. Some corporate sectors, in fact, are beginning to view a Service positively for just this reason.

Alternative Two, an American National Health Service, thus sounds politically naive to some who might read its outlines, and say, "There's too much opposition to it". Yet times and the economy change, and the pressures on working people are increasing for reasons we have already considered, which involve the rest of the world as well as the nation itself. This could lead to greater support for the idea even from the capitalist class, through their motives for it have been spelled out in the previous chapter, as a cost-cutting device. Others could point to the "fear of big government" ideology, yet the support for this is not clear as a refutation.

Consumers don't object to government per se, they object when it doesn't do its job in helping them, when they don't get their money back in terms of services. Yet all the remedies to date short of a national service have failed, and a national health insurance plan does not seem, in our eyes, to be a solution. Still others could point out that the only ones hurt by the present system are the poor, but this evades the twin issues of low medical coverage for many working people and severe exposure to illness conditions at work. And finally, the present patchwork of public and private is definitely costing as much as a well-financed and well-run national service, probably more, and little is coming from it in the way of results.

We do not for a moment think that the proposals presented here are anything but a sketch—a suggestion of what such a system might look like, along with some hints at the internal problems it might have. But any student of health care must consider an American National Health Service as an alternative to the many insurance plans. It is, in fact, about the only alternative we have. Another simple analogy is helpful here. How broken down does our old car have to be before we decide we are spending more to repair it than we would for an entirely new one?

THE CONTEXT PROBLEM AGAIN: CORPORATIONS AND GOVERNMENT

If it is true that the social and political context which surrounds the health-care system in America deeply affects the quality and functioning of the system, then it must also be true that those in control of that wider social and political context ultimately determine the fate of attempts to change the health-care system. If one takes just two examples, the two-class system of care and the causes of environmental disease, the role of corporate power becomes clear, as does the need for its abolition if basic changes are to be made in the pattern of life which creates illness or promotes health. Furthermore, alternative two—an American National Health Service—would have little realistic chance of creation and survival as a chicken within the increasingly hungry den of foxes known as corporate capitalism. On the other hand, replacing corporate dictatorship with bureaucratic totalitarian rule may lead to a situation where some might feel that "efficiency" was purchased at the price of freedom. We need, therefore, to think of the citizen as a "chicken" in two kinds of fox dens: the existing corporate state, and a not-recommended centralized socialist state with an unresponsive bureaucracy. These two parameters, one very real and an enemy of significant change, the other a real danger of nondemocratic trends in socialism (which can be combatted, of course), are the Scylla and Charybdis of the situation at present.

The Need to Abolish Corporate Power

The poisonous atmosphere, the continual maiming of workers in factories, the ongoing perversion and nullification of attempts to regulate dangerous aspects of our existence; all of these phenomena are natural consequences of a system where the corporate capitalist class controls the social context to suit its ends rather than those of consumers. For more than a century one of our dominating political ideologies has been that "the business of America is business", or "what's good for General Motors is good for the country". While these ideologies clearly are pushed by the corporations at the American people, it is beginning to be the case that the people are questioning their basic validity. Once this group of questioners increases in size, and begins to act by electing it *own* representatives to Congress and the Presidency, perhaps some headway can be made in this area. We have recommended the nationalization of the drug, medical technology, biological supply (blood), and insurance systems as a basic part of alternative two. A national health service without such basic internal elements would soon become unmanageable. But we should not stop there, if the issue is to be resources under the control of the people. We might choose to nationalize the large corporations that constitute the main policy-influencing groups, leaving the smaller service sectors and small business in private hands. There is no need to contemplate a society with everyone working for the state. But the power to frustrate legislation and pervert regulation in any area of the society cannot be nullified without removing the separate, interest-group status of the groups themselves, as elements outside the central system.

The need to proceed along these lines is not a steady thing, the same each year. The world is not standing still. Most ordinary citizens are losing ground fast to energy combines, food-processing middle men, real estate trusts, and the corporations for which they work. Ultimately we may have to decide whether what we mean by America is a particular economic order—state capitalism—or a free people. We might begin now with drastic limits on the capacity of private business to lobby in Washington—making this activity illegal, for example. People representing nonbusiness groups should have the right to make their views known, but private influence by private corporations must be limited in a way far more severely than by the control of campaign contributions. Most people are pessimistic about the ability of the people to do any of this, but it is possible to think of the advantages if major production sectors such as automobiles, steel, food distribution, and transportation, in addition to health and welfare, were nationally run. Because they are public is no need for them to be overcentralized, for we could very well have three competing public steel companies, three competing public oil firms. But so much of the overall power to frustrate the will of the majority lies within this broader context that a plan to limit it seems a basic necessity for further reforms.

The Need to Control Government Power

Nothing would be gained were we to exchange one despot (corporate capitalism of the Rockefeller-ITT-Exxon variety) for another (a totalitarian, unresponsive, dictatorial centralized state human service bureaucracy managed by an American "new class"). Technocrats with no controls in command of all our essential supply sectors, including all human services, are at least as frightening a prospect. Therefore, alternative two should be understood as preferable to our present situation *only* if the degree of consumer control and input, as well as ability to reject invasions of privacy and limitations on personal freedom, are built into the new system at the start. Eternal vigilance *is* the price of liberty, and no system, including those set up with the most benevolent or humanitarian of motives, will watch itself, or stay on the track, without constant input and accessibility to the individual consumer, from the outside. The conservative parts company here, and states that with this degree of public ownership and control of essential services, we can wind up nowhere but in a state of greater imprisonment than that which we presently have. But imprisonment is a relative term, especially if freedom, so called, is purchased at the price of poverty and illness, and alternatives are possible which can combine the advantages of public ownership with the dynamics of consumer participation. We do not think that the only alternatives for the future are continuing corporate domination or a totalitarian public state. But to travel the road suggested here is to ask far more of people than any event since the original Revolution in 1776. Like that one, it will have to occur quietly, in peoples' assumptions of the possible and the legitimate, before it becomes a plan for direct action. But a beginning can be made now.

INFORMATION, VALUES, AND ACTION

Introductions are meant to be the beginning, not the end. For health care and social science students, for health workers, and for consumers, for anyone who has read to this point, the next step is to further inform yourself. But information does not come only from books—including this one. It comes as well from direct experience. Every statement and analysis made here should be checked, for accuracy and bias, against the past, present, and future experience of the reader. To those who presently are not involved directly in the delivery of health care, a recommendation is in order—*get* involved! For if one message comes through the chaos it is that without worker and consumer involvement the existing interests will be quite capable of constructing, in the near future, a new health-care system that is beyond repair, even more unresponsive to people's needs than the present one.

A personal word about values is now in order. As stated in the introductory section, "A Point of View", the values of the author have been made explicit throughout. But a dimension was added to them as the work progressed. During the process of writing, much time was spent in a small, well-equipped research library in a medium-sized community general hospital just down the road from my home. It was quiet, the main health care journals were all there, the people were friendly, and the place was open twenty-four hours a day, seven days a week. As time went on, the hospital pathologist, the librarian, the hospital administrator, and a surgeon who was also the head of the hospital's patient-care review board began to strike up conversations with the author. They couldn't miss that pile of books and articles on the politics and economics of health care, and the growing manuscript. It soon became clear that they were not in agreement with one another, and that very few of them were in agreement with me, especially about basic values comparing professional independence with public need. But we could and did have many valuable discussions, and sections of this book are more realistic because of seeing the world, at least in part, from their point of view. If we disagreed as to the recommendations for the future, at least we agreed on the diagnosis, far more than I thought we would. For these were community health workers: the foot soldiers of medicine, as the surgeon once commented, not prestigious professors busy calling famous politicians to give them input on the next piece of national legislation. Their willingness to listen to differing points of view was impressive. Intellectually, I had known, as most of us do, that there are major disagreements and conflicts even within "monolithic" organizations such as the AMA. Most of the analyses describe the groups as political actors, and in fact this book has been so directed, deliberately. But they are also people, people who in most cases want to help the sick. They are hassled constantly, as much as others are in other jobs, if not more. If some of them have other motivations besides providing care—for fame, money, power, self-esteem, total independence from outside control—who among us does not?

If consumers must take an increasingly important and powerful role in building and running the health-care system of the future, and be the ultimate decisionmakers on most critical issues affecting their welfare, let us hope they will not forget to listen to the viewpoints and the daily frustrations of the health-care workers themselves. Although many of our institutions are in need of drastic revision, it is nevertheless likely to be a major mistake if we write off the accumulated experience of the workers themselves. Abstract schemes are often created by those who have not seen what it is like at the other end, who have not faced the conflicting demands of the layers upon layers of systems imposed from above which make the delivery of service increasingly impossible. What is needed, therefore, is a willingness to stop and rebuild from the ground up, as well as from the top down. For the student, the health worker, and the consumer, perhaps this book will help to begin a dialog, one which will eventually result in a better health-care system for us all.

Notes and References

A Point of View

1. Mary O. Furner, *Advocacy and Objectivity. A Crisis in the Professionalization of American Social Science 1865—1905*. (Lexington: University Press of Kentucky, 1975), p. 334.
2. The discussion of the decision was printed in the following day's university student newspaper, *The Harvard Crimson*. The quote of record was from the chairman of the department. Bowles is now a tenured full professor at the University of Massachusetts in Amherst, Leontief left Harvard the next year, in part out of protest concerning the philosophy, and Galbraith retired in June 1975.
3. Marc Pilisuk and Thomas Hayden, "Is There a Military-Industrial Complex Which Prevents Peace?" *Journal of Social Issues* 21 (July 1965): 67–117.
4. C. Wright Mills, *The Sociological Imagination* (New York: Oxford, 1959), p. 71.
5. This issue is even more complex, for the protection of individual privacy retards the gathering of data that might also be useful for exposing the inequities of an existing system. On the other hand, the Public Information Law exists precisely because there is a gap, in health care data as elsewhere,

351

between what the government has gathered and analyzed and that which it is willing to release.

The Historical Context of Health

1. Robert O. Steuer and J. B. Saunders, *Ancient Egyptian and Cnidan Medicine*. (Berkeley: University of California Press, 1959). See also ref. 2.
2. Herodotus, quoted in Henry E. Sigerist, *History of Medicine, Vol. I* (New York: Oxford University Press, 1965).
3. Charles Singer and E. Ashworth Underwood, *A Short History of Medicine*. (New York: Oxford University Press, 1962), pp. 22–27.
4. Sigerist, *History of Medicine*, Ibid.
5. Barbara Ehrenreich and Deidre English, *Witches, Midwives and Nurses* (Old Saybrook, Connecticut: Feminist Press, 1973).
6. Walter Ullmann, *Individual and Society in the Middle Ages* (Baltimore: Johns Hopkins Press, 1966), pp. 2–50 ("The Abstract Thesis")
7. W. S. C. Copeman, *Doctors and Disease in Tudor Times*, (London: Dawsons, 1960).
8. Ibid., p. 39.
9. Ibid., p. 3.
10. Joseph Kett, *The Formation of the American Medical Profession. The Role of Institutions 1780–1860* (New Haven: Yale University Press, 1968), p. 13.
11. In 1848 they were still at war with one another, even when founding the new national association. See Daniel H. Calhoun, *Professional Lives in America. Structure and Aspiration* (New Haven: Yale University Press, 1968).
12. Howard S. Berliner, "A Larger Perspective on the Flexner Report", *International Journal of Health Services* 5, no. 4 (1975): 573–592.
13. See George Rosen, "The Evolution of Social Medicine", in Howard E. Freeman et al., eds., *Handbook of Medical Sociology* (Englewood Cliffs, N.J.: Prentice-Hall, 1963), p. 18.
14. See Richard H. Shryock, *Medicine in America: Historical Essays* (Baltimore: Johns Hopkins Press, 1966).
15. For a valuable summary of the period, see John Scarborough, *Roman Medicine* (Ithaca, N.Y.: Cornell University Press, 1969).
16. Rosen, "The Hospital: Historical Sociology of a Community Institution", in Eliot Friedson, ed., *The Hospital in Modern Society* (New York: Free Press, 1963), p. 3.
17. Copeman, *Doctors and Disease*, p. 175.
18. Rosen, "The Hospital", p. 5. See also George Rosen, "Hospitals, Medical Care and Social Policy in the French Revolution" *Bulletin of the History of Medicine 30* (1956): 124–149.

19. Edwin H. Ackerknecht, *Medicine at the Paris Hospital, 1794–1848* (Baltimore: Johns Hopkins Press, 1967) pp. 149–160.
20. Ibid., p. 17.
21. Ibid., pp. 121–127.
22. Ibid., p. 39.
23. Ibid., p. 15
24. Ibid., pp. 152–153.
25. Ibid., p. 151
26. Ibid., p. 149–160.
27. Karl Marx, *The Eighteenth Brumaire of Louis Bonaparte* (New York: International Publishers, 1963).
28. W. T. Sedgewick, "An Epidemic of Typhoid Fever in Lowell, Mass.", *Boston Medical and Surgical Journal* 124, no. 17: 401.
29. Ibid., p. 398.
30. Barbara G. Rosenkrantz, *Public Health and the State. Changing Views in Massachusetts, 1842–1936* (Cambridge: Harvard University Press, 1972).
31. Stephan Thernstrom, *Poverty and Progress. Social Mobility in a Nineteenth Century City* (Cambridge: Harvard University Press, 1964).
32. For a comparison of the American and European case, see Roy G. Lubove, *The Struggle for Social Security, 1900–1935* (Cambridge: Harvard University Press, 1968), pp. 67–68.
33. Ibid., pp. 66–90.
34.. Ibid., p. 52.
35. See Daniel S. Hirschfield, *The Lost Reform. The Campaign for Compulsory Health Insurance in the U.S. from 1930 to 1943* (Cambridge: Harvard University Press, 1970), pp. 6–41.
36. Ibid., p. 94.
37. For a detailed legislative and political history of the AMA's fight against Medicare, see Richard Harris, *A Sacred Trust* (New York: Pelican, 1969).
38. But see the last section of Harris, *A Sacred Trust*, and my chapter "Action through Law".
39. For a discussion of the issues, see Vicente Navarro, "National Health Insurance and the Strategy for Change" *Health and Society, The Milbank Memorial Fund Quarterly 51*, No. 2 (1973), pp. 223–251.

Chapter 1   Control over Work

1. Harry Braverman, *Labor and Monopoly Capital* (New York: Monthly Review Press, 1975), pp. 11–24.
2. Eliot Freidson, *Profession of Medicine: A Study in the Sociology of Applied Knowledge* (New York: Dodd, Mead, 1970), p. 23.
3. Ibid., pp. 24–25.

4. Everett C. Hughes, *Men and Their Work* (New York: Free Press, 1958), pp. 78–87.
5. U.S. Supreme Court Decision, Russelton Practice Group vs County Medical Society, 1968.
6. For discussions of "profession" see A. M. Carr-Saunders and P. M. Wilson, *The Professions* (Oxford: Claredon Press, 1933), pp. 284–287; and Elliott A. Krause, *The Sociology of Occupations* (Boston: Little, Brown, 1971), pp. 75–79.
7. Freidson, *Profession of Medicine*, pp. 43–49.
8. Osler L. Peterson et al., "An Analytical Study of North Carolina General Practice, 1953–1954", *Journal of Medical Education*, 31 (1956), part 2: 130.
9. President's Report, American College of Surgeons, 1970. See also Robert S. McCleery et al., *One Life—One Physician: An Inquiry into the Medical Profession's Performance in Self-Regulation* (Washington, D.C.; Public Affairs Press, 1971), pp. 8–46.
10. McCleery et al., *One Life—One Physician*, p. 87.
11. Rose L. Coser, "Alienation and the Social Structure", in Eliot Friedson, ed., *The Hospital in Modern Society* (New York: Free Press, 1963), pp. 253–258.
12. Freidson, *Doctoring Together* (New York: Elsevier, 1975).
13. McCleery et al., *One Life—One Physician*, pp. 110–120.
14. Friedson, and Buford Rhea, "Processes of Control in a Company of Equals", *Social Problems*, 11 (1963): 119–131.
15. Lowell E. Bellin, prepared statement before U.S. Senate Finance Committee, 26 May 1976.
16. Julius B. Richmond, *Currents in American Medicine: A Developmental View of Medical Care and Education* (Cambridge: Harvard University Press, 1969), p. 71.
17. For a description (but not a critical evaluation) of the PSRO (Professional Standards Review Organization) program, see Barry Decker and Paul Bonner, *PSRO: Organization for Regional Peer Review* (Cambridge: Ballinger, 1973).
18. See the entire March 1970 issue of *Health PAC Bulletin* on women as workers and as patients in health care.
19. Peter Kong-Ming New, "The Osteopathic Students: A Study in Dilemma", in E. Gartly Jaco, ed., *Patients, Physicians, and Illness* (Glencoe: Free Press, 1957), pp. 413–421.
20. Marjorie White and James K. Skipper, Jr., "The Chiropractic Physician: A Study of Career Contingencies", *Journal of Health and Social Behavior*, 12, no. 4 (December 1971): 300–306.
21. In some states, psychologists have lobbied successfully for the passage of legislation allowing them independent rights to practice psychotherapy.

However, drug prescription and certification as well as other semiofficial activities, and many public administrative jobs in mental health are still primarily under the control of psychiatry.

22. Freidson, *Profession of Medicine*, p. 61.

23. Nursing internships are a natural consequence of another form of training—cooperative work-study—where university training is combined with alternating periods of work and study under joint college-hospital supervision. Northeastern University in Boston has one such program.

24. Anselm Strauss, "The Structure and Ideology of American Nursing", in Fred Davis, ed., *The Nursing Profession: Five Sociological Essays* (New York: Wiley, 1966), pp. 60–108.

25. For a summary article, see *Report of the American Association of Medical Colleges Task Force on Physician's Assistant Programs* (Washington, D.C.: Association of American Medical Colleges, 1970).

26. Dan C. Lortie, "Anaesthesia: From Nurse's Work to Medical Specialty", in E. Gartly Jaco, ed., *Patients, Physicians and Illness* (Glencoe: Free Press, 1958), p. 407.

27. Mark Field, *Soviet Socialized Medicine* (New York: Free Press, 1967), pp. 126–127.

28. Morris A. Horowitz and Harold M. Goldstein, *Hiring Standards for Paramedical Manpower* (Boston: Northeastern University, 1968), pp. ix–xv.

29. Field, *Soviet Socialized Medicine*, p. 128.

30. This pay difference is noted by nursing associates in many areas. It is in line with similar discrimination on grounds of sex in the pay area that is found elsewhere.

31. William J. Curran, "New Paramedical Personnel—To License or Not to License?" *New England Journal of Medicine*, 282 (1970): 1085–1086.

32. D. W. Schiff, C. H. Fraser, and H. L. Walter, "The Pediatric Nurse Practitioner in the Office of Pediatricians in Private Practice", *Pediatrics*, 44 (1969): 65–66.

33. Beyer, "Five Easy Lessons", *Journal of the American Medical Association* (1973–1974).

34. The reader is referred to the collected essays of Everett C. Hughes, *The Sociological Eye* (Chicago: Aldine-Atherton, 1971).

Chapter 2   Unions: The Past or the Future?

1. *Health PAC Bulletin*, July–August, 1970, p. 1

2. Ibid.

3. Leon J. Davis and Moe Foner, "Organization and Unionization of Health Workers in the United States: The Trade Union Perspective", *International*

Journal of Health Services, 5, no. 1 (1975): 24–25.

4. Ibid., p. 22.
5. Elinor Langner, "The Hospital Workers: The Best Contract Anywhere?" *New York Review of Books*, 16, no. 10 (3 June 1971), p. 30.
6. Ibid., p. 36–37.
7. Harold L. Wilensky, "The Professionalization of Everyone?" *American Journal of Sociology*, 70 (September 1964): 137–158.
8. For an example, see Robin F. Badgely and Samuel Wolfe, *Doctor's Strike* (Toronto: Macmillan, 1967).
9. The ability of physicians in Israel to dictate conditions was limited, however, by a strong trade-union leadership and an oversupply of physicians.
10. Langner, "Hospital Workers", pp. 36–37.
11. Thomas Bodenheimer, *Health PAC Bulletin*, July–August 1970, p. 19.
12. David Handel, *Nurses and Collective Bargaining* (Chicago: University of Chicago Graduate Program in Hospital Administration, 1969).
13. Elinor Langner, "Inside the Hospital Workers' Union", *New York Review of Books*, 17, no. 9 (20 May 1971), pp. 26–27.
14. Langner, "Hospital Workers", p. 35.
15. Barbara and John Ehrenreich, "Hospital Workers: Class Conflicts in the Making", *International Journal of Health Services*, 5, no. 1 (1975): 45.
16. Robert K. Match et al., "Unionization, Strikes, Threatened Strikes, and Hospitals—The View from Hospital Management", *International Journal of Health Services*, 5, no. 1 (1975): 30.
17. Ibid.
18. Ehrenreich and Ehrenreich, "Hospital Workers", p. 50.
19. James O'Connor, *The Fiscal Crisis of the State* (New York: St. Martin's Press, 1974).
20. Robert F. Badgely, "Health Worker Strikes: Social and Economic Bases of Conflict", *International Journal of Health Services*, 5, no. 1 (1975): 9.

Chapter 3   The Critique of Service

1. Talcott Parsons, *Social Structure and Personality* (New York: Free Press of Glencoe, 1964), pp. 258–291.
2. Irving K. Zola, "Medicine as an Institution of Social Control", in Caroline Cox and Adrienne Mead, eds., *A Sociology of Medical Practice* (London: Collier-Macmillan, 1975), pp. 170–185; Ivan Illich, *Medical Nemesis* (London: Calder and Boyer, 1974).
3. For a discussion of unnecessary surgery, see Robert S. McCleery et al., *One Life—One Physician: An Inquiry into the Medical Profession's Performance in Self-Regulation* (Washington, D.C.: Public Affairs Press, 1971).

4. Thomas S. Szasz, *The Manufacture of Madness* (New York: Harper and Row, 1970), p. 193.

5. Ibid.

6. Anthony Burgess, *Clockwork Orange* (New York: Norton, 1963).

7. Mark Field, *Doctor and Patient in the Soviet Union* (Cambridge: Harvard University Press, 1957), p. 166.

8. Ibid., p. 166.

9. Szasz, *Manufacture of Madness*, pp. 207–241. And see Michael Foucault, *Madness and Civilization: A History of Insanity in the Age of Reason* (New York: Pantheon, 1965).

10. The "transference" situation is itself, of course, an expression of a superior-inferior relationship, one under criticism by modern radical therapists.

11. Joshua S. Horn, *Away With All Pests: An English Surgeon in People's China 1954–1969* (New York: Monthly Review Press, 1969), p. 53.

12. Ibid.

13. Ellen Frankfort, *Vaginal Politics* (New York: Quadrangle Books, 1972), pp. 35, 65, 204–208.

14. Ibid., p. xii.

15. Ibid., p. xxxv.

16. Ibid., pp. 127–140. But note that each case is different and a radical operation may be necessary in a given case. But what is of primary importance is that the options and risks be stated to the woman; this is not the usual practice.

17. Ibid., p. 105.

18. Boston Women's Health Collective, *Our Bodies, Ourselves*. (New York: Simon and Schuster, 1972).

19. New programs to control health care costs for those on public support, while in the hospital (the PSRO program) often tend to discriminate against the elderly. More likely to be chronically ill and less responsive to treatment, they are more frequently transferred out of hospitals into nursing homes than younger, middle-class patients on private insurance such as Blue Cross. See Chapter 8, "Action through Law".

20. See Emily Mumford, *Interns* (Cambridge: Harvard University Press, 1969) for a discussion of this issue.

21. Julius A. Roth and Elizabeth M. Eddy, *Rehabilitation for the Unwanted* (Chicago: Aldine, 1967).

22. See Mary A. Mendelson, *Tender Loving Greed* (New York: World, 1974).

23. Richard Harris, *A Sacred Trust* (Baltimore: Penguin Books, 1969), pp. 141–143.

24. Lyle Saunders, *Cultural Difference and Medical Care* (New York: Russell Sage, 1954), pp. 237–238.

25. Mark Zborowski, "Cultural Components in Response to Pain", *Journal of Social Issues* 8 (1952): 16–30.

26. Frantz Fanon, *A Dying Colonialism* (New York: Monthly Review Press, 1965), pp. 121–145.
27. Joseph Bensman and Bernard Rosenberg, *Mass, Class and Bureaucracy: The Evolution of Contemporary Society* (Englewood Cliffs, N.J.: Prentice-Hall, 1963), pp. 267–268.
28. Robert Michels, *Political Parties*, trans. E. and C. Paul (Glencoe: Free Press, 1949).
29. Marx's concept was that of "oriental despotism", where the state owns all and oppresses all economically.
30. Peter Blau, *Dynamics of Bureaucracy* (Chicago: University of Chicago Press, 1963).
31. Harry Cohen, *Demonics of Bureaucracy* (Ames, Iowa: Iowa State University Press, 1965), p. 227.
32. Michael Crozier, *The Bureaucratic Phenomenon* (Chicago: University of Chicago Press, 1964).
33. Anselm Strauss et al., "The Hospital as a Negotiated Order", in Eliot Friedson, ed., *The Hospital in Modern Society* (New York: Free Press, 1963), pp. 147–169.
34. Robert K. Merton, *Social Theory and Social Structure* (Glencoe, N.Y.: Free Press, 1968).
35. Rose L. Coser, "Alienation and the Social Structure: A Case Analysis of a Hospital", in Eliot Friedson, ed., *The Hospital in Modern Society*, pp. 231–265.
36. George Annis, *The Rights of Hospital Patients* (New York: Dutton, 1976).
37. Julius A. Roth, *Timetables: Structuring the Passage of Time in Hospitals and Other Careers* (Indianapolis: Bobbs-Merrill, 1963).
38. Illich, *Medical Nemesis*, p. 49.
39. Ibid., p. 50.
40. Ibid., p. 174–208.
41. Vicente Navarro, "The Industrialization of Fetishism or the Fetishism of Industrialization: A Critique of Ivan Illich", *Social Science and Medicine*, 9, no. 7 (1975): 351–363.

Chapter 4 The American System: Ideology and Fact

1. For a discussion of the Social Darwinist ideology ("survival of the fittest"), see Richard Hofstadter, *Social Darwinism in American Thought* (New York: Braziller, 1969).
2. Eli Ginzberg and the Conservation of Human Resources Staff, *Urban Health Services: The Case of New York* (New York: Columbia University Press, 1971), p. 10.
3. Ibid., p. 27.

4. See Jean Meynaud, *Technocracy*, trans. Paul Barnes (New York: Free Press, 1969). And see also Guy Benveniste, *The Politics of Expertise* (Berkeley: Glendessary Press, 1972).

5. David D. Rutstein, *Blueprint for Medical Care* (Cambridge: MIT Press, 1974).

6. Marie R. Haug and Marvin B. Sussman, "Professional Autonomy and the Revolt of the Client", *Social Problems*, 17 (Fall 1969): 153–161.

7. Barbara G. Rosenkrantz, *Public Health and the State. Changing Views in Massachusetts 1842–1936* (Cambridge: Harvard University Press, 1972), pp. 128–176.

8. Dell S. Wright, "Intergovernmental Relations: An Analytical Overview", *American Academy of Political and Social Science*, 416 (November 1974): 1–16.

9. Ibid., p. 16.

10. Floyd Hunter, *Community Power Structure. A Study of Decision Makers* (New York: Doubleday, 1963).

11. Robert A. Dahl, *Who Governs?* (New Haven: Yale University Press, 1961).

12. Edward C. Banfield and James Q. Wilson, *City Politics* (Cambridge: Harvard University Press, 1967).

13. The Joint Commission on the Accreditation of Hospitals has a special division for accrediting community facilities.

14. On the other hand, union support is strong at present for comprehensive national health insurance, of the kind favored in the Kennedy bills of the early 1970s.

15. But the Health Research Group has provided consultative support to local community groups who *do* act in specific local struggles.

16. A discussion on the relationship between population location change and health care systems can be found in the article by Alice M. Yohalem and Charles M. Brecher, "The University Medical Center and the Metropolis: A Working Paper", in Eli Ginzberg and Alice M. Yohalem, eds., *The University Medical Center and the Metropolis* (New York: Macy, 1974), pp. 5–9.

17. See William A. Rushing and George T. Wade, "Community-Structural Constraints on the Distribution of Physicians", *Health Services Research*, 8, no. 4 (Winter 1973): 283–297.

18. Ibid., p. 294.

19. Yohalem and Brecher, in Ginzberg and Yohalem, eds., *University Medical Center*, p. 11.

20. Michel Zuboff, "Emergency Room Services", in Ginzberg et al., eds., *Urban Health Services*, p. 122.

21. Leon S. Robertson et al., *Changing the Medical Care System* (New York: Praeger, 1974), p. 8.

22. Emily Mumford, *Interns* (Cambridge: Harvard University Press, 1969), pp. 54–56, 94–98.

23. Mary Mendelson, *Tender Loving Greed* (New York: World, 1974), p. 29.
24. See Claude Levi-Strauss, *Anthropologie Structurale* (Paris: Adler, 1968).
25. Sol Levine and Paul E. White, "The Community of Health Organizations", in Howard S. Freeman, Sol Levine, and Leo G. Reader, *Handbook of Medical Sociology* (New York: Prentice-Hall, 1963), p. 341.
26. Stephen M. Shortell, "Patterns of Referral Among Internists in Private Practice: A Social Exchange Model", *Journal of Health and Social Behavior*, 14, no. 4 (December 1973): 335–347.

Chapter 5   The American System: Haves and Have-Nots

1. Leon S. Robertson, et al., *Changing the Medical Care System* (New York: Praeger, 1974), p. 9.
2. For a summary of these reasons, see John B. McKinlay, "Some Approaches and Problems in the Study of the Use of Services", *Journal of Health and Social Behavior*, 13, no. 2 (June 1972): 115–151.
3. For a short history of the OEO Neighborhood Health Centers program, see Sar A. Levitan, *The Great Society's Poor Law* (Baltimore: Hopkins, 1969), pp. 191–206.
4. Ibid., p. 194.
5. Ibid., p. 199.
6. Robert M. Hollister, *From Consumer Participation to Community Control of Neighborhood Health Centers*, Ph.D. dissertation, MIT, Department of Urban Planning, 1971.
7. The literature of the radical populist movement is especially relevant to this issue. See the items listed under neighborhood health centers in Ken Rosenberg and Gordon Schiff, eds., *The Politics of Health Care* (Boston: Medical Committee for Human Rights, 1971), pp. 10–12.
8. Langston et al., *Study to Evaluate the OEO Neighborhood Health Center Program at Selected Centers*, vol. II, (Rockville, Md.: Geomet, Inc., 1972), p. vi.
9. George A. Silver, *Family Medical Care. A Report on the Family Health Maintenance Demonstration* (Cambridge: Harvard University Press, 1963), esp. p. 109.
10. Charles H. Goodrich, Margaret C. Olendski, and George G. Reader, *Welfare Medical Care* (Cambridge: Harvard University Press, 1970), p. 214.
11. Robertson et al, *Changing Medical Care*, p. 24.
12. Ibid., pp. v–vi.
13. Robert and Rosemary Stevens, *Welfare Medicine in America. A Case Study of Medicaid* (New York: Free Press, 1974), pp. 73–128.
14. Ibid., p. 114.

15. U.S. Government Statistics, HEW, National Center for Health Services Research, Rockville, Md., 1971.
16. See Lowell E. Bellin, "*Realpolitik* in the Health Care Arena: Standard-setting of Professional Services", *American Journal of Public Health*, 59 (1969): 820–824.
17. Stevens and Stevens, *Welfare Medicine in America*, p. 199.
18. Robertson et al., *Changing Medical Care*, p. 55.
19. Alice M. Yohalem and Charles M. Brecher, "The University Medical Center and the Metropolis: A Working Paper", in Eli Ginzberg and Alice M. Yohalem, eds., *The University Medical Center and the Metropolis* (New York: Macy, 1974), p. 9.
20. This is the arrangement which Health PAC was to describe as "medical empires". See Barbara and John Ehrenreich, *The American Health Empire: Power, Profits, and Politics* (New York: Random House, 1970).
21. For a summary of these problems, see Miriam Ostow, "Affiliation Contracts", in Eli Ginzberg and the Conservation of Human Resources Staff, *Urban Health Services: The Case of New York* (New York: Columbia University Press, 1971), pp. 96–118.
22. Charles M. Brecher, "The Process of Regionalization: The Bronx", in Ginsberg et al., *Urban Health Services*, p. 177.
23. Miriam Ostow, "Affiliation Contracts", in Ginsberg et al., *Urban Health Services*, p. 113.
24. See, for example, Clifford Gurney, "Five Communities: The University of Chicago Medical Center", in Eli Ginsberg and Alice M. Yohalem, eds., *University Medical Center and the Metropolis* (New York: Macy, 1974), pp. 61–64.
25. Ibid., p. 69.

Chapter 6   The American System: Political Economy

1. For a discussion of the monopoly-creation process, and its consequences for the consumer, see Paul Baran and Paul Sweezy, *Monopoly Capital* (New York: Monthly Review Press, 1966).
2. For the nature of licensure as a *monopoly* in medicine, versus its less restrictive character in other occupations, see Office of the Secretary for Health and Scientific Affairs, HEW, *Report on Licensure and Related Health Personnel Credentialling* (Washington, D.C.: HEW, 1971). See also Chapter 8 of this book, on regulation as an approach.
3. For an overall discussion of this strategy, see Aaron Wildavsky, *The Politics of the Budgetary Process*, 2nd ed., (Boston: Little, Brown, 1974).
4. John A. DeLuca, "The Politics of Budget Allocation for Health and Welfare

in San Francisco", in Douglass Cater and Philip R. Lee, *Politics of Health* (New York: Medcom Press, 1972), p. 117.

5. Attempts to control the rising costs of care through regulation are considered in Chapter 8 of this book.

6. An excellent introduction to the group of strategies in use here is Guy Benveniste, *The Politics of Expertise* (Berkeley: Glendessary Press, 1972).

7. Rashi Fein, *The Doctor Shortage* (Washington, D.C.: Brookings Institution, 1967), p. 132.

8. Ibid., p. 97.

9. Ibid., p. 16.

10. Harold M. Goldstein and Morris A. Horowitz, *Restructuring Paramedical Occupations: A Case Study*. Department of Economics, Northeastern University, January 1972, p. 52: "There is indeed a great degree of overlap in the performance of various functions irrespective of the degree of difficulty and the educational exposure, formal or otherwise, by various categories of paramedical personnel (RN's, LPN's, NA's, orderlies) at the Cambridge Hospital".

11. The official viewpoint here by the academic wing of the nursing profession is that this strategy increases the quality of the education. But "birth control" strategies are *usually* justified in this way. Extra information is conveyed in the extra two years of training, but other social consequences follow from such an approach.

12. William J. Bicknell, Diana C. Walsh, and Marsha M. Tanner, "Substantial or Decorative? Physicians' Assistants and Nurse Practitioners in the United States", *Lancet*, 2 (23 November 1974): 1244.

13. Harold Margulies and Lucille S. Bloch, *Foreign Medical Graduates in the United States* (Cambridge: Harvard University Press, 1969), p. 75. From June 1, 1966 to June 30, 1967 there were 8,540 foreign medical graduates in the nation and 7,743 graduates of U.S. medical schools, each group having entered work during this period by immigration or graduation from school.

14. Ibid., pp. 71–72.

15. R. M. Titmuss, *The Gift Relationship. From Human Blood to Social Policy* (New York: Pantheon, 1971), p. 12.

16. J. Garott Allen, "Advantages of Volunteer Blood Donors", *New England Journal of Medicine* 291, no. 25 (1974): 1365.

17. D. M. Surgenor, "Progress Toward a National Blood System", *New England Journal of Medicine*, 291, no. 1 (4 July 1974): 19.

18. This is seemingly a technical point, but it is not in terms of eventual results. If the government asks *others* to do something, the burden is on *them* to do it; if the government accepts direct responsibility (which it did not do here), then it can be held legally accountable. The entire policy is one of the "wouldn't-it-be-lovely" kind, with no teeth and, as events soon indicated, no real willingness to push for results. Longer-term change may come through

new regulations in the area of blood collection and distribution for programs supported with government money. But the problems here—of the limits of regulation—are always important. Again, see Chapter 8.

19. Drug companies make their main profits in this area through obtaining blood fractions—plasma, platelets, etc., from outdated blood, which is, of course, more available in an inefficient system than an efficient one.

20. Surgenor, *National Blood System*, p. 22.

21. Ibid., p. 19.

22. *American Medical News*, 4 November 1974, p. 18.

23. U.S. Congress, House Committee on Interstate and Foreign Commerce. *An Overview of Medical Malpractice 94th Congress*, 1st Session (Washington, D.C.: U.S. Government Printing Office, 1975).

24. *American Medical News*, 4 November 1974, p. 18.

25. U.S. Congress, *An Overview of Medical Malpractice*, pp. 11–12.

26. "Medical Liability Outlook Bleak: Rising Premiums, Fewer Insurers, and More Suits", *American Medical News*, 17, no. 43 (4 November 1974): 20.

27. *American Medical News*, 3 February 1975, p. 8.

28. "Malpractice Problems Widen", *American Medical News*, 18, no. 5 (3 February 1975): 8.

29. George J. Annas, "Medical Malpractice: Are the Doctors Right?" *Trial*, 10, no. 4 (July–August 1974): 59–63.

30. R. Kirschner, letter to *American Medical News*, 18, no. 2 (13 January 1975).

31. *American Medical News*, 13 January 1975, p. 4.

32. *American Medical News*, 3 February 1975, p. 1, 8.

33. See Summary, Final Report of the National Commission on Workmen's Compensation Laws, *Congressional Record*, 1 August 1972, at § 12332.

34. For a good article on the development of prepaid group practice, see Tom Bodenheimer, "Patterns of American Ambulatory Care", *Inquiry*, 7, no. 3: 26–37.

35. David Mechanic, "A Note on the Concept of Health Maintenance Organizations", in D. Mechanic, *Public Expectations and Health Care: Essays on the Changing Organization of Health Services* (New York: Wiley, 1972) p. 107.

36. Robert W. Geist, "Incentive Bonuses in Repayment Plans", *New England Journal of Medicine*, 291, no. 24 (December 1974): 12.

37. Doris L. Wagner, "Issues in the Provision of Health Care for All", *American Journal of Public Health*, 63, no. 6 (June 1973): 481.

38. See, for example, "Harvard Health Plan Blushes Crimson", *Health PAC Bulletin*, January 1971, pp. 2–5.

39. For an earlier example of this ostracism, see Roy Penchansky, Beryl Safford, and Henry Simmons, "Medical Practice in a Group Setting: The Russelton Experiment", in Roy Penchansky, ed., *Health Services Administration: Policy Cases and the Case Method* (Cambridge: Harvard University Press, 1968), p. 194.

40. Source: HEW, National Center for Health Service Research, Rockville, Md.
41. Mechanic, "Health Maintenance Organizations", pp. 102–111.
42. Ibid., p. 110.
43. For a general discussion of the medical-industrial complex, see Elliott A. Krause, "Health and the Politics of Technology", *Inquiry*, 8 (September 1971): 51–59.
44. Myers, quoted in Krause, "Health and Politics of Technology", p. 52.
45. Green, quoted in Krause, "Health and Politics of Technology", p. 59.
46. See International Commission on Radiological Protection, Committee III, *Protection of the Patient in X-ray Diagnosis; A Report* (New York: Pergamon Press, 1970).
47. *Harvard Gazette*, 14 February 1975, p. 1.
48. *Harvard Crimson*, 161, no. 11 (14 February 1975): 1.

Chapter 7   Power, Participation, and Planning

1. See Max Rheinstein, ed., *Max Weber on Law in Economy and Society*, translated by Edward Shils and Max Rheinstein (Cambridge: Harvard University Press, 1966): 334–338.
2. Ibid., pp. 341.
3. For his discussion of the "ideal type" analytical approach, see Max Weber, *The Methodology of the Social Sciences*, translated and edited by Edward A. Shils and Henry A. Finch (N.Y.: Free Press, 1949).
4. See Nicos P. Mouzelis, *Organisation and Bureaucracy* (Chicago: Aldine, 1968), pp. 7–8.
5.. See Raymond Vernon, ed., *Big Business and The State: Changing Relations in Western Europe* (Cambridge: Harvard University Press, 1974).
6. For a discussion of this process in the area of the regulation of health care, see Chapter 8.
7. Charles C. Edwards, "The Federal Involvement in Health: A Personal View of Current Problems and Future Needs", *New England Journal of Medicine*, 292, no. 11 (13 March 1975): 559–562.
8. For a basic discussion of this essential difference between the English parliamentary form and the American form, see Samuel Beer, *Modern British Politics; A Study of Parties and Pressure Groups* 2nd ed. (London: Faber, 1969).
9. There has been a recent trend to exert greater control on spending within the National Health Service, with special attention to equalizing spending between urban and rural areas, but not on regulating the profits of the English

drug industry. See "Capital Spending on the Health Service", *Lancet*, 1, no. 7907 (1975): 625.

10. For a discussion of labor unions under Soviet conditions, see Alex Inkeles, *Social Change in Soviet Russia* (Cambridge: Harvard University Press, 1968).

11. Mark V. Nadel, *The Unorganized Interests: Consumers in the Policy Process* (Baltimore: Hopkins, 1970), dissertation summary, p. 1.

12. Peter K-M New, Richard N. Hessler, and Phillis Y. Bagwell, "Consumer Control and Public Accountability", paper presented before the American Anthropological Association, Toronto, Canada, December 1972, p. 15.

13. W. I. Thomas, Morris Janowitz, ed., *On Social Organization and Social Personality* (Chicago: University of Chicago Press, 1966).

14. Jean Meynaud, *Technocracy*, trans Paul Barnes (New York: Free Press, 1969), pp. 21–70.

15. Ibid., pp. 184–186.

16. C. Wright Mills, *The Power Elite* (New York: Oxford University Press, 1956).

17. Daniel P. Moynihan, *Maximum Feasible Misunderstanding. Community Action in the War on Poverty* (New York: Free Press, 1969) pp. 22–23.

18. A. M. Carr-Saunders and P. M. Wilson, *The Professions* (Oxford: Clarendon Press, 1933).

19. Eliot Freidson, *Profession of Medicine: A Study in the Sociology of Applied Knowledge* (New York: Dodd, Mead, 1970), p. 24.

20. Alan Altshuler, *The Planning Process*, unpublished mss, MIT, pp. 455–470.

21. Bernard J. Frieden and James Peters, "Urban Planning and Health Services: Opportunities for Cooperation", *Journal of the American Institute of Planners*, 36, no. 2 (1970): 82–95.

22. Richard C. Wood and V. V. Almendinger, *1400 Governments. The Political Economy of the New York Metropolitan Region* (Cambridge: Harvard University Press, 1961).

23. Robert R. Alford, "The Political Economy of Health Care: Dynamics Without Change", *Politics and Society*, 2, no. 1 (1972): 143–145.

24. Elliott A. Krause, "Health and the Politics of Technology", *Inquiry*, 8 (September 1971): 51–59.

25. Frieden and Peters, "Urban Planning and Health Services".

26. Ibid., pp. 86, 88, 90.

27. U.S. Congress, "Hospital Construction: Presidential Veto Overridden", *Congressional Quarterly Almanac* (1970): 223.

28. Minnesota Legislative Research Committee, *The Minnesota Use of Hill-Burton Funds 1948–1962* (St. Paul: State of Minnesota, 1962), p. 12.

29. U.S. Supreme Court Decision, 1 November 1963, upholding decision of U.S. Court of Appeals, by refusal to consider appeal.

30. M. G. Rose, "The Hill-Burton Act—The Interim Regulation and Service to the Poor: A Study in Public Interest Litigation", *Clearinghouse Review*, 6, no. 6 (1972): 309–315.

31. Charles Singer and E. A. Underwood, *A Short History of Medicine* (New York: Oxford University Press, 1962).

32. Edward M. Kennedy, Testimony, Hearings, U.S. Senate Committee on Labor and Public Welfare, Subcommittee on Health on S.2182, Medical Care Facilities Construction and Modernization Act of 1969 (Washington, D.C.: U.S. Government Printing Office, 1969), pp. 191–196.

33. U.S. Department of Health, Education, and Welfare, *Hill-Burton Highlights* (Washington, D.C.: U.S. Government Printing Office, 1969), pp. 5, 15, 19.

34. Singer and Underwood, *A Short History of Medicine*, pp. 494–515.

35. Joint Commission on Mental Illness and Health, *Action for Mental Health*, Final Report, 1961 (New York: Basic Books, 1961).

36. U.S. Department of Health, Education, and Welfare, Public Health Service, "Guidelines for the Federal Grant-in-Aid Program to Support Mental Health Planning", in *Digest: State Mental Health Planning Grant Proposals* (Bethesda, Maryland: National Institute of Mental Health, 22 January 1963), pp. 54–62.

37. Public Law 88–164, Section 204 (3), 88th Congress, 31 October 1963.

38. Don C. Klein, *Community Dynamics and Mental Health* (New York: John Wiley and Sons, 1968).

39. Ibid., p. 199.

40. Meynaud, *Technocracy*, pp. 207–247.

41. H. P. Halpert, *Comprehensive Mental Health Planning in Six States* (Chevy Chase, Maryland: National Institute of Mental Health, 1967), pp. 2–46.

42. Ibid., pp. 42–46.

43. See Moynihan, *Maximum Feasible Misunderstanding*, pp. 75–101.

44. Edgar S. Kahn and Barry A. Passett, eds., *Citizens Participation: Effecting Community Change* (New York: Praeger, 1971).

45. Office of Economic Opportunity, Office of Health Affairs, *History of the OEO Comprehensive Health Service Program* (Washington, D.C.: Office of Economic Opportunity, January 1971), pp. 1–2.

46. Barbara and John Ehrenreich, *The American Health Empire: Power, Profits, and Politics* (New York: Random House, 1970), pp. 214–231.

47. The same dynamics operate here as with the physician in the doctor-patient relationship. We have discussed this previously under the topic of "professional dominance".

48. Economic Opportunity Act of 1964, Section 222a (4), as amended on 23 December 1967.
49. Ehrenreich and Ehrenreich, *The American Health Empire*, p. 299.
50. Arthur D. Little, Inc., *A Study of the Regional Medical Program* (Cambridge: Arthur D. Little, November 1970), p. 12.
51. Public Law 39–239, § 900c, 89th Congress, 6 October 1965.
52. *U.S. Code and Administrative News*, 89th Congress, First Session, p. 904, 1966.
53. Regional Medical Program Service, *Statement of Mission and Priorities: Regional Medical Program*. Proceedings, Conference of Coordinators and Chairmen of Regional Medical Programs. (Regional Medical Programs Service, Health Services and Mental Health Administration, Rockville, Maryland, 1969).
54. Ibid., p. 165.
55. Ibid., mission statement, Introduction.
56. Ibid., p. 195.
57. Arthur D. Little, Inc., *Regional Medical Program*, p. 12.
58. Ibid., p. 34.
59. Public Law 89–749, § 2a.
60. Charles Roseman, "Problems and Prospects for Comprehensive Health Planning", *American Journal of Public Health*, 62 (1972): 16–19.
61. Public Law 89-749, § 3a–2–b.
62. D. Anderson and N. N. Anderson, *Comprehensive Health Planning in the States: A Current Status Report* (Minneapolis: Health Services Research Center, American Rehabilitation Foundation, 1969), p. 3.
63. Organization for Social and Technological Innovation (OSTI), *Surveys of Selected 314 (a) and Areawide 314 (b) Comprehensive Health Planning Agencies* (OSTI: Cambridge, 1971), pp. 6–7.
64. Donald B. Ardell, "Public Regional Councils and Comprehensive Health Planning: A Partnership?", *Journal of the American Institute of Planners*, 36 (1970): 393–404.
65. OSTI, *Health Planning Agencies*, pp. 19–20.
66. R. Morris and G. Eggert, "Does Comprehensive Health Planning Exist?", unpublished paper, MIT student assignment, 1971, p. 11.
67. Robert Hollister and W. Shapiro, *Boston Area Health Care Services and Facilities Planning*, unpublished, n.d.
68. William J. Curran, "Health Planning Agencies: A Legal Crisis?", *American Journal of Public Health* 60, no. 2 (1970): 359–360.
69. Community Health, Inc., *Comprehensive Health Planning Expectations Project*, working paper, Meeting V, p. 2.
70. OSTI, *Health Planning Agencies*, pp. 213, 229.

71. Linton, Mields, and Coston, Inc., *Factors Affecting Health Planning in Large Urban Areas* (Washington, D.C.: Linton, Mields and Coston, 1972), p. 23.

72. Community Health, Inc., *Comprehensive Health Planning Expectations Project*, p. 27.

73. Gwynn Williams, as quoted in Eugene Genovese, "On Antonio Gramsci", in Eugene Genovese [collected essays] *In Red and Black: Marxian Explorations in Southern and Afro-American History*. (New York: Pantheon, 1968), p. 406.

74. Elliott A. Krause, "Recent Trends in Planning as Ideology: A Critique of Anderson and Robins". *International Journal of Health Services*, 6, no. 4 (1976, in press).

75. Genovese, "On Antonio Gramsci", p. 407.

Chapter 8   Action through Law

1. The Nader reports, often accused of being "sensational" in style, are usually written with this media impact in mind, to be "quotable" for a mass audience which then in turn can help put leverage on politicians to do something about the problems. Also, the facts sometimes *are* sensational and shocking.

2. See Daniel Callahan, *Abortion: Law, Choice and Morality* (New York: Macmillan, 1970) and John T. Noonan, *The Morality of Abortion: Legal and Historical Perspectives* (Cambridge: Harvard University Press, 1970).

3. For the role of the women's movement in abortion law reform, see Boston Women's Health Book Collective, *Our Bodies, Ourselves*, 2nd ed., revised (New York: Simon and Schuster, 1976).

4. Papal Encyclical, Pope Paul 23rd, "Humanae Vitae".

5. U.S. Supreme Court Reports, Roe vs Wade, 35 L Ed 2d, p. 148.

6. News reports on the Edelin case, on day of announcement of verdict, *Boston Globe, New York Times, Washington Post*.

7. F. J. Ingelfinger, "The Edelin Trial Fiasco", *New England Journal of Medicine*, 292, no. 13 (1975): 697.

8. Stephen P. Strickland, "Medical Research: Public Policy and Power Politics", in Douglass Cater and Philip R. Lee, eds., *Politics of Health* (New York: Medcom Press, 1973), p. 78.

9. Ibid., p. 79.

10. Stephen P. Strickland, *Politics, Science, and Dread Disease. A Short History of United States Medical Research Policy* (Cambridge: Harvard University Press, 1972), p. 278.

11. Ibid., p. 283.

12. Daniel S. Greenberg, "Progress in Cancer Research: Don't Say It Isn't So", *New England Journal of Medicine*, 292, no. 13 (1975): 708.
13. Ibid.
14. R. Noll, *Reforming Regulation. An Evaluation of the Ash Council Proposals* (Washington, D.C.: Brookings Institution, 1971).
15. L. Jaffe and N. Nathanson, *Administrative Law: Cases and Materials* (Boston: Little, Brown, 1968).
16. H. Friendly, *The Federal Administrative Agencies: The Need for Better Definition of Standards* (Cambridge: Harvard University Press, 1962).
17. R. Fellmeth, ed., *The Interstate Commerce Omission: Ralph Nader's Study Group Report on the Interstate Commerce Commission and Transportation* (New York: Grossman 1969); M. Green, B. Moore Jr., and B. Wasserstein, *The Closed Enterprise System: Ralph Nader's Study Group Report on Antitrust Enforcement* (New York: Grossman, 1972); M. Green, ed., *The Monopoly Makers. Ralph Nader's Study Group Report on Regulation and Competition* (New York: Grossman, 1973).
18. J. Goulden, *The Superlawyers. The Small and Powerful World of the Great Washington Law Firms* (New York: Weybright and Talley, 1971).
19. Eliot Freidson, *Profession of Medicine. A Study in the Sociology of Applied Knowledge* (New York: Dodd, Mead, 1970).
20. Elton Rayack, *Professional Power and American Medicine: The Economics of the American Medical Association* (Cleveland, Ohio: World Publishing Co., 1967).
21. Robert R. Alford, "The Political Economy of Health Care: Dynamics Without Change", *Politics and Society*, 2, no. 1 (1972): 143–145. See also Robert R. Alford, *Health Care Politics. Ideological and Interest Group Barriers to Reform* (Chicago: University of Chicago Press, 1975). See especially his discussion in Chapter 1, "Health Care Reform and Structural Interests", pp. 1–20.
22. C. Schlicke, "American Surgery's Noblest Experiment". President's Address, 80th Annual Meeting, Western Surgical Association, Rochester, Minnesota, Nov. 16, 1972.
23. J. Hoppock, "The Joint Commission's Role", paper presented to the New Jersey Hospital Association, North Brunswick, New Jersey, 28 February 1973.
24. Massachusetts House Bill 6120 (1973), on centralized regulation in a division of "health systems regulation" at state level. Defeated.
25. Elliott A. Krause, "Health and the Politics of Technology", *Inquiry*, 8 (September 1971): 51–59.
26. Elliott A. Krause, *The Sociology of Occupations*, Chapter 6 (Boston: Little, Brown, 1971).

27. R. Derbyshire, *Medical Licensure and Discipline in the United States* (Baltimore: Johns Hopkins, 1969).
28. Robert S. McCleery et al., *One Life—One Physician. An Inquiry into the Medical Profession's Performance in Self-Regulation* (Washington, D.C.: Public Affairs Press, 1971).
29. Office of the Assistant Secretary for Health and Scientific Affairs, HEW, *Report on Licensure and Related Health Personnel Credentialling* (Washington, D.C.: HEW, 1971).
30. Derbyshire, *Medical Licensure*, p. 35.
31. Harris Cohen, "Professional Licensure, Organizational Behavior, and the Public Interest", paper delivered at the Annual Meeting, American Public Health Association, Atlantic City, New Jersey, 14 November 1972.
32. Harris Cohen and L. Miike, "Toward a More Responsive System of Professional Licensure", *International Journal of Health Services*, 4 (1974): 267.
33. Ibid., p. 268.
34. Ibid.
35. Joint Commission on the Accreditation of Hospitals, Procedure for Retrospective Medical Care Audit in Hospitals. *Trustee-Administrator-Physician Institutes*. Joint Commission, Chicago, 1972.
36. Joseph A. Page and Mary-win O'Brien, *Bitter Wages. Ralph Nader's Study Group Report on Disease and Injury on the Job* (New York: Grossman, 1973).
37. Paul Brodeur, *The Expendable Americans* (New York: Viking, 1974).
38. Rachel Scott, *Muscle and Blood* (New York: Dutton, 1974).
39. Elliott A. Krause, "Health Planning as a Managerial Ideology", *International Journal of Health Services*, 3, no. 3 (1973): 445–463. [This is reprinted here with minor changes as Chapter 7].
40. Harris Cohen, "Regulating Health Care Facilities: The Certificate of Need Process Reexamined", *Inquiry*, 10 (September 1973): 3–9.
41. William J. Curran, *National Survey and Analysis of Certification-of-Need Laws: Health Planning and Regulation in State Legislatures, 1972* (Chicago: American Hospital Association, 1973), p. 27. See also C. Havighurst, "Regulation of Health Facilities and Services by 'Certificate of Need'", *Virginia Law Review*, 59 (October 1973): 1143–1232.
42. See Elliott A. Krause, "Planning as Ideology: A Critique of Anderson and Robins", *International Journal of Health Services*, 6, no. 4 (fall 1976, in press).
43. J. Turner, *The Chemical Feast: Ralph Nader's Study Group Report on the Food and Drug Administration* (New York: Grossman, 1970).
44. M. Silverman and P. Lee, *Pills, Profits and Politics* (Berkeley: University of California Press, 1974).
45. R. M. Titmuss, *The Gift Relationship. From Human Blood to Social Policy* (New York: Pantheon, 1971).

46. D. M. Surgenor, "Progress toward a National Blood System", *New England Journal of Medicine*, 291, no. 1 (4 July 1974): 17–22.
47. Staff estimate, National Center for Health Service Research, HEW, 31 January 1975.
48. Public Law 92–603, Section 1152 (a).
49. Harris Cohen, "Regulatory Politics: The Case of Medical Care Review and Public Law 92–603", paper presented at the Annual Meeting, American Political Science Association, 5 September 1973.
50. Staff estimate, Office of Professional Standards Review, HEW, 31 January 1975.
51. Three separate, informal, and "not-for-attribution" opinions by staffers at HEW, Office of Professional Standards Review, the Bureau of Quality Assurance, and Legal Division, 31 January 1975.
52. Association of American Physicians and Surgeons et al. v. Caspar Weinberger (HEW), U.S. District Court, Northern Illinois, Civil 73 C 1653, 1973; Texas Medical Association v. Caspar Weinberger (HEW), U.S. District Court, Western Texas, Civil A–74–CA–102, 1974.
53. Office of the Secretary of Health, Education, and Welfare, Legislative History of Professional Standards Review Organization, Provisions of the Social Security Act Amendments, November 1973.
54. P. Caper, "The Meaning of Quality in Medical Care", *New England Journal of Medicine*, 291 (21 November 1974): 1136–1137.

Chapter 9   The Sickening Environment

1. Frances Fox Piven and Richard A. Cloward, *Regulating the Poor: The Functions of Public Relief* (New York: Pantheon, 1971), p. xiii.
2. Ibid., Entire book, esp. concluding chapter.
3. Monroe Lerner, "Social Differences in Physical Health", in John Kosa, Aaron Antonovsky, and Irving K. Zola, *Poverty and Health. A Sociological Analysis*. (Cambridge: Harvard University Press, 1969), pp. 69–112.
4. Marc Fried, "Social Differences in Mental Health", in Kosa, Antonovsky, and Zola, *Poverty and Health*, p. 113.
5. Elie Shenour, *The Malnourished Mind* (New York: Doubleday, 1974), p. 52.
6. Nick Kotz, *Let Them Eat Promises: The Politics of Hunger in America* (New York: Doubleday, 1971), p. 35.
7. See especially Kotz, *Let Them Eat Promises*, pp. 80–97.
8. Ibid., p. 24.
9. Ibid., p. 163.
10. The political role of the FBI in such domestic issues is, as of 1976, becoming

clearer as more such instances come to light. For the Study itself see Citizens' Board of Inquiry into Hunger and Malnutrition in the United States, *Hunger USA* (Washington, D.C.: New Community Press, 1968).

11. For an example of a screening program, see Massachusetts Advocacy Center, *State of Danger: Childhood Lead Paint Poisoning in Massachusetts* (Boston: Mass. Advocacy Center, 1974).

12. Robert Coles, *The South Goes North* (Boston: Little, Brown, 1971), p. 27.

13. M. Harvey Brenner, *Mental Illness and the Economy* (Cambridge: Harvard University Press, 1973).

14. Lerner, "Social Differences in Physical Health", in Kosa, Antonovsky, and Zola, *Poverty and Health*, pp. 79–91.

15. J. A. Page and M. W. O'Brien, *Bitter Wages. Ralph Nader's Study Group Report on Disease and Injury on the Job* (New York: Grossman, 1973), p. 3.

16. U.S. House of Representatives, Hearings on HR 14816, The Occupational Health and Safety Act of 1968, pp. 1292–1293.

17. HEW, *Occupational Disease. The Silent Enemy* (Washington, D.C.: HEW, 1968), p. 1.

18. Commerce Clearing House, *President's Report on Occupational Safety and Health* (1972), p. 111.

19. Page and O'Brien, *Bitter Wages*, pp. xi–xii, 15–17, 165–166.

20. Ibid., p. 27.

21. Ibid., p. 31.

22. Ibid., pp. 32–37.

23. Ibid., pp. 41–43.

24. Anna Baetjer, *Women in Industry: Their Health and Efficiency* (Philadelphia: Saunders, 1946), p. 255.

25. Ibid.

26. Harry Levinson, *Executive Stress* (New York: Harper and Row, 1970).

27. For a survey of these issues, see Joseph Eyer, "Hypertension as a Disease of Modern Society", *International Journal of Health Services*, 5, no. 4 (1975): p. 539.

28. For a listing and analysis of these work-related diseases, see Special Task Force to the Secretary of HEW, *Work in America* (Cambridge: MIT Press, 1973), pp. 76–91.

29. Studs, Turkel, *Working* (New York: Random House, 1972), pp. 159–163.

30. For the most recent instances of the Workmen's Compensation system, see *Summary, Final Report of the National Commission on State Workmen's Compensation Laws. Congressional Record*, 1 August 1972, at § 12332. See also Elliott A. Krause, "The Political Sociology of Rehabilitation" in Gary Albrecht, ed., *The Sociology and Social Psychology of Disability* (Pittsburgh: University of Pittsburgh Press, 1976).

31. William P. Shepard, *The Physician in Industry*, (New York: Blakiston, 1961), p. 6.

32. Page and O'Brien, *Bitter Wages*, pp. 115–136.
33. Ibid., p. 71.
34. Ibid., pp. 47–85.
35. Ibid., pp. 181–182.
36. For studies of particular industries, more in the popular vein, see Paul Brodeur, *The Expendable Americans* (New York: Viking, 1974); and Rachel Scott, *Muscle and Blood* (New York: Dutton, 1974).
37. Page and O'Brien, *Bitter Wages*, pp. 210–221. As of 1976, OSHA gathers its disease statistics by questionnaires sent to management.
38. Urban Planning Aid, Cambridge, Massachusetts, Pamphlets on occupational injury.
39. T. R. Lewis et al., "Long-Term Exposure to Auto Exhaust and Other Pollutant Mixtures", *Archives of Environmental Health*, 29, no. 2 (August 1974): 102–106.
40. John E. Esposito, *Vanishing Air: The Nader Report on Air Pollution* (New York: Grossman, 1970).
41. Constance Holden, "Environmental Action Organizations Are Suffering from Money Shortages, Lack of Commitment", *Science*, 175 (1972): 395.
42. James O'Connor, *The Fiscal Crisis of the State* (New York: St. Martin's Press, 1973).
43. Ian Gough, "State Expenditure in Advanced Capitalism", *New Left Review*, 92 (1975): 53–92.
44. For a more extensive discussion see Vicente Navarro, "Social Class, Political Power and the State, and their Implications in Medicine", Paper presented at Colloque Internationale de Sociologie Medicale, Paris, France, 6 July 1976.

Chapter 10   Who Will Make the Future?

1. Victor R. Fuchs, *Who Shall Live?* (New York: Basic Books, 1975), p. 25.
2. Sylvia Law and the Health Law Project of the University of Pennsylvania, *Blue Cross: What Went Wrong?* (New Haven: Yale University Press, 1974), pp. 59–114.
3. Ibid., pp. 31–50.
4. The Health Law project, for example, had to sue the government under the Public Information Act in order to get them to release details on the nature of the government-Blue Cross relationship in public programs for which the government had subcontracted administrative functions to Blue Cross.
5. Administrative Cost Data, 1975, Blue Cross National Headquarters, Accounting Division, Chicago, Illinois.
6. Law, *Blue Cross: What Went Wrong?*, p. xx.

7. Blue Cross National Headquarters, Chicago Office of Public Information, "What Went Wrong With *What Went Wrong?*, 1974, mimeo.

8. For a good comparative discussion of seven proposed national insurance plans, see Karen Davis, *National Health Insurance: Benefits, Costs, and Consequences* (Washington, D.C.: Brookings Institution, 1975). See also Spyros Andreopoulos, ed., *National Health Insurance: Can We Learn from Canada?* (New York: John Wiley, 1975). Of course, the author, for reasons spelled out through the book, is not as optimistic as these authors that *any* insurance plan will be a solution.

9. *American Medical News*, 3 (March 1975): 19.

10. Health Rights and Community Services Act, Draft of 27 February 1975. As of June 1975 this is the preliminary draft of a proposal for an American National Health Service, in preparation at the Institute for Policy Studies, which is intended for introduction into Congress early in 1977.

11. Ibid., "Findings and Declarations of Purpose", pp. 1–2.

Index

O'Brien, Mary-Win, 287–8
Occupational disease, 307–19
Occupational Health and Safety Act of 1970, 313–9
Office of Economic Opportunity (OEO), 159, 300; Community Action Program, 129, 160; New Careers Program, 63–4; Neighborhood Health Centers, 125, 159–63, 233, 246–8, 252
Oil, Chemical, and Atomic Worker's Union, 317
Organization for Social and Technological Innovation Inc., 253, 254, 255–6
Osteopaths, 43–4, 54

Page, Joseph A., 287–8
Paraprofessionals, 56–64
Peters, James, 240, 255
Peterson, Osler, 38
Physician Assistant, 57; versus Nurse Associate, 59–61
Pilisuk, Marc, 5
Priven, Frances F., 297–8
Planning, Health, 39, 237–59; as occupation, 237–9; as process, 239–41; federal planning programs, 241–58, in a National Health Service, 339–44
Pneumoconiosis, 309
Poisoning, industrial solvents and metals, 310–1
Pope Paul VI, 268
Poverty: and health, 296–307; and type of care delivered, 144–55, 156–79; see also Ageism, Racism, Medicare, Medicaid, Office of Economic Opportunity
Power: definition of, 224–5; and

legitimacy, 225–6; and medical profession, 226; and ownership, 227; see also Marx, and Marxian critique
Prejudice, 101–2, 102–5, 105, 107, 107–10; future of, 327
Profession: definition of, 36; as an ideology, 36–7; and dominance, 35–41
Professionalization: and control over work, 33–67; and unionization, 74–87
Professional Standards Review Organizations (PSRO), 281, 286, 291–3, 340
Program (of health service): definition of, 123; examples, 124–5
Psychological work pressures, 311–2
Public Health: in ancient Rome, 16–7, in Massachusetts during 1842–1936, 25, 132; and Hill-Burton program, 242; home environment, 303–7; occupational hygiene, 307–12; environmental health, 319–23, 308
Public laws, U.S. Federal, 89–7; Medicare, 29; Manpower Development and Training Act, Nurse Training Act, Health Manpower Training Act, 190; Health Maintenance Organization Act of 1973, 211; Hospital Survey and Construction Act of 1946 (Hill-Burton), 241–3; Community Mental Health Centers Act of 1963, 243–6; Office of Economic Opportunity Act of 1964, 246–7; Regional Medical Program (P.L. 89–239), 248–52; Partnership for Health Act of 1966 (Comprehensive

Public laws (*cont'd*)
Health Planning P.L. 89–749),
252–7; Health Planning and
Resources Development Act of 1974
(P.L. 93–641), 258–9, 280–1,
288–9; Occupational Health and
Safety Act of 1970, 287–8; 313–9;
National Cancer Act of 1971, 270–4

Racism: in service relationship,
101–2; in patterns of service,
156–80; *see also* Poverty, Office of
Economic Opportunity
Regional Medical Program, 248–52
Regulation, 274–95; definition of,
274–6; politics of, 279–83;
credentialling, 284–5; of places for
health service, 285–9; of things,
289–90; of costs, 290–1, 315
Robertson, Leon, 147–8, 167, 172
Rome, ancient, health and service in,
15–7
Roosevelt administration, 28, 298
Rosenberg, Bernard, 111
Rosenkrantz, Barbara G., 25, 132
Roth, Julius, 106, 116–7
Rushing, William A., 145
Rutstein, David, 128

Schiff, D. W., 64
Schlicke, C., 280
Science for the People, 144, 235
Scott, Rachel, 288
Second World War, and health care,
28–9
Securities and Exchange Commission,
254, 276
Sedgewick, W. T., 24–5
Service Employees Industrial Union,
71

Service systems, history of, 15–23
Sex discrimination: and health careers,
12, 56, 59–60, 61, 64, 72; and
treatment relationship, 102–10,
236; and service system, 110, 236;
and health products, 236; *see also*
Women's Health Movement
Shadid, Michael, 206
Shapiro, W., 67
Shenour, Elie, 300
Silver, George, 164–5
Silverman, M., 289
Social Darwinism, 127
Social Insurance, American, 26–30
Social Security, and Medicare, 29
Soviet Union: Feldshers, 58; extension
courses in health, 62; physician
maldistribution, 65; political
pressure on diagnosis of illness,
92–3; state exploitation, 112; labor
unions and occupational health, 231
Stevens, Robert and Rosemary,
169–70, 171
Strauss, Anselm, 113–4
Strickland, Stephen P., 271, 273
Supreme Court, U.S., 35–36; on
abortion, 104, 268; on physician
monopoly, 211; comparison of
education with health decisions,
268–9, 316
Surgenor, D. M., 196, 289–90
Szasz, Thomas, 91–2, 94

Taft-Hartley law, 69–70
Technocrats, 128, 237–8, 243, 246,
250–1, 257
Technology: and health care, 19,
23–4, 37, 39, 52–3, 55, 65–7,
117–20, 136, 140–1, 213–8; as a
source of disease, 307–20.

382

James H. Price